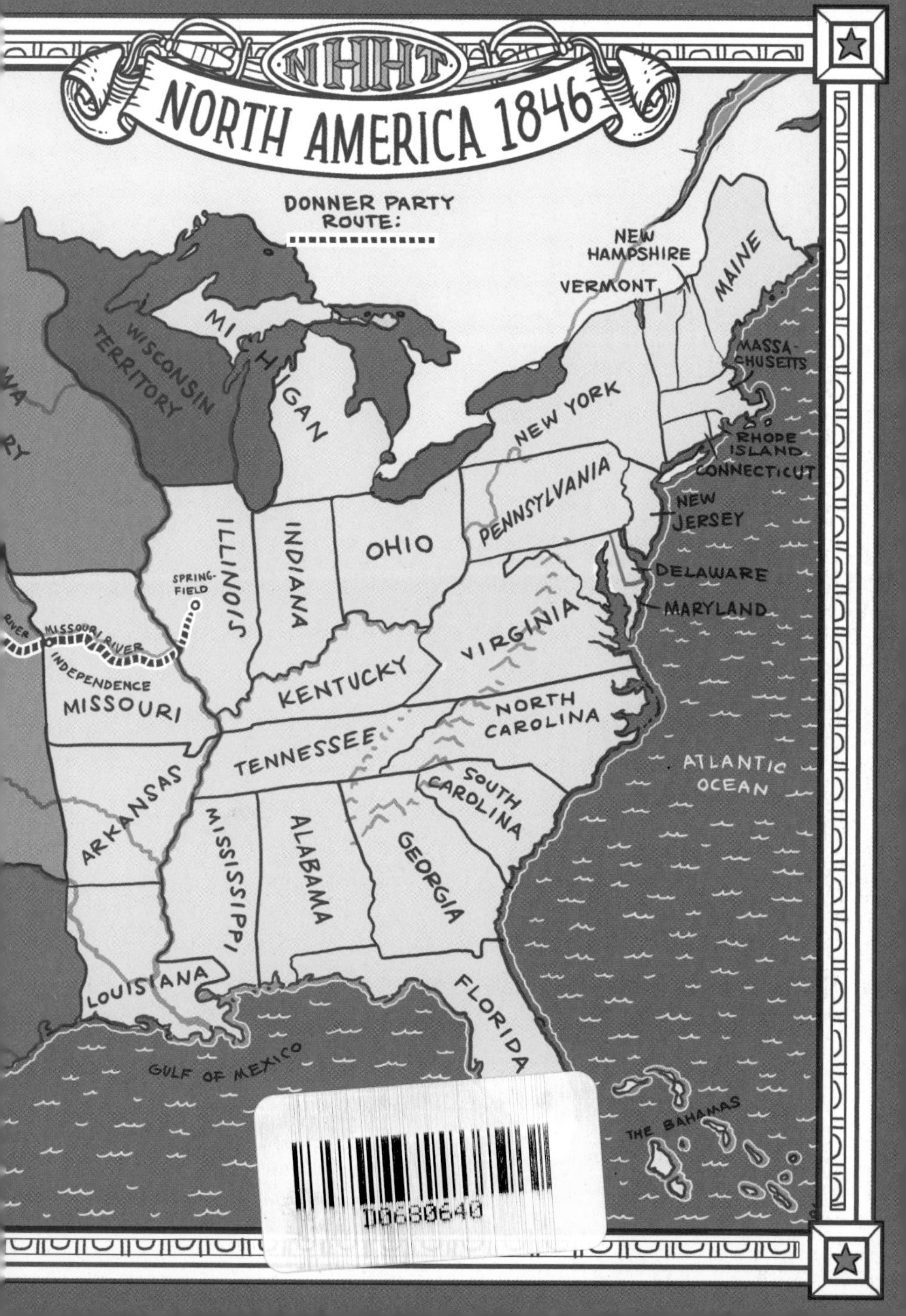
NHHT
NORTH AMERICA 1846
DONNER PARTY ROUTE:
NEW HAMPSHIRE
VERMONT
MAINE
MASSACHUSETTS
NEW YORK
RHODE ISLAND
CONNECTICUT
WISCONSIN TERRITORY
MICHIGAN
PENNSYLVANIA
NEW JERSEY
ILLINOIS
INDIANA
OHIO
DELAWARE
SPRINGFIELD
MARYLAND
MISSOURI RIVER
VIRGINIA
INDEPENDENCE
KENTUCKY
MISSOURI
NORTH CAROLINA
TENNESSEE
ATLANTIC OCEAN
ARKANSAS
SOUTH CAROLINA
MISSISSIPPI
ALABAMA
GEORGIA
LOUISIANA
FLORIDA
GULF OF MEXICO
THE BAHAMAS

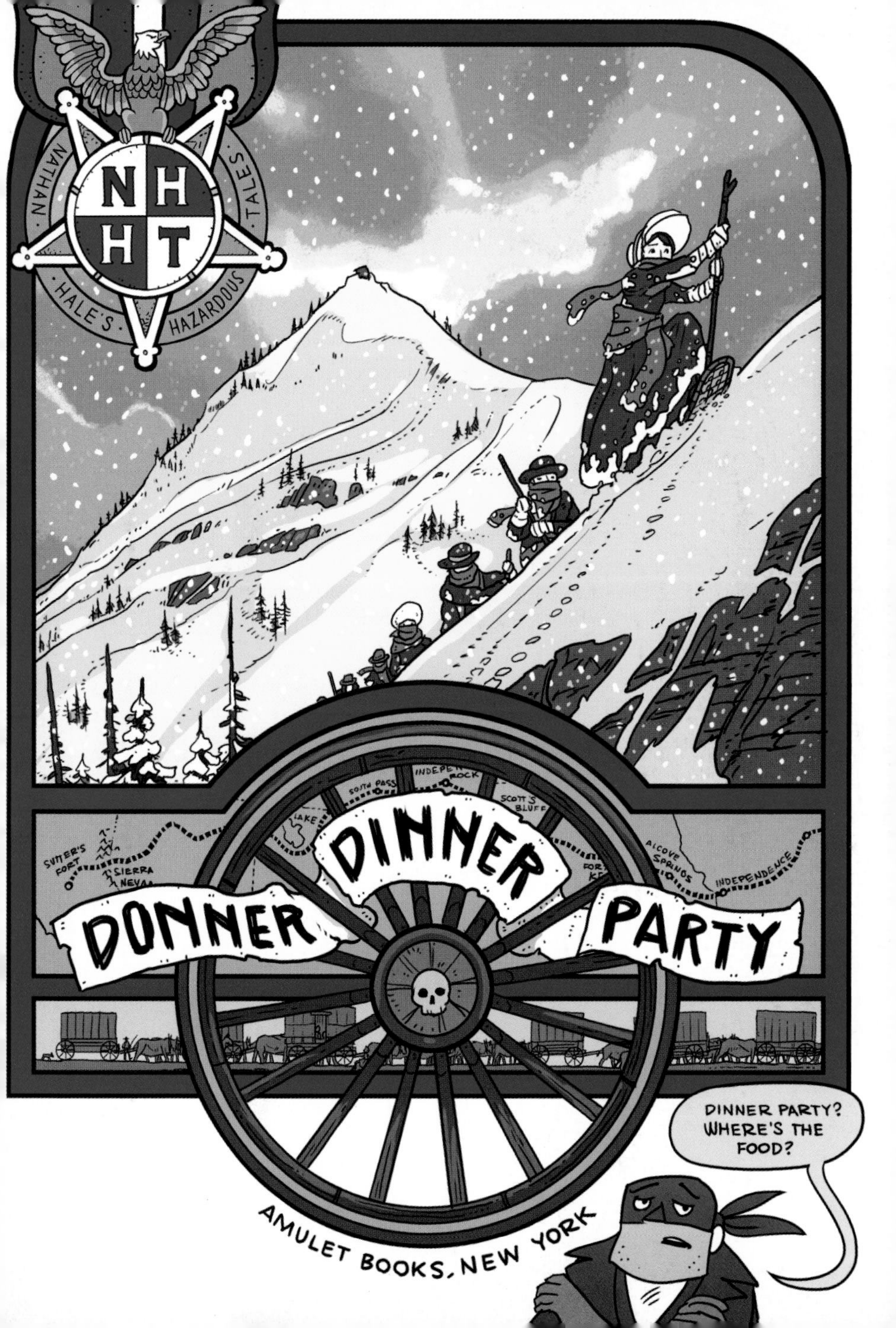

NATHAN HALE'S HAZARDOUS TALES
NH
HT
SOUTH PASS
SCOTT'S BLUFF
SUTTER'S FORT
SIERRA
ALCOVE SPRINGS
INDEPENDENCE
DONNER
DINNER
PARTY
DINNER PARTY? WHERE'S THE FOOD?
AMULET BOOKS, NEW YORK

CATALOGING-IN-PUBLICATION DATA HAS BEEN APPLIED FOR
AND MAY BE OBTAINED FROM THE LIBRARY OF CONGRESS.

ISBN: 978-1-4197-0856-5

PRINTED AND BOUND IN CHINA
15 14 13 12 11 10

AMULET BOOKS ARE AVAILABLE AT SPECIAL DISCOUNTS WHEN
PURCHASED IN QUANTITY FOR PREMIUMS AND PROMOTIONS
AS WELL AS FUNDRAISING OR EDUCATIONAL USE. SPECIAL
EDITIONS CAN ALSO BE CREATED TO SPECIFICATION. FOR
DETAILS, CONTACT SPECIALSALES@ABRAMSBOOKS.COM OR THE
ADDRESS BELOW.

ABRAMS The Art of Books
195 Broadway, New York, NY 10007
abramsbooks.com

TO THE MEMORY OF MY
GREAT-GREAT-GREAT-GRANDFATHER EPH HANKS,
A RESCUER OF SNOWBOUND PIONEERS

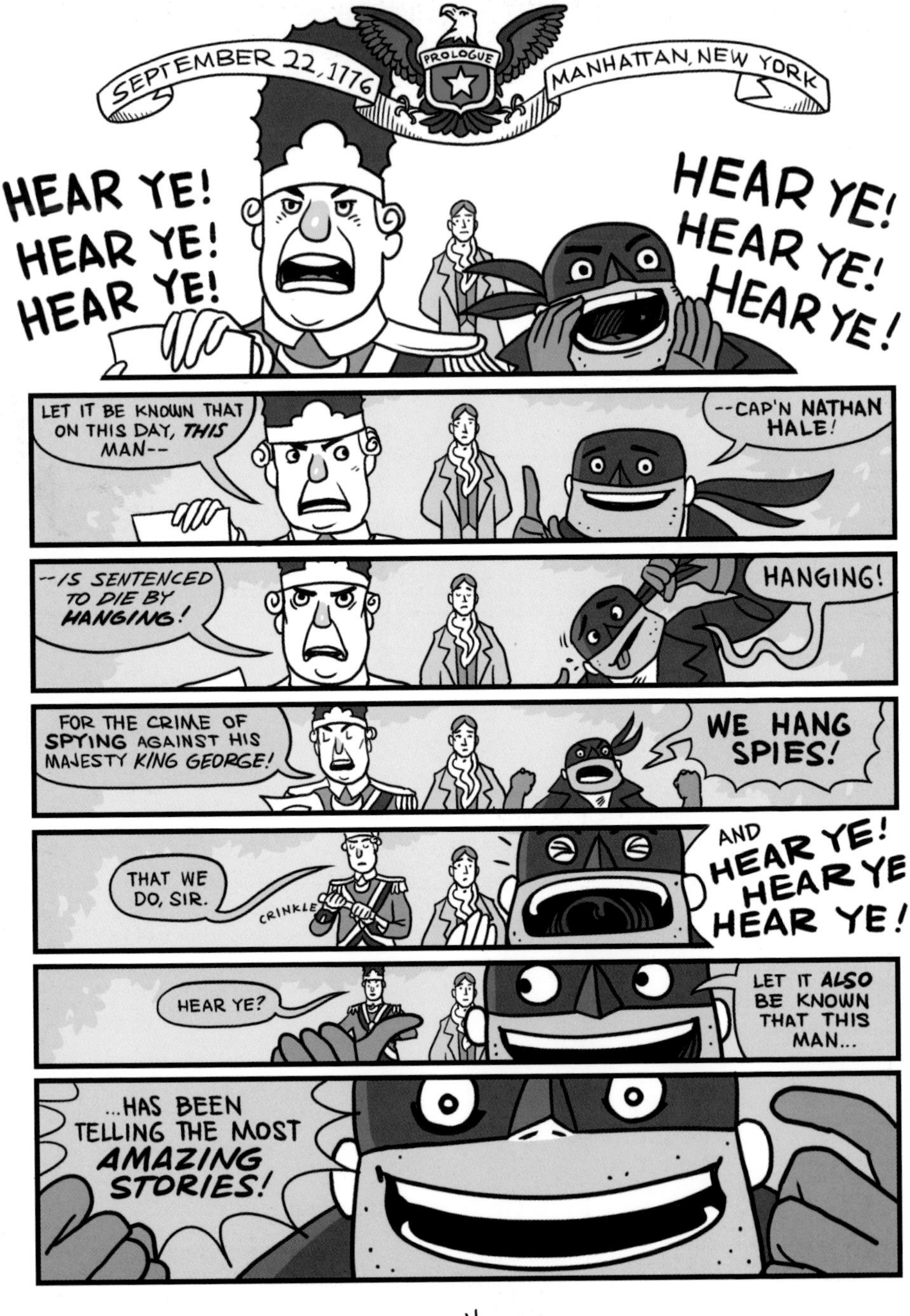
SEPTEMBER 22, 1776
PROLOGUE
MANHATTAN, NEW YORK
HEAR YE! HEAR YE! HEAR YE!
HEAR YE! HEAR YE! HEAR YE!
LET IT BE KNOWN THAT ON THIS DAY, THIS MAN--
--CAP'N NATHAN HALE!
--IS SENTENCED TO DIE BY HANGING!
HANGING!
FOR THE CRIME OF SPYING AGAINST HIS MAJESTY KING GEORGE!
WE HANG SPIES!
THAT WE DO, SIR.
CRINKLE
AND HEAR YE! HEAR YE! HEAR YE!
HEAR YE?
LET IT ALSO BE KNOWN THAT THIS MAN...
...HAS BEEN TELLING THE MOST AMAZING STORIES!

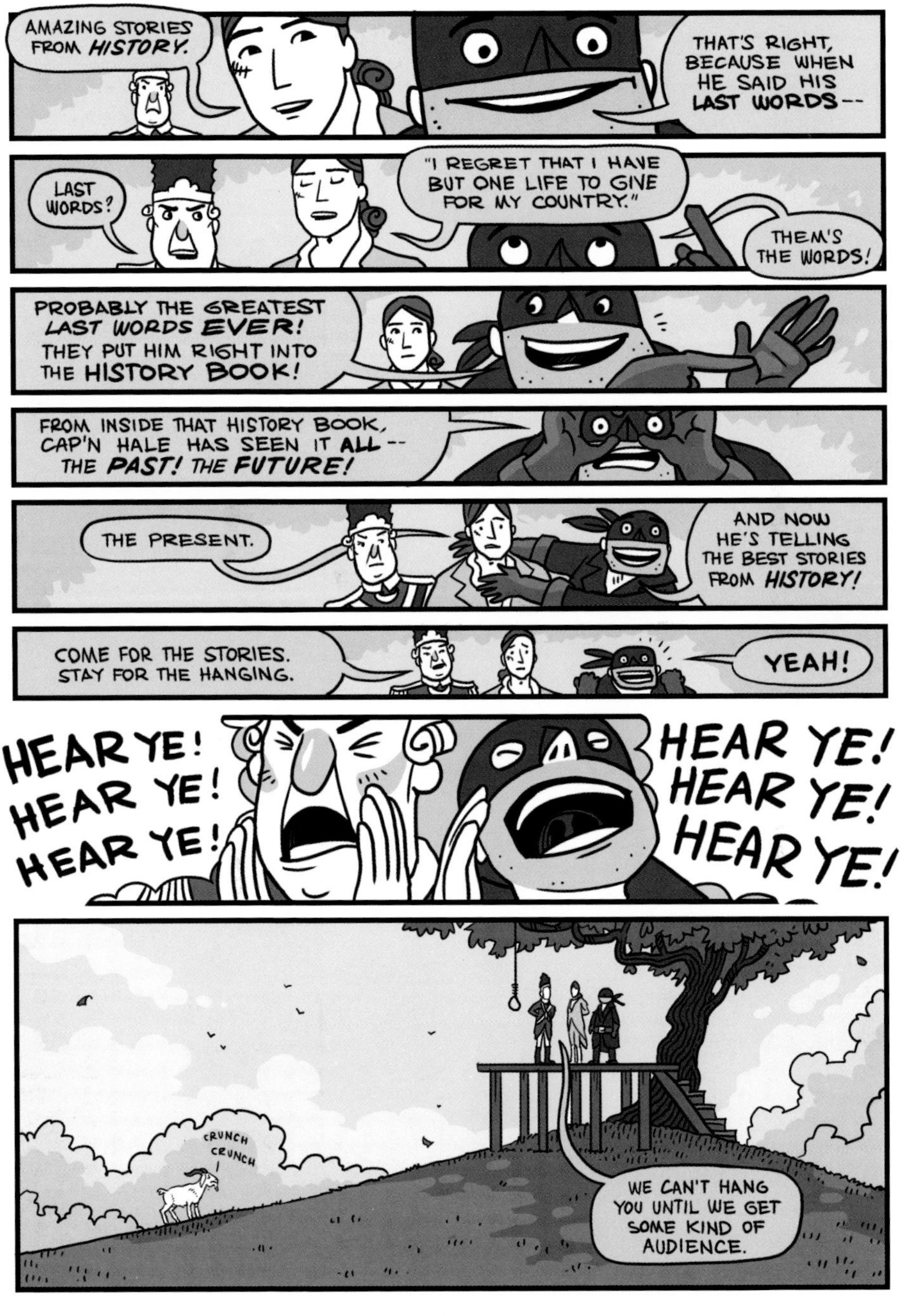

AMAZING STORIES FROM HISTORY.
THAT'S RIGHT, BECAUSE WHEN HE SAID HIS LAST WORDS--
LAST WORDS?
"I REGRET THAT I HAVE BUT ONE LIFE TO GIVE FOR MY COUNTRY."
THEM'S THE WORDS!
PROBABLY THE GREATEST LAST WORDS EVER! THEY PUT HIM RIGHT INTO THE HISTORY BOOK!
FROM INSIDE THAT HISTORY BOOK, CAP'N HALE HAS SEEN IT ALL-- THE PAST! THE FUTURE!
THE PRESENT.
AND NOW HE'S TELLING THE BEST STORIES FROM HISTORY!
COME FOR THE STORIES. STAY FOR THE HANGING.
YEAH!
HEAR YE! HEAR YE! HEAR YE!
HEAR YE! HEAR YE! HEAR YE!
CRUNCH CRUNCH
WE CAN'T HANG YOU UNTIL WE GET SOME KIND OF AUDIENCE.

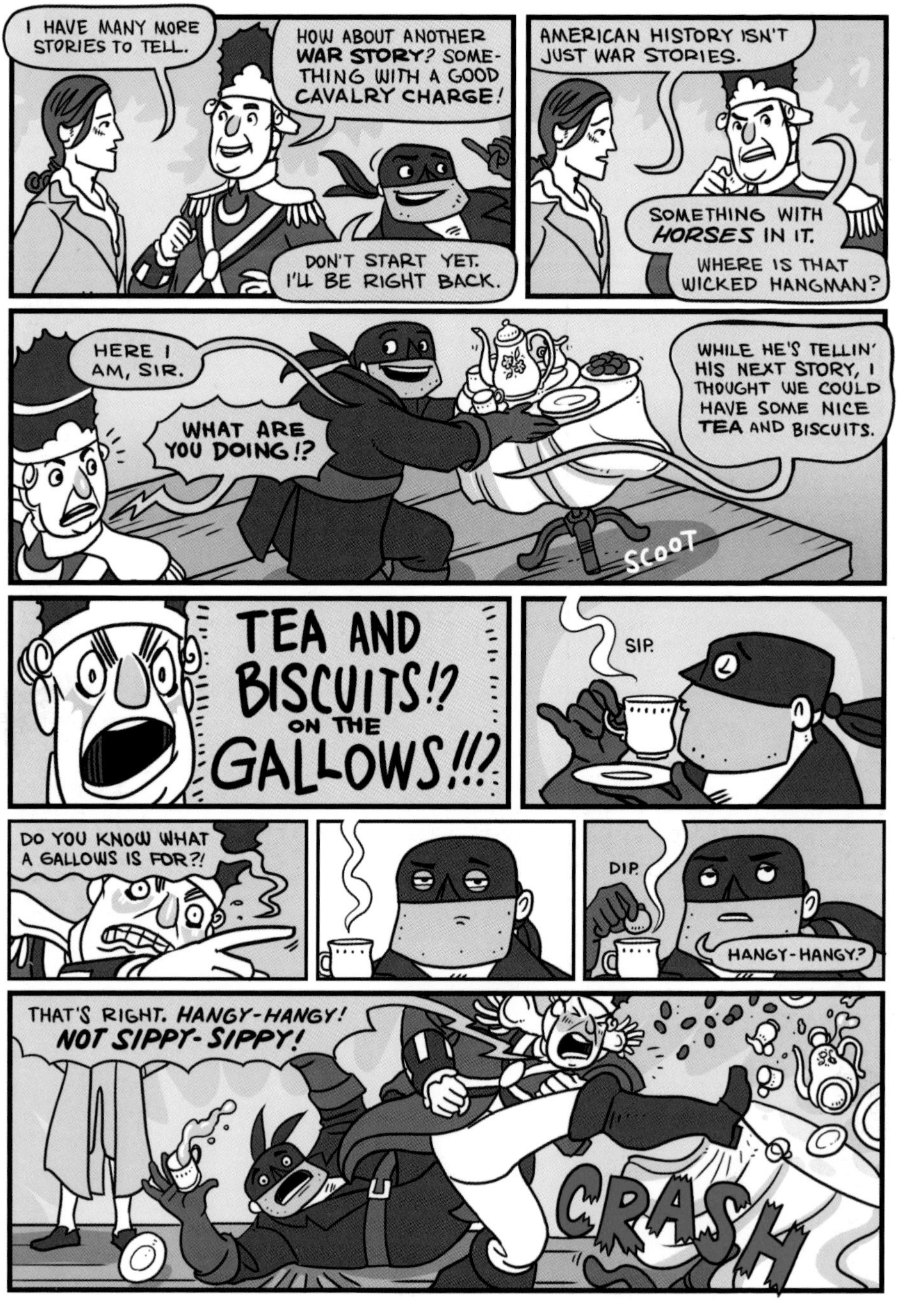
I HAVE MANY MORE STORIES TO TELL.
HOW ABOUT ANOTHER WAR STORY? SOMETHING WITH A GOOD CAVALRY CHARGE!
DON'T START YET. I'LL BE RIGHT BACK.
AMERICAN HISTORY ISN'T JUST WAR STORIES.
SOMETHING WITH HORSES IN IT.
WHERE IS THAT WICKED HANGMAN?
HERE I AM, SIR.
WHAT ARE YOU DOING!?
WHILE HE'S TELLIN' HIS NEXT STORY, I THOUGHT WE COULD HAVE SOME NICE TEA AND BISCUITS.
SCOOT
TEA AND BISCUITS!? ON THE GALLOWS!!?
SIP.
DO YOU KNOW WHAT A GALLOWS IS FOR?!
DIP.
HANGY-HANGY?
THAT'S RIGHT. HANGY-HANGY! NOT SIPPY-SIPPY!
CRASH

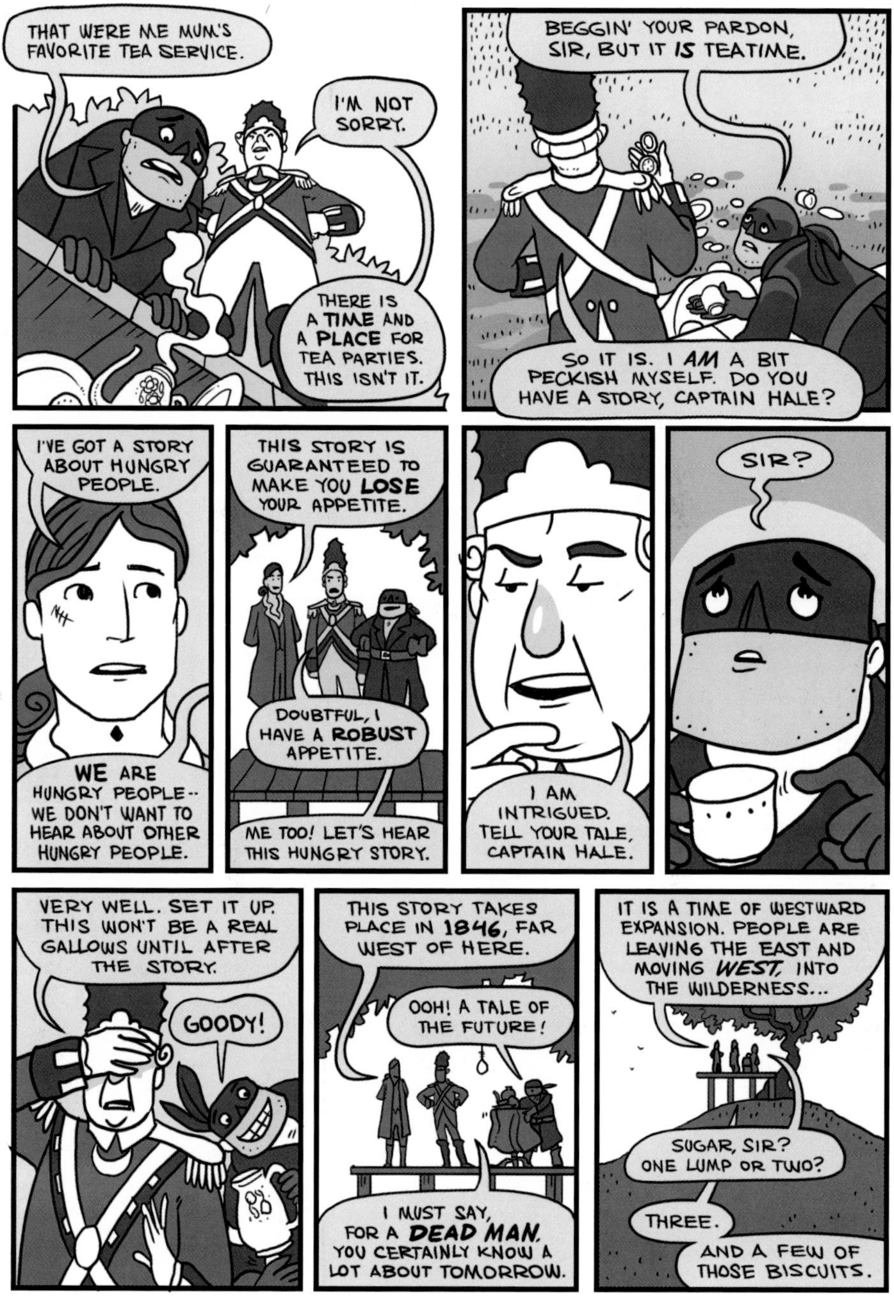

THAT WERE ME MUM'S FAVORITE TEA SERVICE.
I'M NOT SORRY.
THERE IS A **TIME** AND A **PLACE** FOR TEA PARTIES. THIS ISN'T IT.
BEGGIN' YOUR PARDON, SIR, BUT IT ***IS*** TEATIME.
SO IT IS. I ***AM*** A BIT PECKISH MYSELF. DO YOU HAVE A STORY, CAPTAIN HALE?
I'VE GOT A STORY ABOUT HUNGRY PEOPLE.
WE ARE HUNGRY PEOPLE-- WE DON'T WANT TO HEAR ABOUT OTHER HUNGRY PEOPLE.
THIS STORY IS GUARANTEED TO MAKE YOU **LOSE** YOUR APPETITE.
DOUBTFUL, I HAVE A **ROBUST** APPETITE.
ME TOO! LET'S HEAR THIS HUNGRY STORY.
I AM INTRIGUED. TELL YOUR TALE, CAPTAIN HALE.
SIR?
VERY WELL. SET IT UP. THIS WON'T BE A REAL GALLOWS UNTIL AFTER THE STORY.
GOODY!
THIS STORY TAKES PLACE IN **1846**, FAR WEST OF HERE.
OOH! A TALE OF THE FUTURE!
I MUST SAY, FOR A ***DEAD MAN***, YOU CERTAINLY KNOW A LOT ABOUT TOMORROW.
IT IS A TIME OF WESTWARD EXPANSION. PEOPLE ARE LEAVING THE EAST AND MOVING ***WEST***, INTO THE WILDERNESS...
SUGAR, SIR? ONE LUMP OR TWO?
THREE.
AND A FEW OF THOSE BISCUITS.

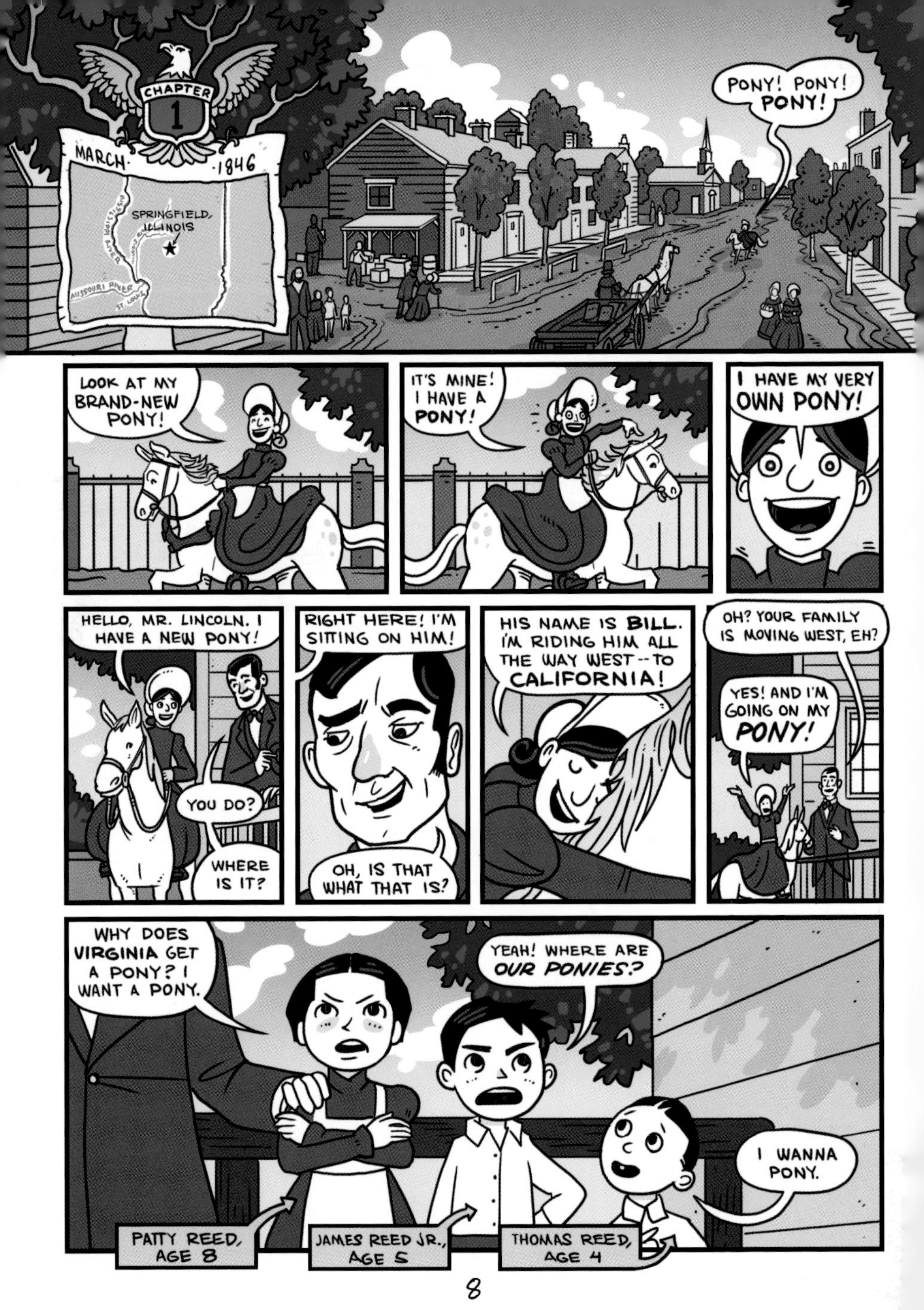
CHAPTER 1
MARCH · 1846
SPRINGFIELD, ILLINOIS
MISSOURI RIVER
ST. LOUIS
PONY! PONY! PONY!
LOOK AT MY BRAND-NEW PONY!
IT'S MINE! I HAVE A PONY!
I HAVE MY VERY OWN PONY!
HELLO, MR. LINCOLN. I HAVE A NEW PONY!
YOU DO?
WHERE IS IT?
RIGHT HERE! I'M SITTING ON HIM!
OH, IS THAT WHAT THAT IS?
HIS NAME IS BILL. I'M RIDING HIM ALL THE WAY WEST -- TO CALIFORNIA!
OH? YOUR FAMILY IS MOVING WEST, EH?
YES! AND I'M GOING ON MY PONY!
WHY DOES VIRGINIA GET A PONY? I WANT A PONY.
YEAH! WHERE ARE OUR PONIES?
I WANNA PONY.
PATTY REED, AGE 8
JAMES REED JR., AGE 5
THOMAS REED, AGE 4

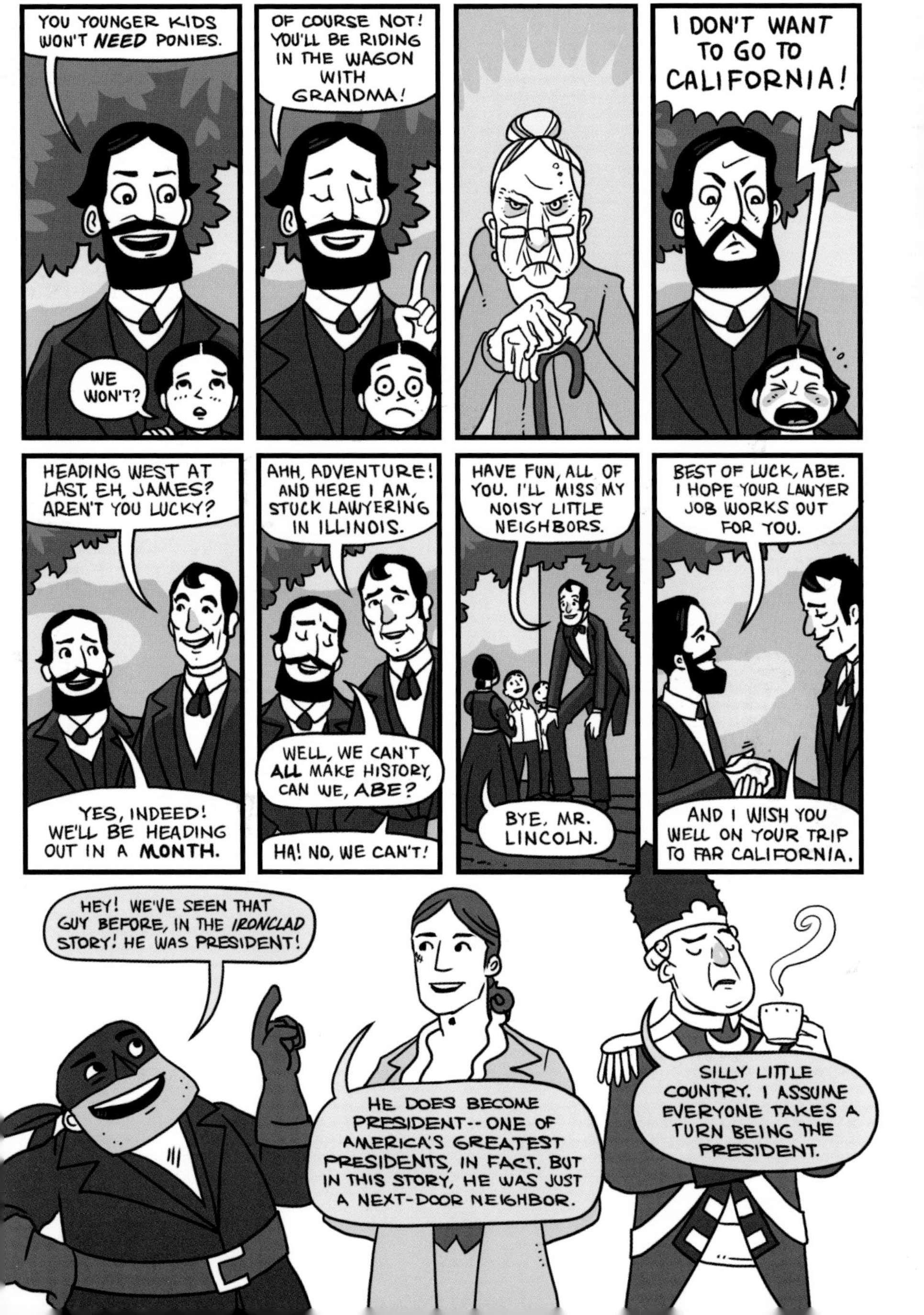
YOU YOUNGER KIDS WON'T NEED PONIES.
WE WON'T?
OF COURSE NOT! YOU'LL BE RIDING IN THE WAGON WITH GRANDMA!
I DON'T WANT TO GO TO CALIFORNIA!
HEADING WEST AT LAST, EH, JAMES? AREN'T YOU LUCKY?
YES, INDEED! WE'LL BE HEADING OUT IN A MONTH.
AHH, ADVENTURE! AND HERE I AM, STUCK LAWYERING IN ILLINOIS.
WELL, WE CAN'T ALL MAKE HISTORY, CAN WE, ABE?
HA! NO, WE CAN'T!
HAVE FUN, ALL OF YOU. I'LL MISS MY NOISY LITTLE NEIGHBORS.
BYE, MR. LINCOLN.
BEST OF LUCK, ABE. I HOPE YOUR LAWYER JOB WORKS OUT FOR YOU.
AND I WISH YOU WELL ON YOUR TRIP TO FAR CALIFORNIA.
HEY! WE'VE SEEN THAT GUY BEFORE, IN THE IRONCLAD STORY! HE WAS PRESIDENT!
HE DOES BECOME PRESIDENT-- ONE OF AMERICA'S GREATEST PRESIDENTS, IN FACT. BUT IN THIS STORY, HE WAS JUST A NEXT-DOOR NEIGHBOR.
SILLY LITTLE COUNTRY. I ASSUME EVERYONE TAKES A TURN BEING THE PRESIDENT.

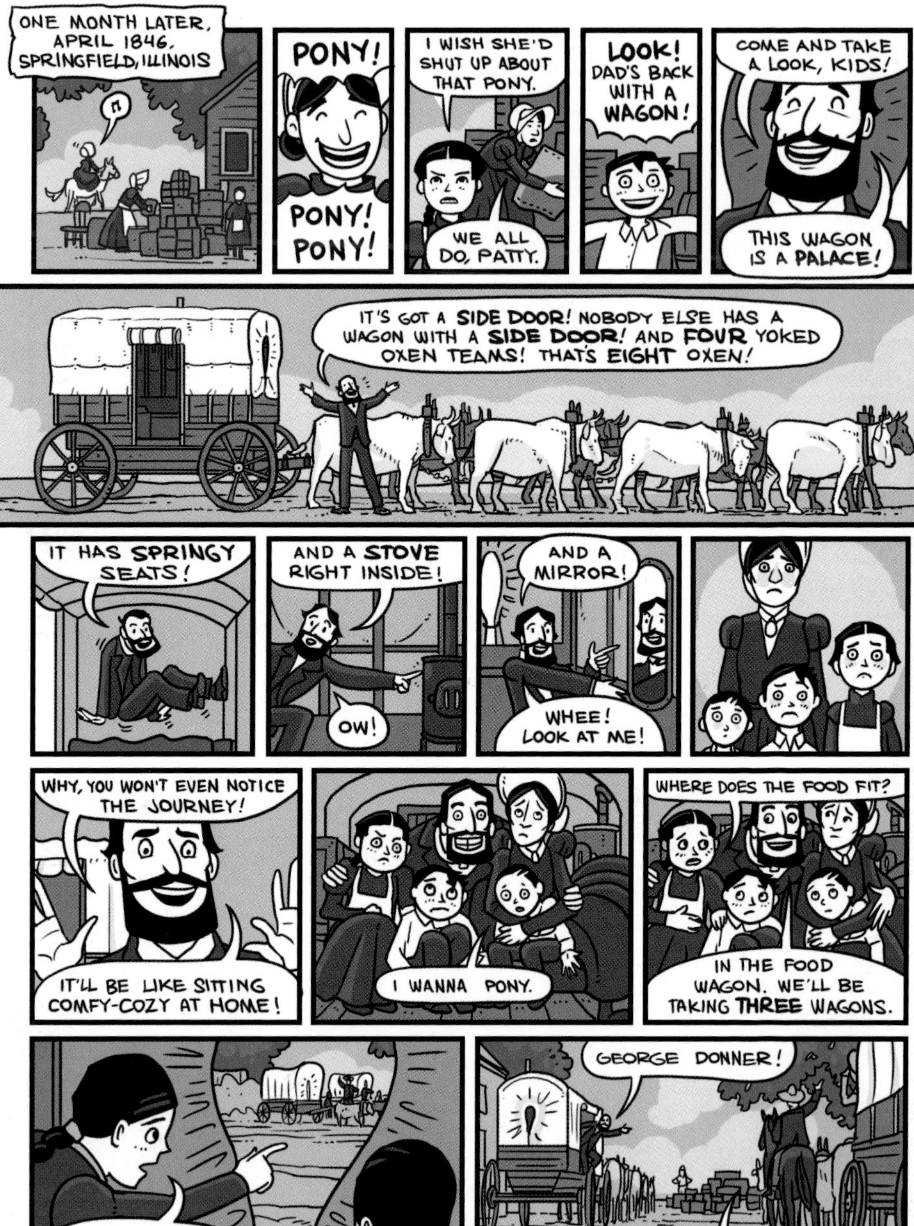

ONE MONTH LATER, APRIL 1846, SPRINGFIELD, ILLINOIS
PONY!
PONY! PONY!
I WISH SHE'D SHUT UP ABOUT THAT PONY.
WE ALL DO, PATTY.
LOOK! DAD'S BACK WITH A WAGON!
COME AND TAKE A LOOK, KIDS!
THIS WAGON IS A PALACE!
IT'S GOT A SIDE DOOR! NOBODY ELSE HAS A WAGON WITH A SIDE DOOR! AND FOUR YOKED OXEN TEAMS! THAT'S EIGHT OXEN!
IT HAS SPRINGY SEATS!
AND A STOVE RIGHT INSIDE!
OW!
AND A MIRROR!
WHEE! LOOK AT ME!
WHY, YOU WON'T EVEN NOTICE THE JOURNEY!
IT'LL BE LIKE SITTING COMFY-COZY AT HOME!
I WANNA PONY.
WHERE DOES THE FOOD FIT?
IN THE FOOD WAGON. WE'LL BE TAKING THREE WAGONS.
HERE COME THE DONNERS!
GEORGE DONNER!
HURRY AND FINISH YOUR PACKING, JAMES REED! IT'S TIME TO GO!

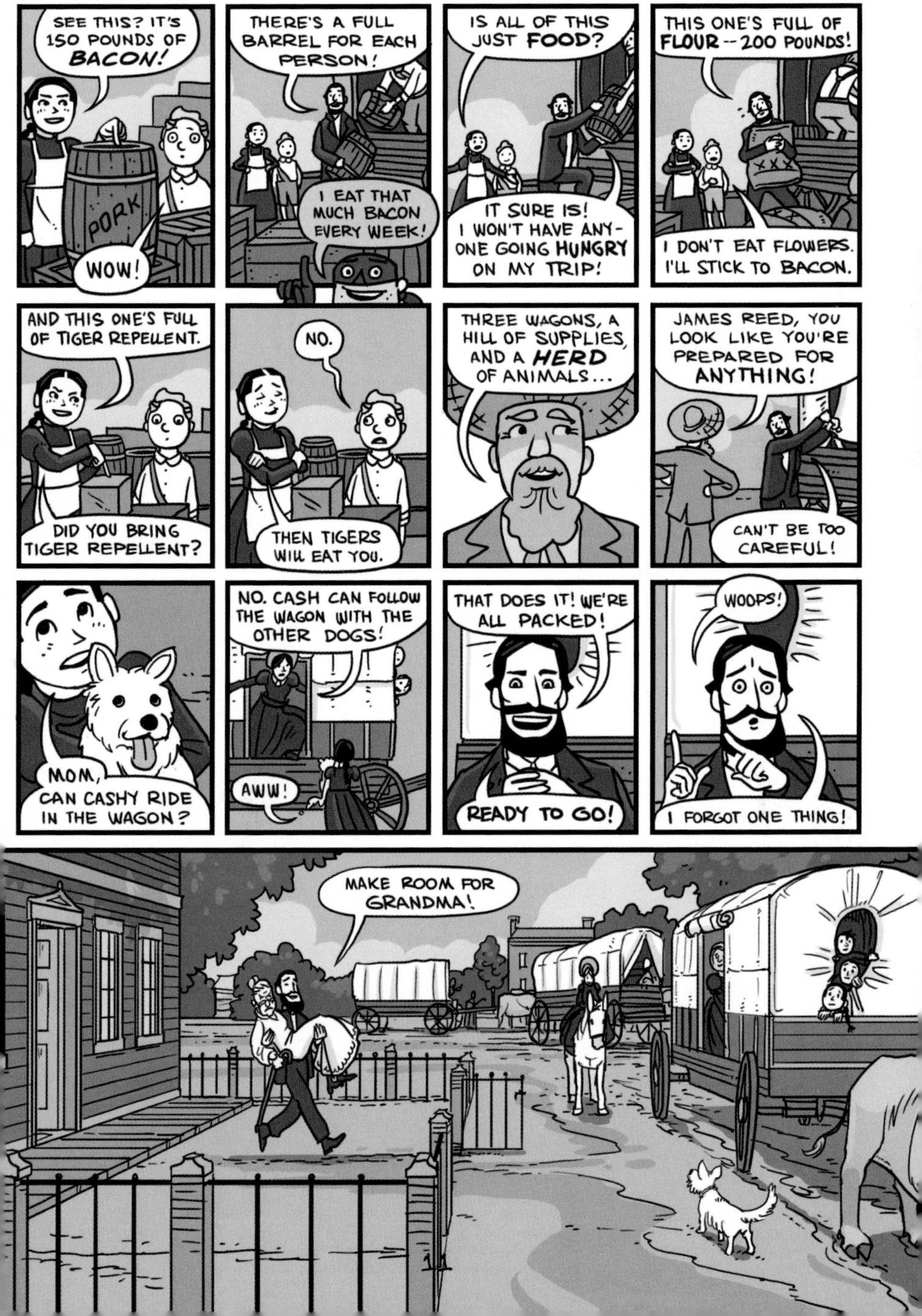
SEE THIS? IT'S 150 POUNDS OF BACON!
WOW!
THERE'S A FULL BARREL FOR EACH PERSON!
I EAT THAT MUCH BACON EVERY WEEK!
IS ALL OF THIS JUST FOOD?
IT SURE IS! I WON'T HAVE ANY-ONE GOING HUNGRY ON MY TRIP!
THIS ONE'S FULL OF FLOUR--200 POUNDS!
I DON'T EAT FLOWERS. I'LL STICK TO BACON.
AND THIS ONE'S FULL OF TIGER REPELLENT.
DID YOU BRING TIGER REPELLENT?
NO.
THEN TIGERS WILL EAT YOU.
THREE WAGONS, A HILL OF SUPPLIES, AND A HERD OF ANIMALS...
JAMES REED, YOU LOOK LIKE YOU'RE PREPARED FOR ANYTHING!
CAN'T BE TOO CAREFUL!
MOM, CAN CASHY RIDE IN THE WAGON?
NO. CASH CAN FOLLOW THE WAGON WITH THE OTHER DOGS!
AWW!
THAT DOES IT! WE'RE ALL PACKED!
READY TO GO!
WOOPS!
I FORGOT ONE THING!
MAKE ROOM FOR GRANDMA!

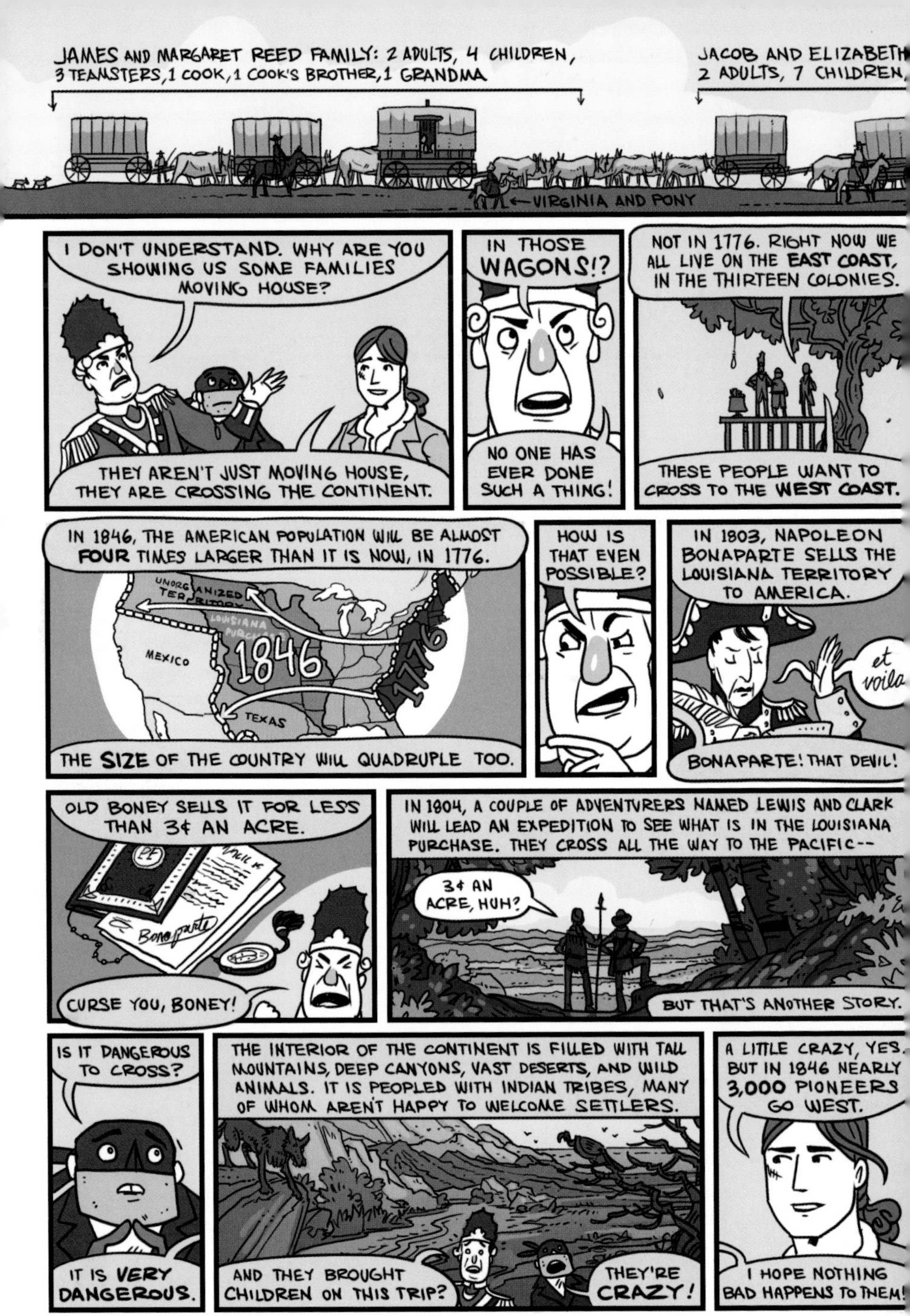
JAMES AND MARGARET REED FAMILY: 2 ADULTS, 4 CHILDREN, 3 TEAMSTERS, 1 COOK, 1 COOK'S BROTHER, 1 GRANDMA
JACOB AND ELIZABETH
2 ADULTS, 7 CHILDREN,
VIRGINIA AND PONY
I DON'T UNDERSTAND. WHY ARE YOU SHOWING US SOME FAMILIES MOVING HOUSE?
THEY AREN'T JUST MOVING HOUSE, THEY ARE CROSSING THE CONTINENT.
IN THOSE WAGONS!?
NO ONE HAS EVER DONE SUCH A THING!
NOT IN 1776. RIGHT NOW WE ALL LIVE ON THE EAST COAST, IN THE THIRTEEN COLONIES.
THESE PEOPLE WANT TO CROSS TO THE WEST COAST.
IN 1846, THE AMERICAN POPULATION WILL BE ALMOST FOUR TIMES LARGER THAN IT IS NOW, IN 1776.
UNORGANIZED TERRITORY
LOUISIANA PURCHASE
MEXICO
1846
1776
TEXAS
THE SIZE OF THE COUNTRY WILL QUADRUPLE TOO.
HOW IS THAT EVEN POSSIBLE?
IN 1803, NAPOLEON BONAPARTE SELLS THE LOUISIANA TERRITORY TO AMERICA.
et voila
BONAPARTE! THAT DEVIL!
OLD BONEY SELLS IT FOR LESS THAN 3¢ AN ACRE.
Bonaparte
CURSE YOU, BONEY!
IN 1804, A COUPLE OF ADVENTURERS NAMED LEWIS AND CLARK WILL LEAD AN EXPEDITION TO SEE WHAT IS IN THE LOUISIANA PURCHASE. THEY CROSS ALL THE WAY TO THE PACIFIC--
3¢ AN ACRE, HUH?
BUT THAT'S ANOTHER STORY.
IS IT DANGEROUS TO CROSS?
IT IS VERY DANGEROUS.
THE INTERIOR OF THE CONTINENT IS FILLED WITH TALL MOUNTAINS, DEEP CANYONS, VAST DESERTS, AND WILD ANIMALS. IT IS PEOPLED WITH INDIAN TRIBES, MANY OF WHOM AREN'T HAPPY TO WELCOME SETTLERS.
AND THEY BROUGHT CHILDREN ON THIS TRIP?
THEY'RE CRAZY!
A LITTLE CRAZY, YES. BUT IN 1846 NEARLY 3,000 PIONEERS GO WEST.
I HOPE NOTHING BAD HAPPENS TO THEM!

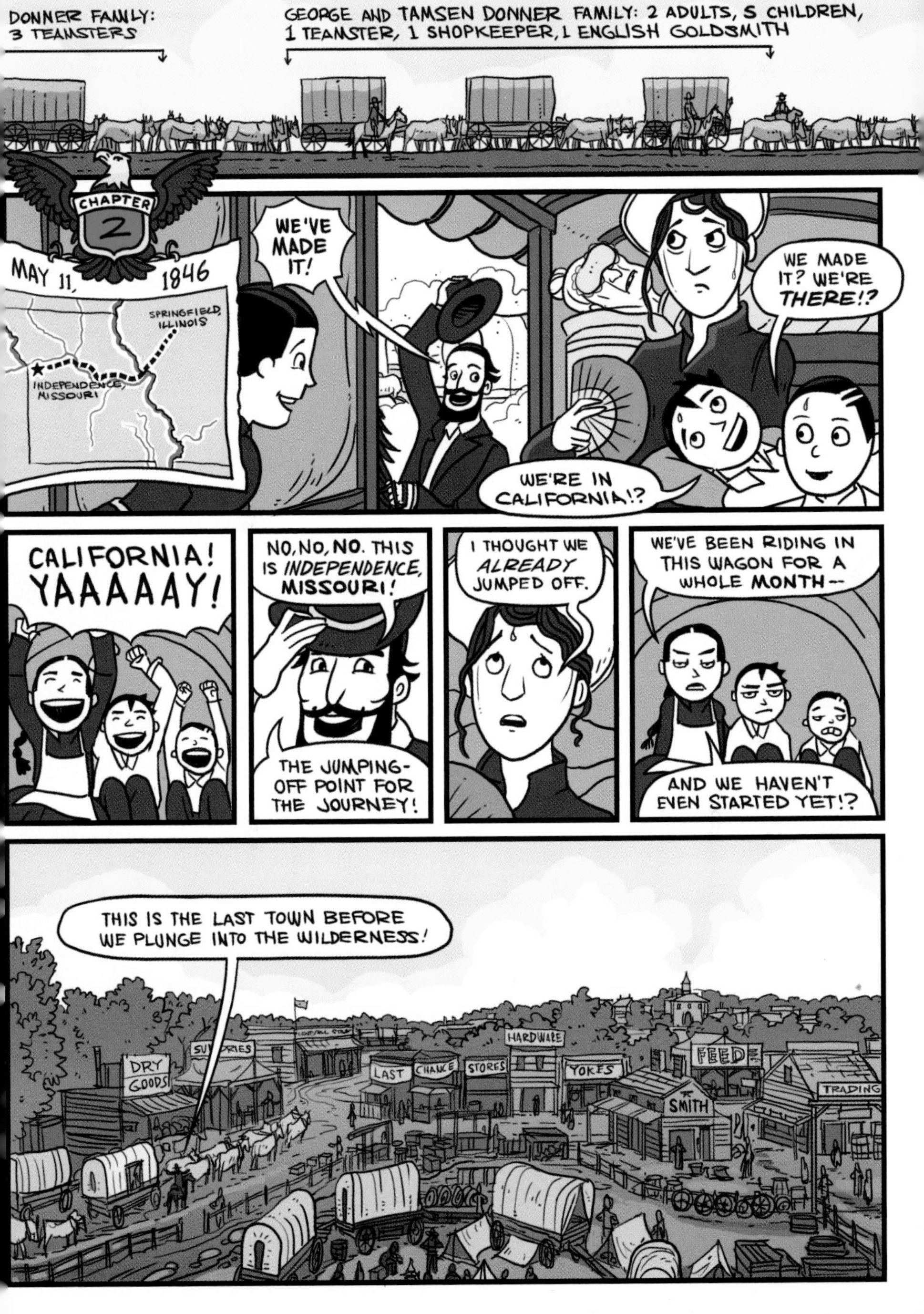
DONNER FAMILY: 3 TEAMSTERS
GEORGE AND TAMSEN DONNER FAMILY: 2 ADULTS, 5 CHILDREN, 1 TEAMSTER, 1 SHOPKEEPER, 1 ENGLISH GOLDSMITH
CHAPTER 2
MAY 11, 1846
SPRINGFIELD, ILLINOIS
INDEPENDENCE, MISSOURI
WE'VE MADE IT!
WE MADE IT? WE'RE THERE!?
WE'RE IN CALIFORNIA!?
CALIFORNIA! YAAAAAY!
NO, NO, NO. THIS IS INDEPENDENCE, MISSOURI!
THE JUMPING-OFF POINT FOR THE JOURNEY!
I THOUGHT WE ALREADY JUMPED OFF.
WE'VE BEEN RIDING IN THIS WAGON FOR A WHOLE MONTH--
AND WE HAVEN'T EVEN STARTED YET!?
THIS IS THE LAST TOWN BEFORE WE PLUNGE INTO THE WILDERNESS!
DRY GOODS
SUPPLIES
HARDWARE
LAST CHANCE STORES
YOKES
FEED
SMITH
TRADING

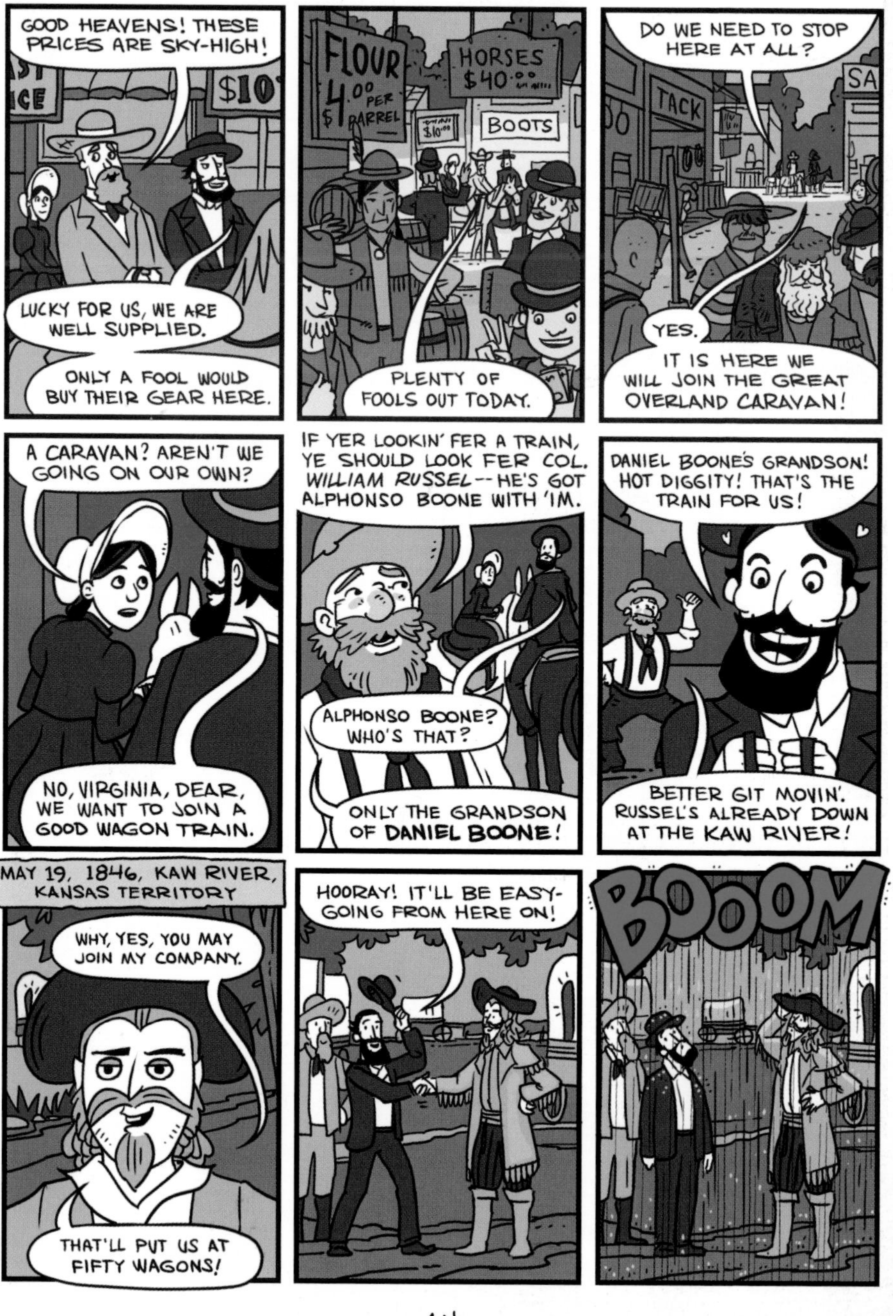
GOOD HEAVENS! THESE PRICES ARE SKY-HIGH!
LUCKY FOR US, WE ARE WELL SUPPLIED.
ONLY A FOOL WOULD BUY THEIR GEAR HERE.
FLOUR $4.00 PER BARREL
HORSES $40.00
BOOTS
PLENTY OF FOOLS OUT TODAY.
TACK
DO WE NEED TO STOP HERE AT ALL?
YES.
IT IS HERE WE WILL JOIN THE GREAT OVERLAND CARAVAN!
A CARAVAN? AREN'T WE GOING ON OUR OWN?
NO, VIRGINIA, DEAR, WE WANT TO JOIN A GOOD WAGON TRAIN.
IF YER LOOKIN' FER A TRAIN, YE SHOULD LOOK FER COL. WILLIAM RUSSEL-- HE'S GOT ALPHONSO BOONE WITH 'IM.
ALPHONSO BOONE? WHO'S THAT?
ONLY THE GRANDSON OF DANIEL BOONE!
DANIEL BOONE'S GRANDSON! HOT DIGGITY! THAT'S THE TRAIN FOR US!
BETTER GIT MOVIN'. RUSSEL'S ALREADY DOWN AT THE KAW RIVER!
MAY 19, 1846, KAW RIVER, KANSAS TERRITORY
WHY, YES, YOU MAY JOIN MY COMPANY.
THAT'LL PUT US AT FIFTY WAGONS!
HOORAY! IT'LL BE EASY-GOING FROM HERE ON!
BOOOM

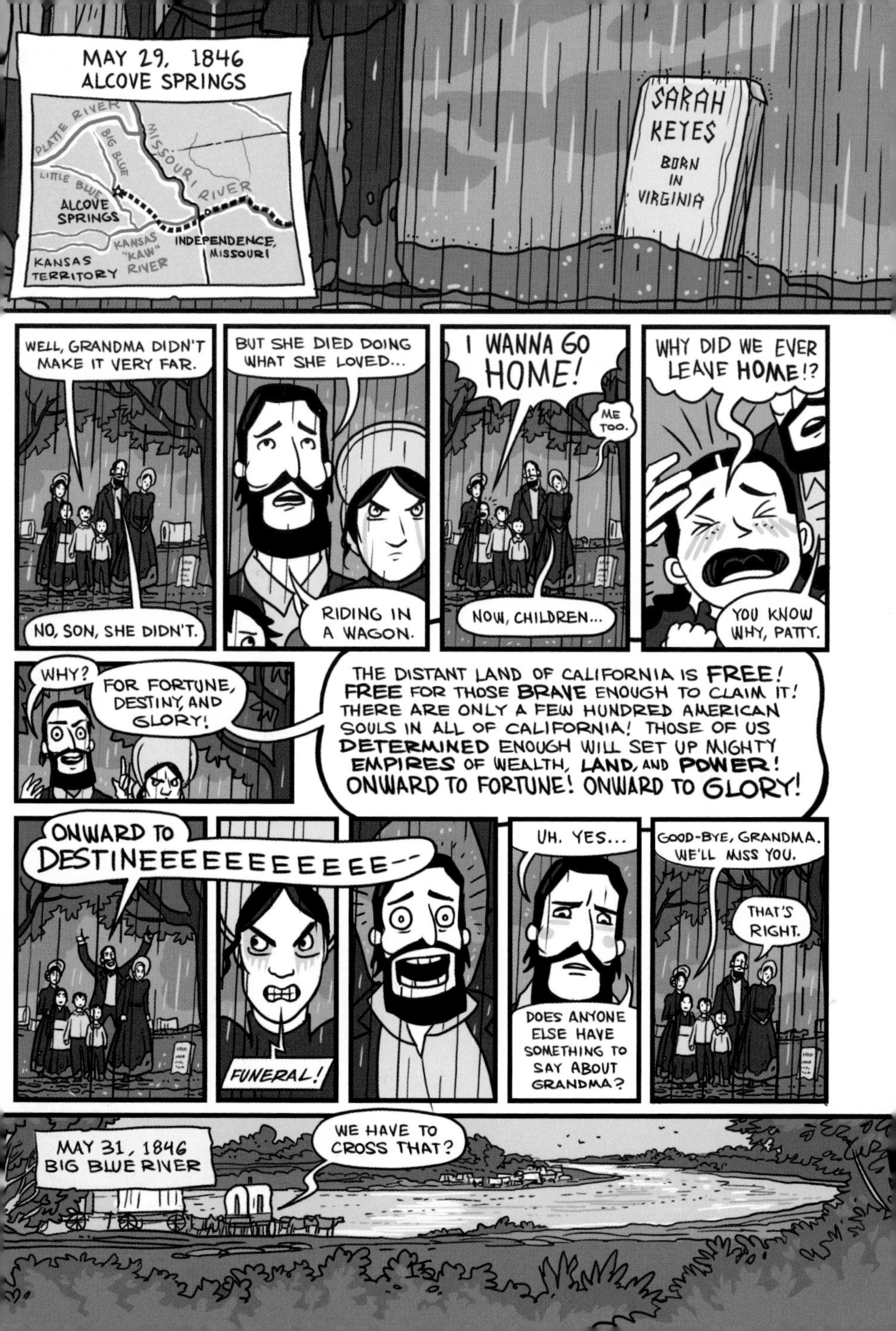
MAY 29, 1846
ALCOVE SPRINGS
PLATTE RIVER
BIG BLUE
MISSOURI RIVER
LITTLE BLUE
ALCOVE SPRINGS
KANSAS "KAW" RIVER
INDEPENDENCE, MISSOURI
KANSAS TERRITORY
SARAH KEYES
BORN IN VIRGINIA
WELL, GRANDMA DIDN'T MAKE IT VERY FAR.
NO, SON, SHE DIDN'T.
BUT SHE DIED DOING WHAT SHE LOVED...
RIDING IN A WAGON.
I WANNA GO HOME!
ME TOO.
NOW, CHILDREN...
WHY DID WE EVER LEAVE HOME!?
YOU KNOW WHY, PATTY.
WHY?
FOR FORTUNE, DESTINY, AND GLORY!
THE DISTANT LAND OF CALIFORNIA IS FREE! FREE FOR THOSE BRAVE ENOUGH TO CLAIM IT! THERE ARE ONLY A FEW HUNDRED AMERICAN SOULS IN ALL OF CALIFORNIA! THOSE OF US DETERMINED ENOUGH WILL SET UP MIGHTY EMPIRES OF WEALTH, LAND, AND POWER! ONWARD TO FORTUNE! ONWARD TO GLORY!
ONWARD TO DESTINEEEEEEEEEEEE--
FUNERAL!
UH. YES...
DOES ANYONE ELSE HAVE SOMETHING TO SAY ABOUT GRANDMA?
GOOD-BYE, GRANDMA. WE'LL MISS YOU.
THAT'S RIGHT.
MAY 31, 1846
BIG BLUE RIVER
WE HAVE TO CROSS THAT?

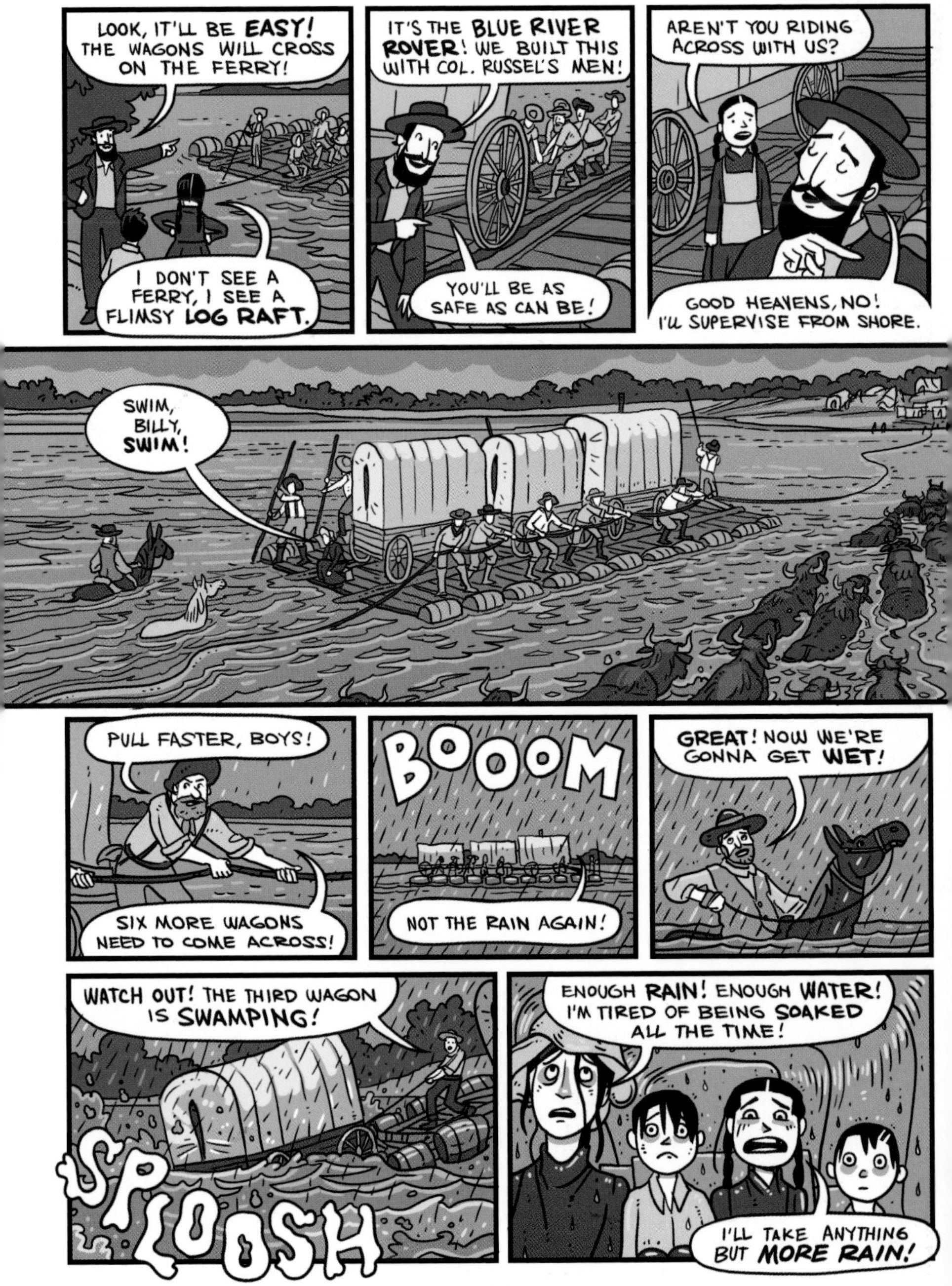
LOOK, IT'LL BE EASY! THE WAGONS WILL CROSS ON THE FERRY!
I DON'T SEE A FERRY, I SEE A FLIMSY LOG RAFT.
IT'S THE BLUE RIVER ROVER! WE BUILT THIS WITH COL. RUSSEL'S MEN!
YOU'LL BE AS SAFE AS CAN BE!
AREN'T YOU RIDING ACROSS WITH US?
GOOD HEAVENS, NO! I'LL SUPERVISE FROM SHORE.
SWIM, BILLY, SWIM!
PULL FASTER, BOYS!
SIX MORE WAGONS NEED TO COME ACROSS!
BOOOM
NOT THE RAIN AGAIN!
GREAT! NOW WE'RE GONNA GET WET!
WATCH OUT! THE THIRD WAGON IS SWAMPING!
SPLOOSH
ENOUGH RAIN! ENOUGH WATER! I'M TIRED OF BEING SOAKED ALL THE TIME!
I'LL TAKE ANYTHING BUT MORE RAIN!

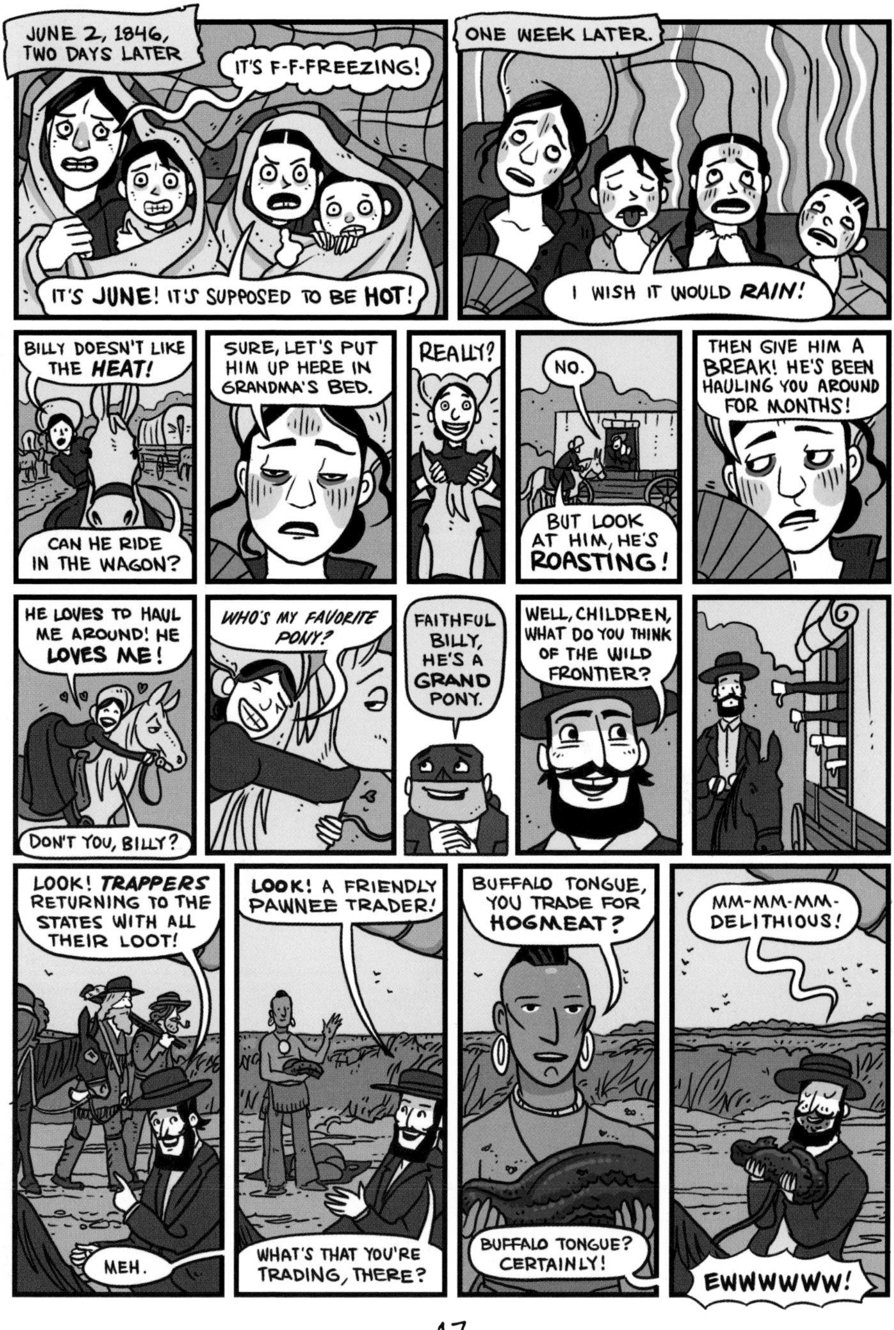
JUNE 2, 1846, TWO DAYS LATER
IT'S F-F-FREEZING!
IT'S JUNE! IT'S SUPPOSED TO BE HOT!
ONE WEEK LATER.
I WISH IT WOULD RAIN!
BILLY DOESN'T LIKE THE HEAT!
CAN HE RIDE IN THE WAGON?
SURE, LET'S PUT HIM UP HERE IN GRANDMA'S BED.
REALLY?
NO.
BUT LOOK AT HIM, HE'S ROASTING!
THEN GIVE HIM A BREAK! HE'S BEEN HAULING YOU AROUND FOR MONTHS!
HE LOVES TO HAUL ME AROUND! HE LOVES ME!
DON'T YOU, BILLY?
WHO'S MY FAVORITE PONY?
FAITHFUL BILLY, HE'S A GRAND PONY.
WELL, CHILDREN, WHAT DO YOU THINK OF THE WILD FRONTIER?
LOOK! TRAPPERS RETURNING TO THE STATES WITH ALL THEIR LOOT!
MEH.
LOOK! A FRIENDLY PAWNEE TRADER!
WHAT'S THAT YOU'RE TRADING, THERE?
BUFFALO TONGUE, YOU TRADE FOR HOGMEAT?
BUFFALO TONGUE? CERTAINLY!
MM-MM-MM-DELITHIOUS!
EWWWWWW!

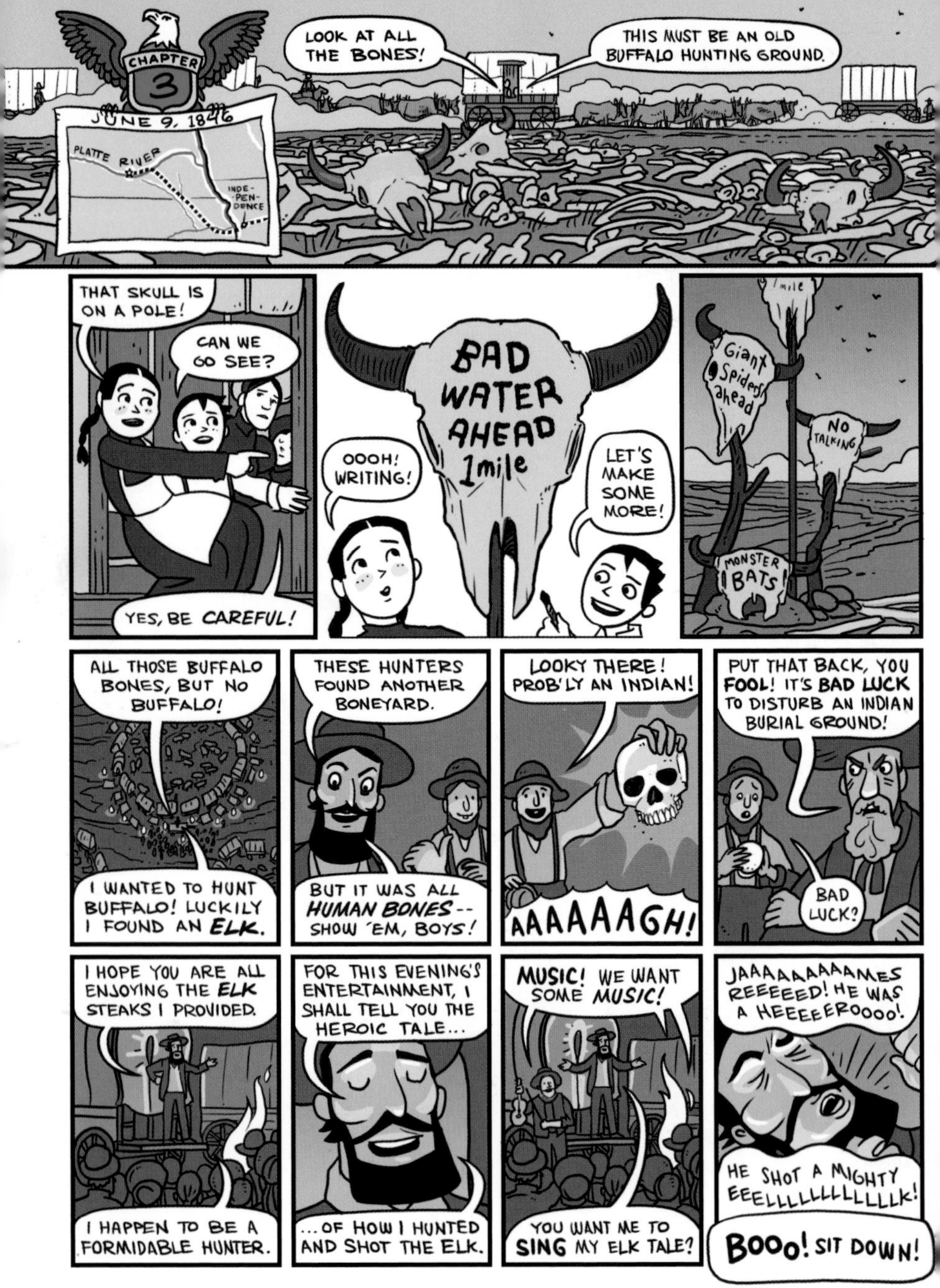
CHAPTER
3
JUNE 9, 1846
PLATTE RIVER
INDE-PEN-DENCE
LOOK AT ALL THE BONES!
THIS MUST BE AN OLD BUFFALO HUNTING GROUND.
THAT SKULL IS ON A POLE!
CAN WE GO SEE?
YES, BE CAREFUL!
BAD WATER AHEAD 1mile
OOOH! WRITING!
LET'S MAKE SOME MORE!
Giant Spiders ahead
NO TALKING
MONSTER BATS!
ALL THOSE BUFFALO BONES, BUT NO BUFFALO!
I WANTED TO HUNT BUFFALO! LUCKILY I FOUND AN ELK.
THESE HUNTERS FOUND ANOTHER BONEYARD.
BUT IT WAS ALL HUMAN BONES-- SHOW 'EM, BOYS!
LOOKY THERE! PROB'LY AN INDIAN!
AAAAAAGH!
PUT THAT BACK, YOU FOOL! IT'S BAD LUCK TO DISTURB AN INDIAN BURIAL GROUND!
BAD LUCK?
I HOPE YOU ARE ALL ENJOYING THE ELK STEAKS I PROVIDED.
I HAPPEN TO BE A FORMIDABLE HUNTER.
FOR THIS EVENING'S ENTERTAINMENT, I SHALL TELL YOU THE HEROIC TALE...
...OF HOW I HUNTED AND SHOT THE ELK.
MUSIC! WE WANT SOME MUSIC!
YOU WANT ME TO SING MY ELK TALE?
JAAAAAAAAAMES REEEEEED! HE WAS A HEEEEEROooo!
HE SHOT A MIGHTY EEELLLLLLLLLLLK!
BOOo! SIT DOWN!

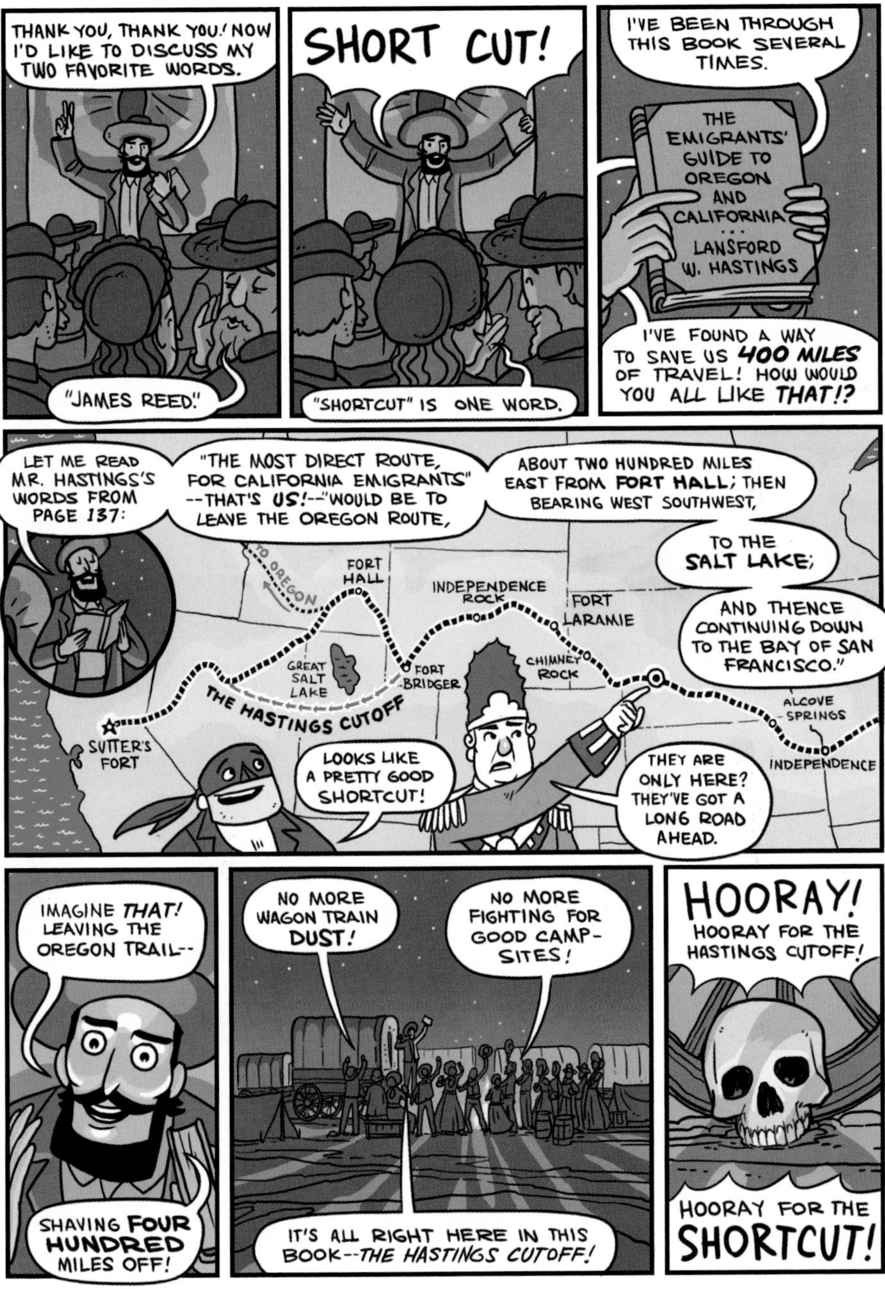
THANK YOU, THANK YOU! NOW I'D LIKE TO DISCUSS MY TWO FAVORITE WORDS.
"JAMES REED."
SHORT CUT!
"SHORTCUT" IS ONE WORD.
I'VE BEEN THROUGH THIS BOOK SEVERAL TIMES.
THE EMIGRANTS' GUIDE TO OREGON AND CALIFORNIA . . . LANSFORD W. HASTINGS
I'VE FOUND A WAY TO SAVE US 400 MILES OF TRAVEL! HOW WOULD YOU ALL LIKE THAT!?
LET ME READ MR. HASTINGS'S WORDS FROM PAGE 137:
"THE MOST DIRECT ROUTE, FOR CALIFORNIA EMIGRANTS" --THAT'S US!--"WOULD BE TO LEAVE THE OREGON ROUTE,
ABOUT TWO HUNDRED MILES EAST FROM FORT HALL; THEN BEARING WEST SOUTHWEST,
TO THE SALT LAKE;
AND THENCE CONTINUING DOWN TO THE BAY OF SAN FRANCISCO."
TO OREGON
FORT HALL
INDEPENDENCE ROCK
FORT LARAMIE
CHIMNEY ROCK
GREAT SALT LAKE
FORT BRIDGER
THE HASTINGS CUTOFF
SUTTER'S FORT
ALCOVE SPRINGS
INDEPENDENCE
LOOKS LIKE A PRETTY GOOD SHORTCUT!
THEY ARE ONLY HERE? THEY'VE GOT A LONG ROAD AHEAD.
IMAGINE THAT! LEAVING THE OREGON TRAIL--
SHAVING FOUR HUNDRED MILES OFF!
NO MORE WAGON TRAIN DUST!
NO MORE FIGHTING FOR GOOD CAMP-SITES!
IT'S ALL RIGHT HERE IN THIS BOOK--THE HASTINGS CUTOFF!
HOORAY!
HOORAY FOR THE HASTINGS CUTOFF!
HOORAY FOR THE SHORTCUT!

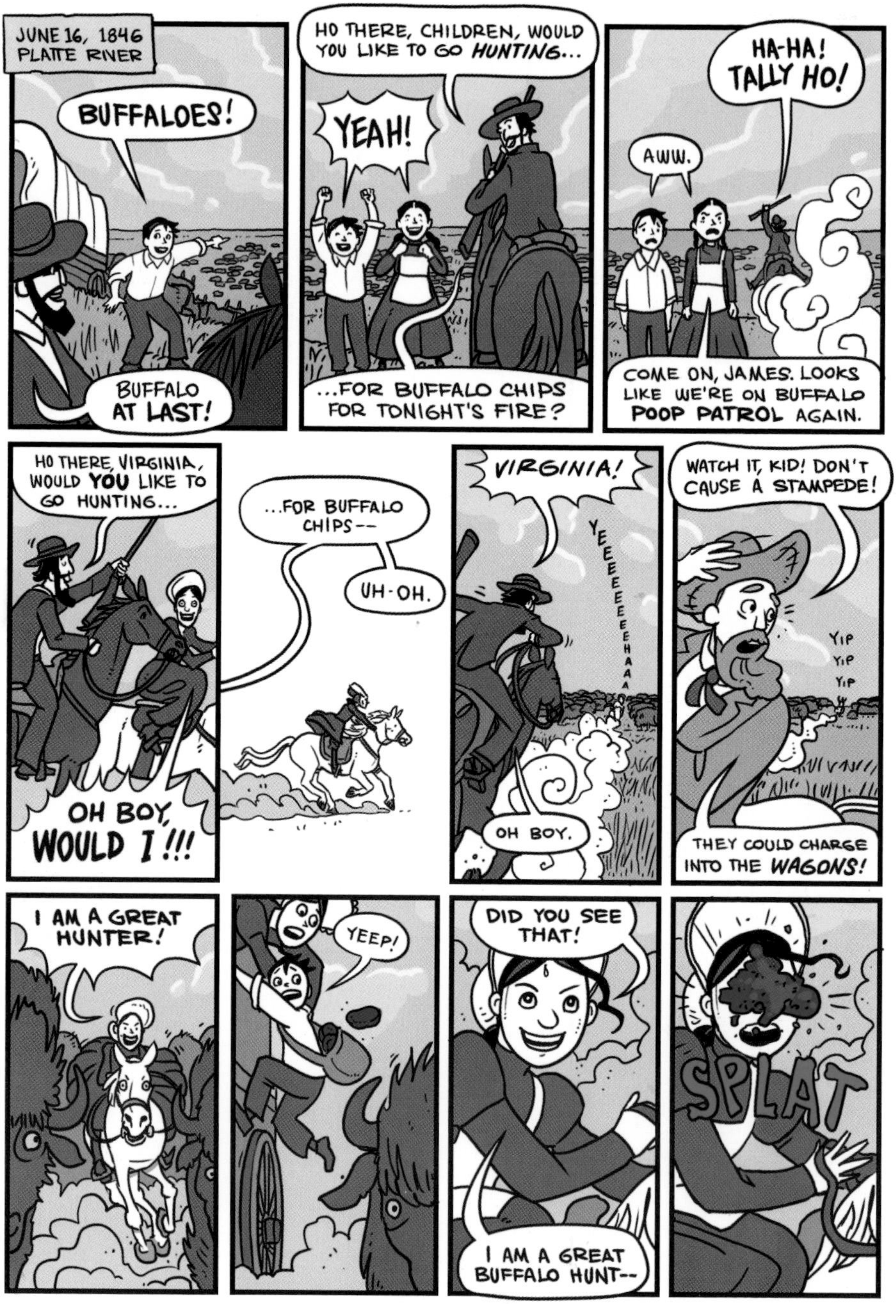
JUNE 16, 1846
PLATTE RIVER
BUFFALOES!
BUFFALO AT LAST!
HO THERE, CHILDREN, WOULD YOU LIKE TO GO HUNTING...
YEAH!
...FOR BUFFALO CHIPS FOR TONIGHT'S FIRE?
HA-HA! TALLY HO!
AWW.
COME ON, JAMES. LOOKS LIKE WE'RE ON BUFFALO POOP PATROL AGAIN.
HO THERE, VIRGINIA, WOULD YOU LIKE TO GO HUNTING...
...FOR BUFFALO CHIPS--
UH-OH.
OH BOY, WOULD I!!!
VIRGINIA!
YEEEEEEEEEHAAA
OH BOY.
WATCH IT, KID! DON'T CAUSE A STAMPEDE!
YIP
YIP
YIP
THEY COULD CHARGE INTO THE WAGONS!
I AM A GREAT HUNTER!
YEEP!
DID YOU SEE THAT!
I AM A GREAT BUFFALO HUNT--
SPLAT

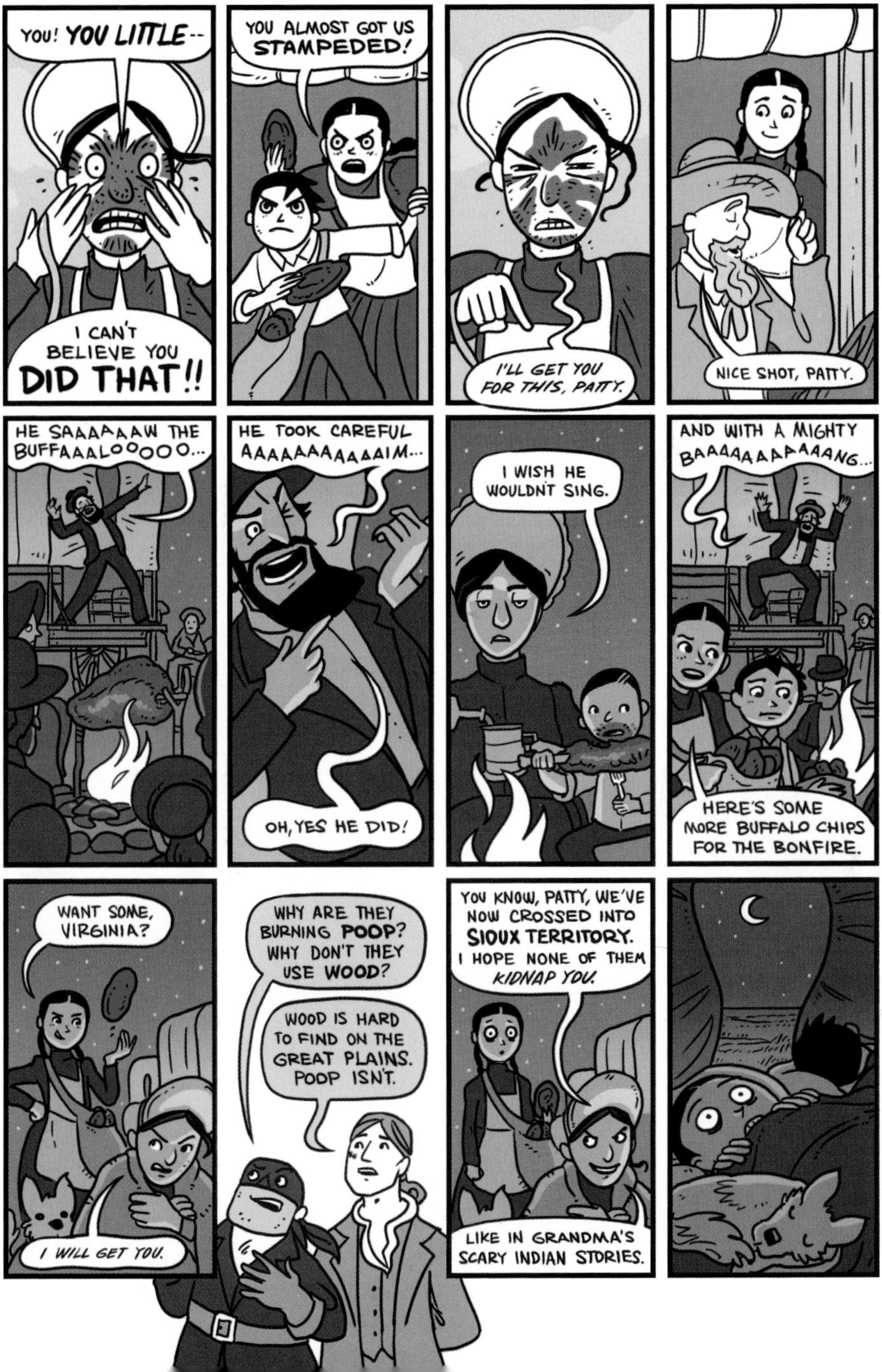
YOU! YOU LITTLE--
I CAN'T BELIEVE YOU DID THAT!!
YOU ALMOST GOT US STAMPEDED!
I'LL GET YOU FOR THIS, PATTY.
NICE SHOT, PATTY.
HE SAAAAAAW THE BUFFAAALOOOOO...
HE TOOK CAREFUL AAAAAAAAAAAIM...
OH, YES HE DID!
I WISH HE WOULDN'T SING.
AND WITH A MIGHTY BAAAAAAAAAAANG...
HERE'S SOME MORE BUFFALO CHIPS FOR THE BONFIRE.
WANT SOME, VIRGINIA?
I WILL GET YOU.
WHY ARE THEY BURNING POOP? WHY DON'T THEY USE WOOD?
WOOD IS HARD TO FIND ON THE GREAT PLAINS. POOP ISN'T.
YOU KNOW, PATTY, WE'VE NOW CROSSED INTO SIOUX TERRITORY. I HOPE NONE OF THEM KIDNAP YOU.
LIKE IN GRANDMA'S SCARY INDIAN STORIES.

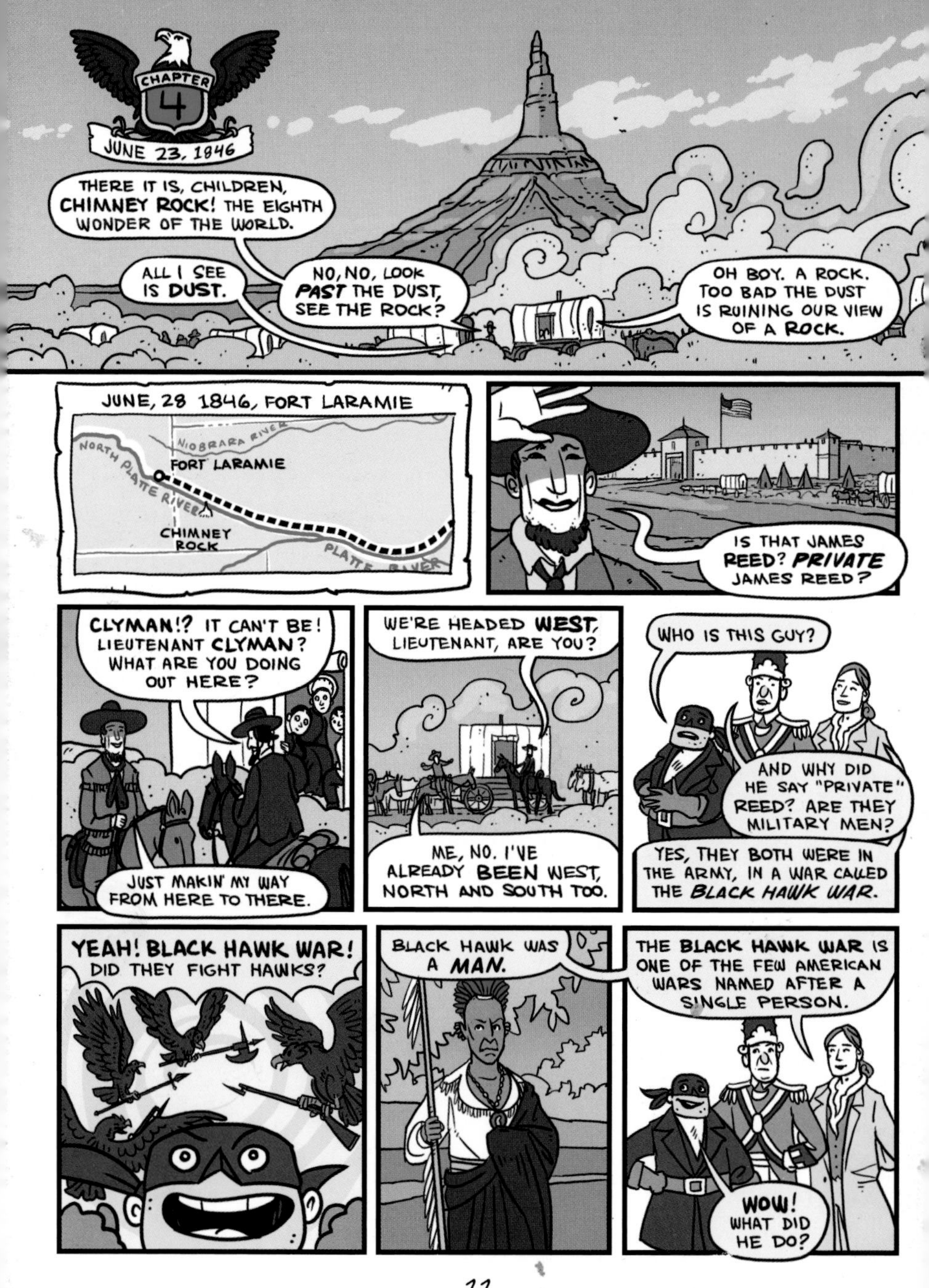
CHAPTER 4
JUNE 23, 1846
THERE IT IS, CHILDREN, CHIMNEY ROCK! THE EIGHTH WONDER OF THE WORLD.
ALL I SEE IS DUST.
NO, NO, LOOK PAST THE DUST, SEE THE ROCK?
OH BOY. A ROCK. TOO BAD THE DUST IS RUINING OUR VIEW OF A ROCK.
JUNE, 28 1846, FORT LARAMIE
NIOBRARA RIVER
NORTH PLATTE RIVER
FORT LARAMIE
CHIMNEY ROCK
PLATTE RIVER
IS THAT JAMES REED? PRIVATE JAMES REED?
CLYMAN!? IT CAN'T BE! LIEUTENANT CLYMAN? WHAT ARE YOU DOING OUT HERE?
JUST MAKIN' MY WAY FROM HERE TO THERE.
WE'RE HEADED WEST, LIEUTENANT, ARE YOU?
ME, NO. I'VE ALREADY BEEN WEST, NORTH AND SOUTH TOO.
WHO IS THIS GUY?
AND WHY DID HE SAY "PRIVATE" REED? ARE THEY MILITARY MEN?
YES, THEY BOTH WERE IN THE ARMY, IN A WAR CALLED THE BLACK HAWK WAR.
YEAH! BLACK HAWK WAR! DID THEY FIGHT HAWKS?
BLACK HAWK WAS A MAN.
THE BLACK HAWK WAR IS ONE OF THE FEW AMERICAN WARS NAMED AFTER A SINGLE PERSON.
WOW! WHAT DID HE DO?

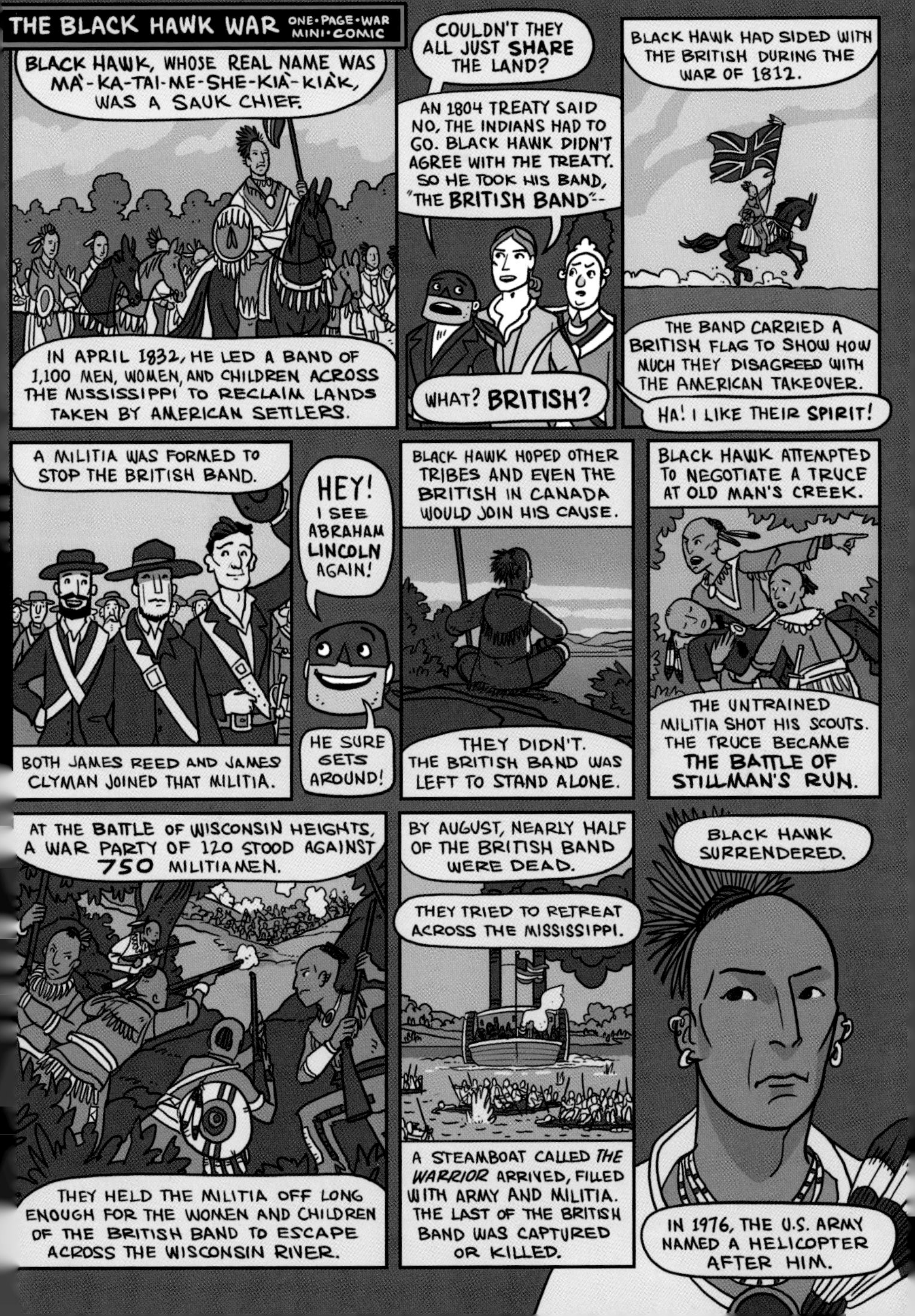
THE BLACK HAWK WAR
ONE•PAGE•WAR MINI•COMIC
BLACK HAWK, WHOSE REAL NAME WAS MÀ-KA-TAI-ME-SHE-KIÀ-KIÀK, WAS A SAUK CHIEF.
IN APRIL 1832, HE LED A BAND OF 1,100 MEN, WOMEN, AND CHILDREN ACROSS THE MISSISSIPPI TO RECLAIM LANDS TAKEN BY AMERICAN SETTLERS.
COULDN'T THEY ALL JUST SHARE THE LAND?
AN 1804 TREATY SAID NO, THE INDIANS HAD TO GO. BLACK HAWK DIDN'T AGREE WITH THE TREATY. SO HE TOOK HIS BAND, "THE BRITISH BAND"-
WHAT? BRITISH?
BLACK HAWK HAD SIDED WITH THE BRITISH DURING THE WAR OF 1812.
THE BAND CARRIED A BRITISH FLAG TO SHOW HOW MUCH THEY DISAGREED WITH THE AMERICAN TAKEOVER.
HA! I LIKE THEIR SPIRIT!
A MILITIA WAS FORMED TO STOP THE BRITISH BAND.
BOTH JAMES REED AND JAMES CLYMAN JOINED THAT MILITIA.
HEY! I SEE ABRAHAM LINCOLN AGAIN!
HE SURE GETS AROUND!
BLACK HAWK HOPED OTHER TRIBES AND EVEN THE BRITISH IN CANADA WOULD JOIN HIS CAUSE.
THEY DIDN'T. THE BRITISH BAND WAS LEFT TO STAND ALONE.
BLACK HAWK ATTEMPTED TO NEGOTIATE A TRUCE AT OLD MAN'S CREEK.
THE UNTRAINED MILITIA SHOT HIS SCOUTS. THE TRUCE BECAME THE BATTLE OF STILLMAN'S RUN.
AT THE BATTLE OF WISCONSIN HEIGHTS, A WAR PARTY OF 120 STOOD AGAINST 750 MILITIAMEN.
THEY HELD THE MILITIA OFF LONG ENOUGH FOR THE WOMEN AND CHILDREN OF THE BRITISH BAND TO ESCAPE ACROSS THE WISCONSIN RIVER.
BY AUGUST, NEARLY HALF OF THE BRITISH BAND WERE DEAD.
THEY TRIED TO RETREAT ACROSS THE MISSISSIPPI.
A STEAMBOAT CALLED THE WARRIOR ARRIVED, FILLED WITH ARMY AND MILITIA. THE LAST OF THE BRITISH BAND WAS CAPTURED OR KILLED.
BLACK HAWK SURRENDERED.
IN 1976, THE U.S. ARMY NAMED A HELICOPTER AFTER HIM.

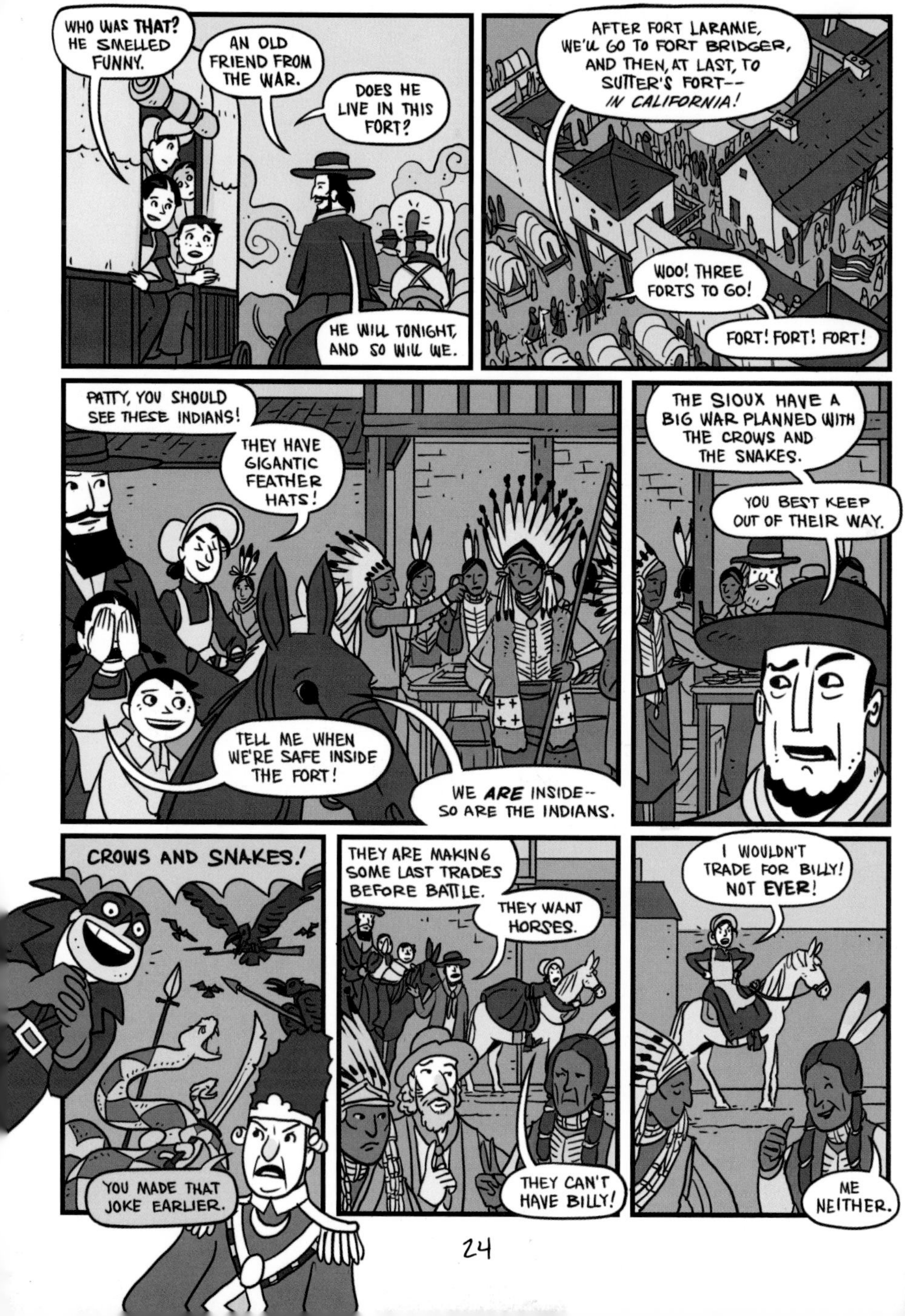

WHO WAS THAT? HE SMELLED FUNNY.
AN OLD FRIEND FROM THE WAR.
DOES HE LIVE IN THIS FORT?
HE WILL TONIGHT, AND SO WILL WE.
AFTER FORT LARAMIE, WE'LL GO TO FORT BRIDGER, AND THEN, AT LAST, TO SUTTER'S FORT-- IN CALIFORNIA!
WOO! THREE FORTS TO GO!
FORT! FORT! FORT!
PATTY, YOU SHOULD SEE THESE INDIANS!
THEY HAVE GIGANTIC FEATHER HATS!
TELL ME WHEN WE'RE SAFE INSIDE THE FORT!
WE ARE INSIDE-- SO ARE THE INDIANS.
THE SIOUX HAVE A BIG WAR PLANNED WITH THE CROWS AND THE SNAKES.
YOU BEST KEEP OUT OF THEIR WAY.
CROWS AND SNAKES!
YOU MADE THAT JOKE EARLIER.
THEY ARE MAKING SOME LAST TRADES BEFORE BATTLE.
THEY WANT HORSES.
THEY CAN'T HAVE BILLY!
I WOULDN'T TRADE FOR BILLY! NOT EVER!
ME NEITHER.

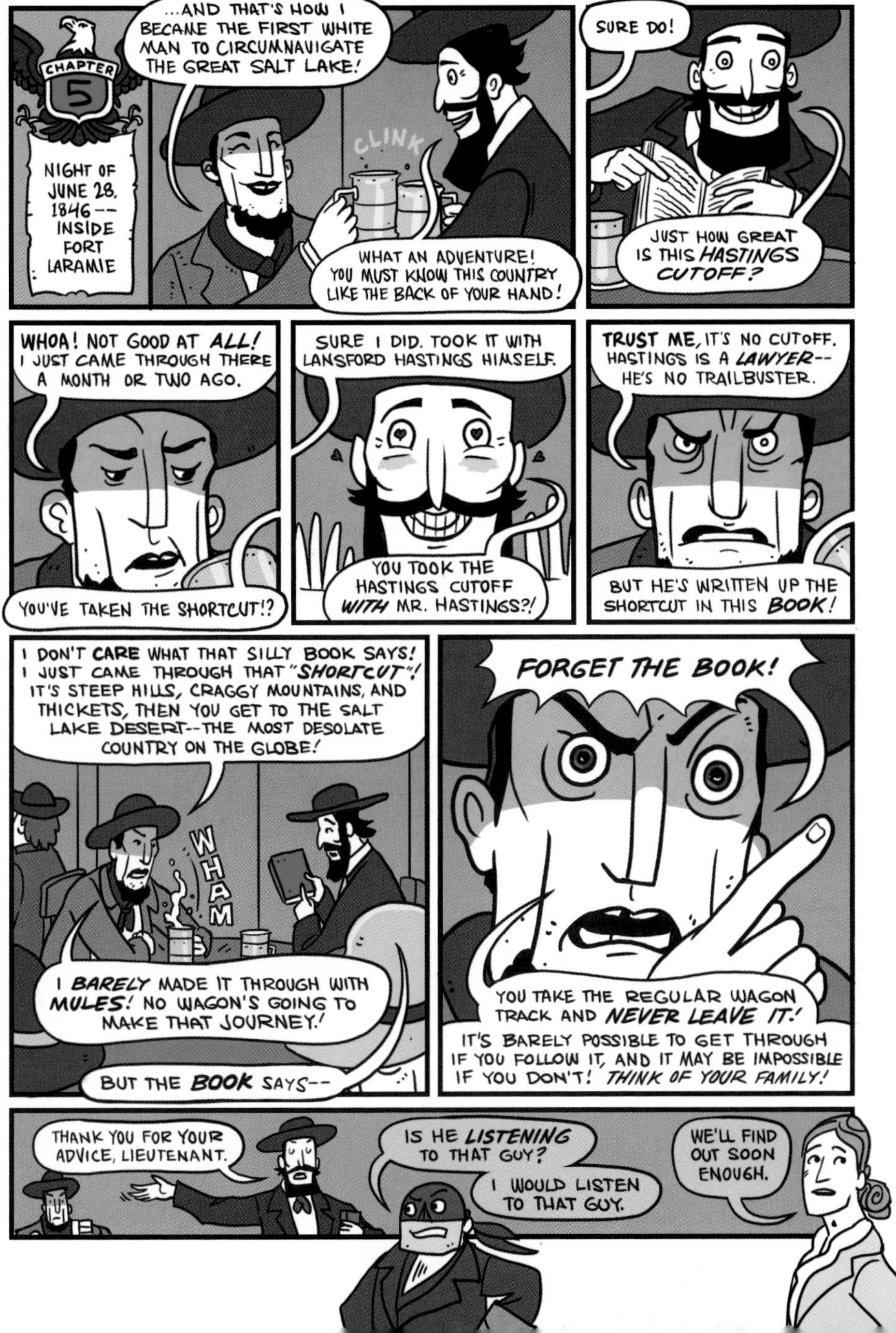
CHAPTER 5
NIGHT OF JUNE 28, 1846-- INSIDE FORT LARAMIE
...AND THAT'S HOW I BECAME THE FIRST WHITE MAN TO CIRCUMNAVIGATE THE GREAT SALT LAKE!
CLINK
WHAT AN ADVENTURE! YOU MUST KNOW THIS COUNTRY LIKE THE BACK OF YOUR HAND!
SURE DO!
JUST HOW GREAT IS THIS HASTINGS CUTOFF?
WHOA! NOT GOOD AT ALL! I JUST CAME THROUGH THERE A MONTH OR TWO AGO.
YOU'VE TAKEN THE SHORTCUT!?
SURE I DID. TOOK IT WITH LANSFORD HASTINGS HIMSELF.
YOU TOOK THE HASTINGS CUTOFF WITH MR. HASTINGS?!
TRUST ME, IT'S NO CUTOFF. HASTINGS IS A LAWYER-- HE'S NO TRAILBUSTER.
BUT HE'S WRITTEN UP THE SHORTCUT IN THIS BOOK!
I DON'T CARE WHAT THAT SILLY BOOK SAYS! I JUST CAME THROUGH THAT "SHORTCUT"! IT'S STEEP HILLS, CRAGGY MOUNTAINS, AND THICKETS, THEN YOU GET TO THE SALT LAKE DESERT--THE MOST DESOLATE COUNTRY ON THE GLOBE!
WHAM
I BARELY MADE IT THROUGH WITH MULES! NO WAGON'S GOING TO MAKE THAT JOURNEY!
BUT THE BOOK SAYS--
FORGET THE BOOK!
YOU TAKE THE REGULAR WAGON TRACK AND NEVER LEAVE IT!
IT'S BARELY POSSIBLE TO GET THROUGH IF YOU FOLLOW IT, AND IT MAY BE IMPOSSIBLE IF YOU DON'T! THINK OF YOUR FAMILY!
THANK YOU FOR YOUR ADVICE, LIEUTENANT.
IS HE LISTENING TO THAT GUY?
I WOULD LISTEN TO THAT GUY.
WE'LL FIND OUT SOON ENOUGH.

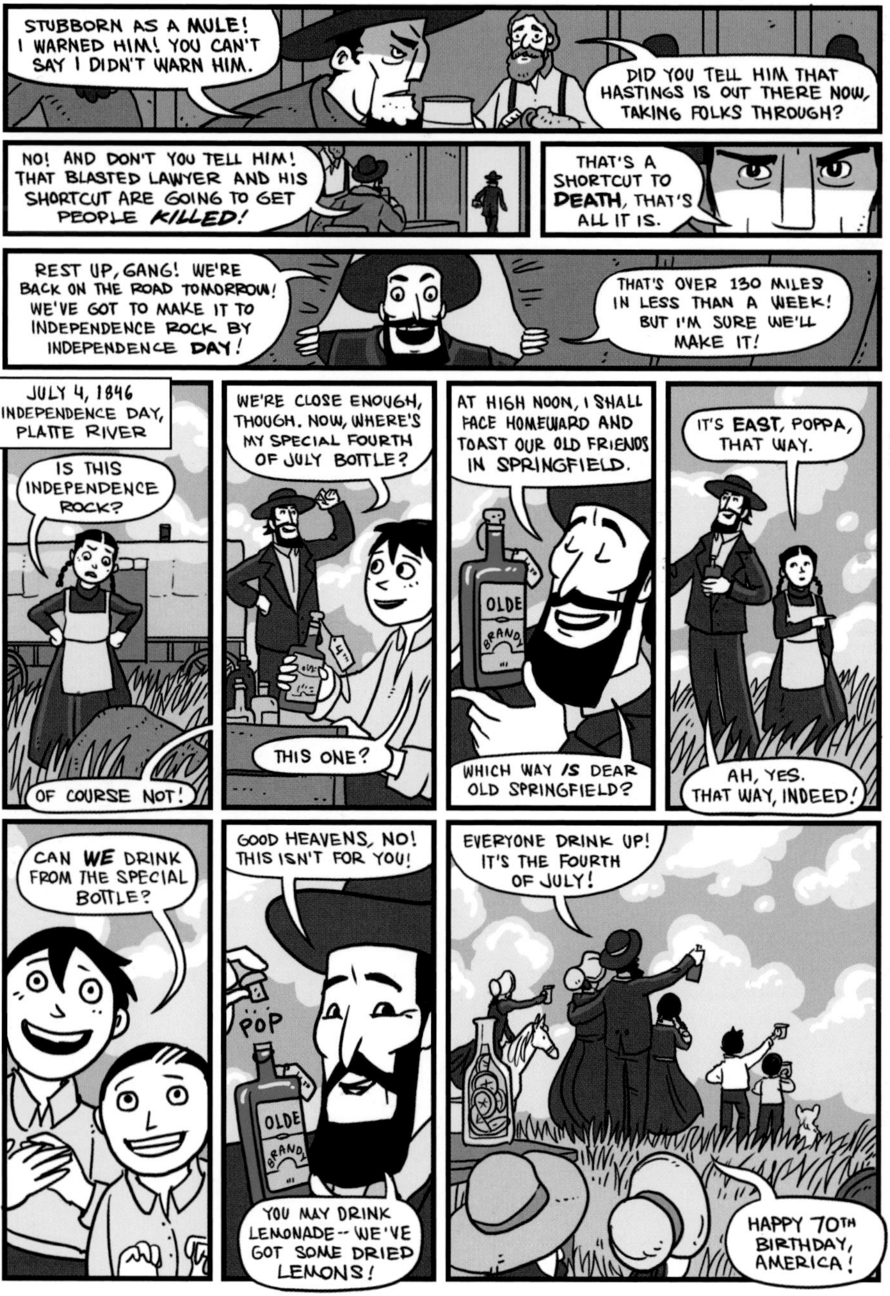
STUBBORN AS A MULE! I WARNED HIM! YOU CAN'T SAY I DIDN'T WARN HIM.
DID YOU TELL HIM THAT HASTINGS IS OUT THERE NOW, TAKING FOLKS THROUGH?
NO! AND DON'T YOU TELL HIM! THAT BLASTED LAWYER AND HIS SHORTCUT ARE GOING TO GET PEOPLE KILLED!
THAT'S A SHORTCUT TO DEATH, THAT'S ALL IT IS.
REST UP, GANG! WE'RE BACK ON THE ROAD TOMORROW! WE'VE GOT TO MAKE IT TO INDEPENDENCE ROCK BY INDEPENDENCE DAY!
THAT'S OVER 130 MILES IN LESS THAN A WEEK! BUT I'M SURE WE'LL MAKE IT!
JULY 4, 1846 INDEPENDENCE DAY, PLATTE RIVER
IS THIS INDEPENDENCE ROCK?
OF COURSE NOT!
WE'RE CLOSE ENOUGH, THOUGH. NOW, WHERE'S MY SPECIAL FOURTH OF JULY BOTTLE?
THIS ONE?
AT HIGH NOON, I SHALL FACE HOMEWARD AND TOAST OUR OLD FRIENDS IN SPRINGFIELD.
OLDE BRANDY
WHICH WAY IS DEAR OLD SPRINGFIELD?
IT'S EAST, POPPA, THAT WAY.
AH, YES. THAT WAY, INDEED!
CAN WE DRINK FROM THE SPECIAL BOTTLE?
GOOD HEAVENS, NO! THIS ISN'T FOR YOU!
POP
OLDE BRANDY
YOU MAY DRINK LEMONADE-- WE'VE GOT SOME DRIED LEMONS!
EVERYONE DRINK UP! IT'S THE FOURTH OF JULY!
HAPPY 70TH BIRTHDAY, AMERICA!

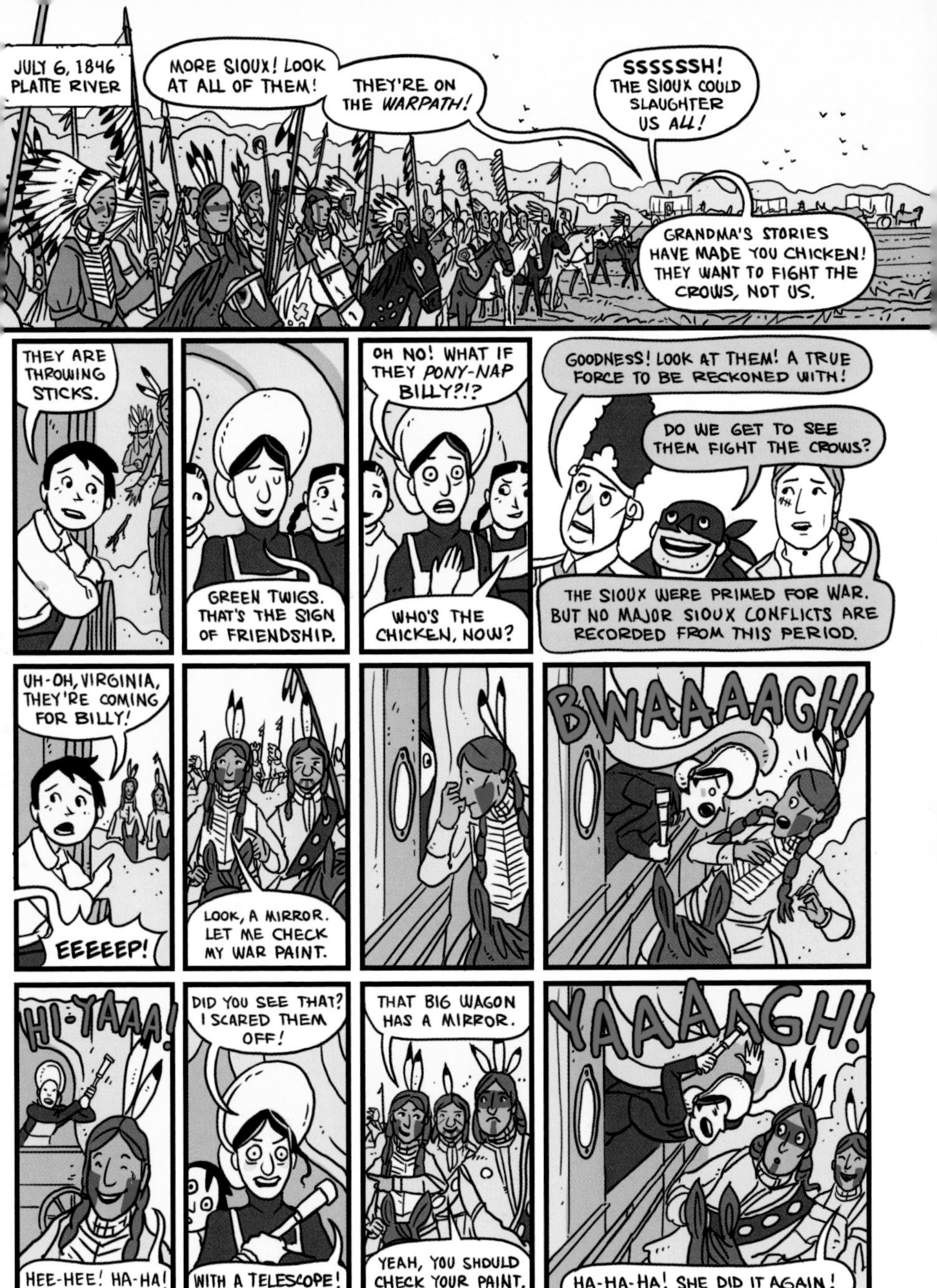
JULY 6, 1846
PLATTE RIVER
MORE SIOUX! LOOK AT ALL OF THEM!
THEY'RE ON THE WARPATH!
SSSSSSH! THE SIOUX COULD SLAUGHTER US ALL!
GRANDMA'S STORIES HAVE MADE YOU CHICKEN! THEY WANT TO FIGHT THE CROWS, NOT US.
THEY ARE THROWING STICKS.
GREEN TWIGS. THAT'S THE SIGN OF FRIENDSHIP.
OH NO! WHAT IF THEY PONY-NAP BILLY?!?
WHO'S THE CHICKEN, NOW?
GOODNESS! LOOK AT THEM! A TRUE FORCE TO BE RECKONED WITH!
DO WE GET TO SEE THEM FIGHT THE CROWS?
THE SIOUX WERE PRIMED FOR WAR. BUT NO MAJOR SIOUX CONFLICTS ARE RECORDED FROM THIS PERIOD.
UH-OH, VIRGINIA, THEY'RE COMING FOR BILLY!
EEEEEP!
LOOK, A MIRROR. LET ME CHECK MY WAR PAINT.
BWAAAAAGH!
HI-YAAA!
HEE-HEE! HA-HA!
DID YOU SEE THAT? I SCARED THEM OFF!
WITH A TELESCOPE!
THAT BIG WAGON HAS A MIRROR.
YEAH, YOU SHOULD CHECK YOUR PAINT.
YAAAAGH!
HA-HA-HA! SHE DID IT AGAIN!

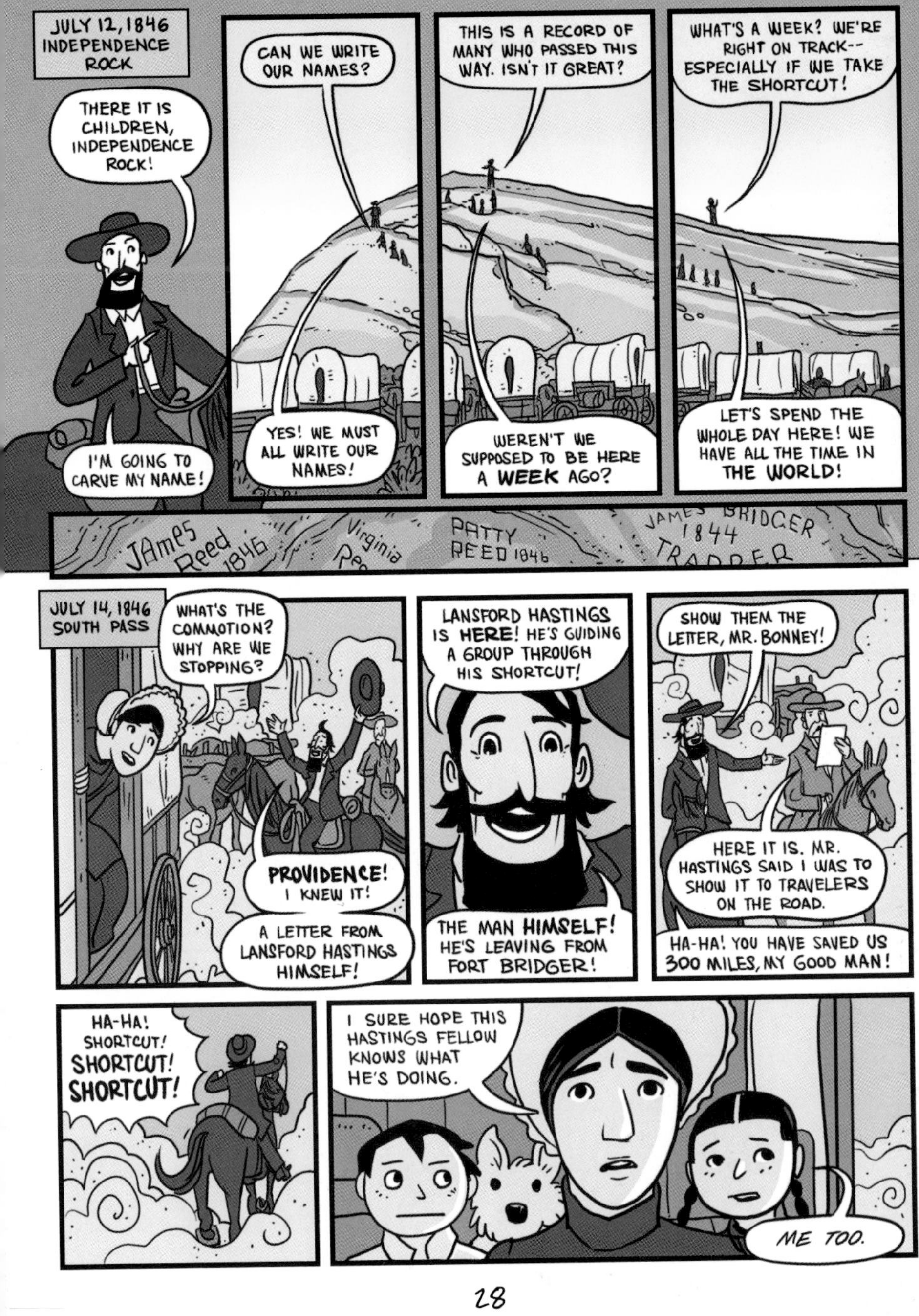

JULY 12, 1846 INDEPENDENCE ROCK
THERE IT IS CHILDREN, INDEPENDENCE ROCK!
I'M GOING TO CARVE MY NAME!
CAN WE WRITE OUR NAMES?
YES! WE MUST ALL WRITE OUR NAMES!
THIS IS A RECORD OF MANY WHO PASSED THIS WAY. ISN'T IT GREAT?
WEREN'T WE SUPPOSED TO BE HERE A WEEK AGO?
WHAT'S A WEEK? WE'RE RIGHT ON TRACK-- ESPECIALLY IF WE TAKE THE SHORTCUT!
LET'S SPEND THE WHOLE DAY HERE! WE HAVE ALL THE TIME IN THE WORLD!
JAmes Reed 1846
Virginia Ree
PATTY REED 1846
JAMES BRIDGER 1844 TRAPPER
JULY 14, 1846 SOUTH PASS
WHAT'S THE COMMOTION? WHY ARE WE STOPPING?
PROVIDENCE! I KNEW IT!
A LETTER FROM LANSFORD HASTINGS HIMSELF!
LANSFORD HASTINGS IS HERE! HE'S GUIDING A GROUP THROUGH HIS SHORTCUT!
THE MAN HIMSELF! HE'S LEAVING FROM FORT BRIDGER!
SHOW THEM THE LETTER, MR. BONNEY!
HERE IT IS. MR. HASTINGS SAID I WAS TO SHOW IT TO TRAVELERS ON THE ROAD.
HA-HA! YOU HAVE SAVED US 300 MILES, MY GOOD MAN!
HA-HA! SHORTCUT! SHORTCUT! SHORTCUT!
I SURE HOPE THIS HASTINGS FELLOW KNOWS WHAT HE'S DOING.
ME TOO.

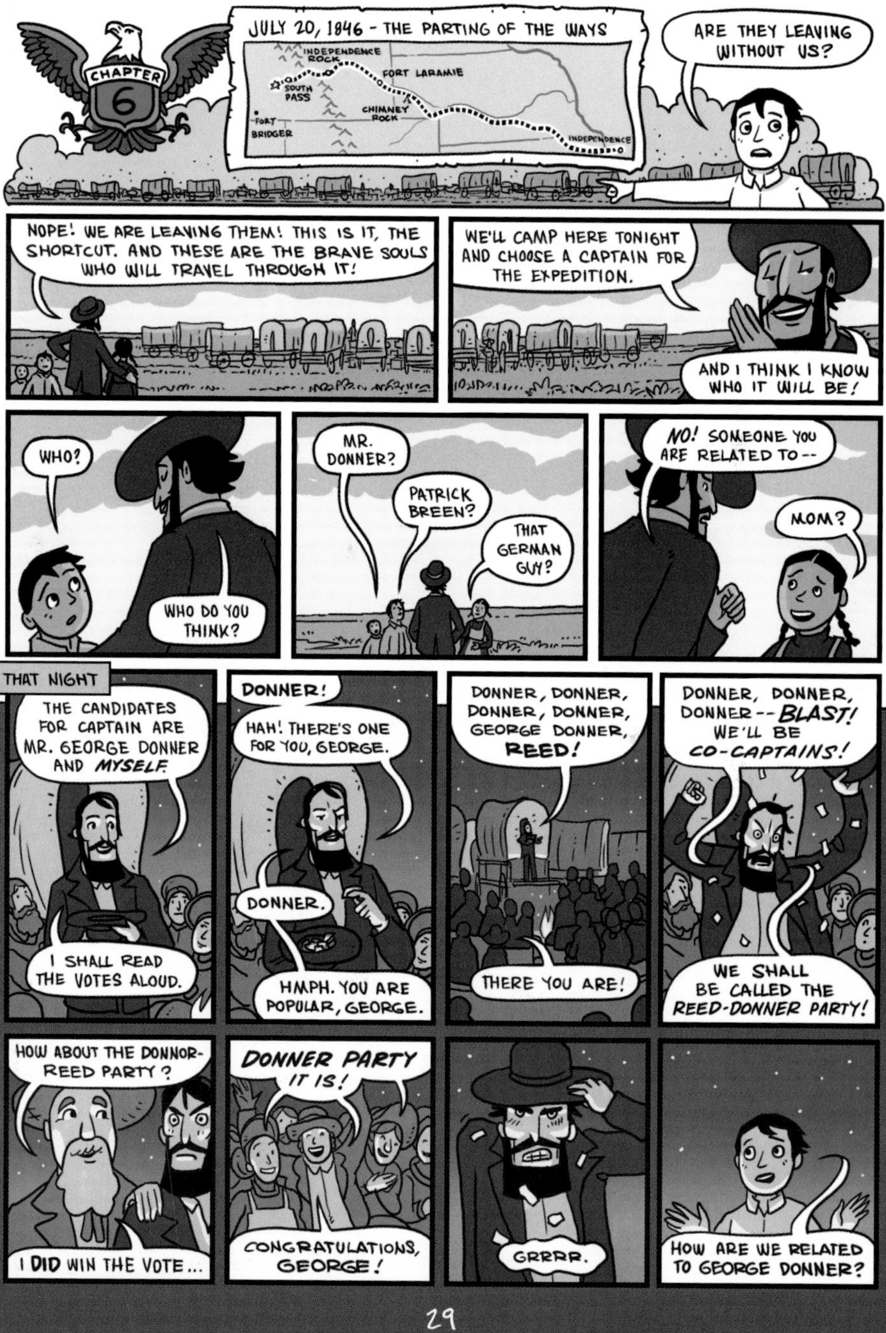
CHAPTER 6
JULY 20, 1846 - THE PARTING OF THE WAYS
INDEPENDENCE ROCK
FORT LARAMIE
SOUTH PASS
CHIMNEY ROCK
FORT BRIDGER
INDEPENDENCE
ARE THEY LEAVING WITHOUT US?
NOPE! WE ARE LEAVING THEM! THIS IS IT, THE SHORTCUT. AND THESE ARE THE BRAVE SOULS WHO WILL TRAVEL THROUGH IT!
WE'LL CAMP HERE TONIGHT AND CHOOSE A CAPTAIN FOR THE EXPEDITION.
AND I THINK I KNOW WHO IT WILL BE!
WHO?
WHO DO YOU THINK?
MR. DONNER?
PATRICK BREEN?
THAT GERMAN GUY?
NO! SOMEONE YOU ARE RELATED TO--
MOM?
THAT NIGHT
THE CANDIDATES FOR CAPTAIN ARE MR. GEORGE DONNER AND MYSELF.
I SHALL READ THE VOTES ALOUD.
DONNER!
HAH! THERE'S ONE FOR YOU, GEORGE.
DONNER.
HMPH. YOU ARE POPULAR, GEORGE.
DONNER, DONNER, DONNER, DONNER, GEORGE DONNER, REED!
THERE YOU ARE!
DONNER, DONNER, DONNER--BLAST! WE'LL BE CO-CAPTAINS!
WE SHALL BE CALLED THE REED-DONNER PARTY!
HOW ABOUT THE DONNOR-REED PARTY?
I DID WIN THE VOTE...
DONNER PARTY IT IS!
CONGRATULATIONS, GEORGE!
GRRRR.
HOW ARE WE RELATED TO GEORGE DONNER?

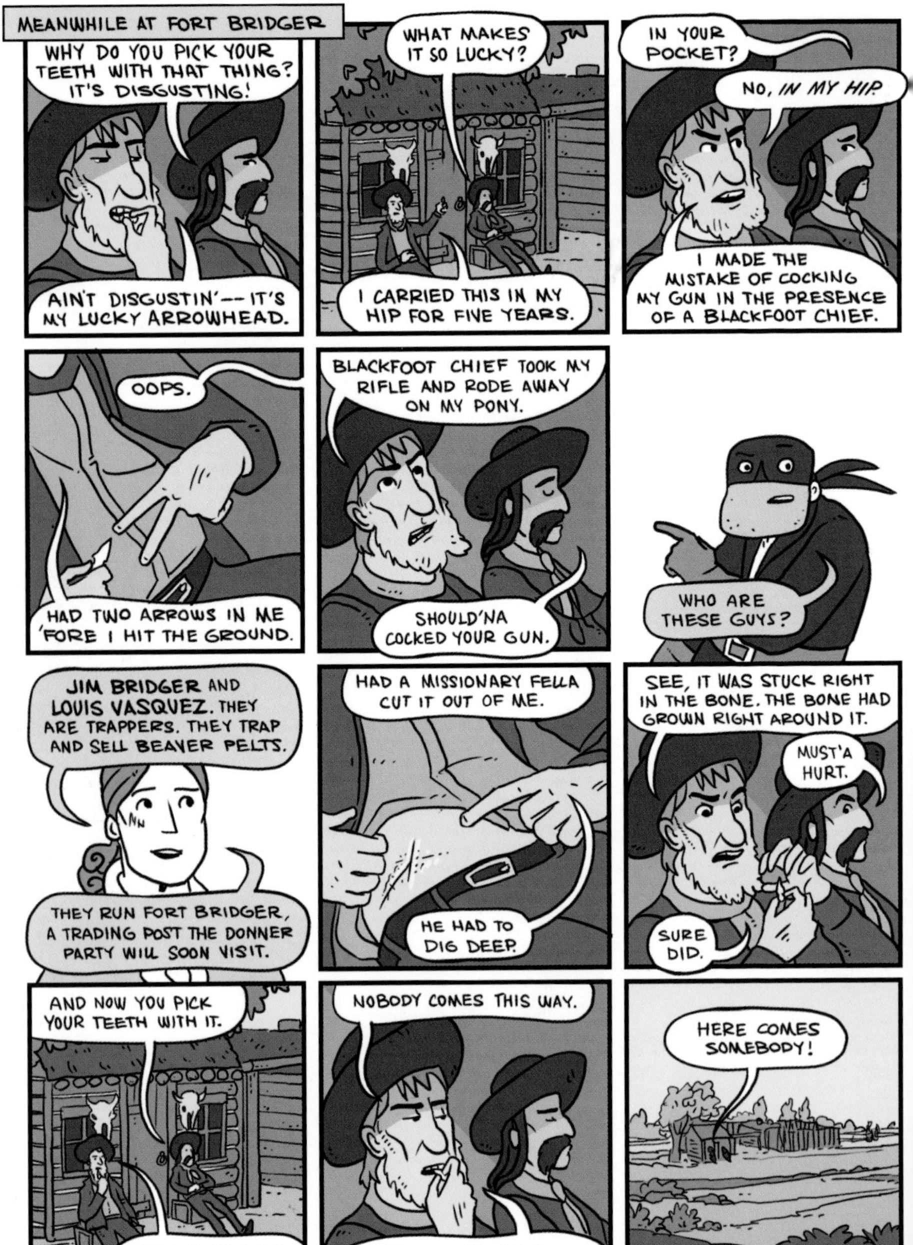
MEANWHILE AT FORT BRIDGER
WHY DO YOU PICK YOUR TEETH WITH THAT THING? IT'S DISGUSTING!
AIN'T DISGUSTIN'-- IT'S MY LUCKY ARROWHEAD.
WHAT MAKES IT SO LUCKY?
I CARRIED THIS IN MY HIP FOR FIVE YEARS.
IN YOUR POCKET?
NO, *IN MY HIP.*
I MADE THE MISTAKE OF COCKING MY GUN IN THE PRESENCE OF A BLACKFOOT CHIEF.
OOPS.
HAD TWO ARROWS IN ME 'FORE I HIT THE GROUND.
BLACKFOOT CHIEF TOOK MY RIFLE AND RODE AWAY ON MY PONY.
SHOULD'NA COCKED YOUR GUN.
WHO ARE THESE GUYS?
JIM BRIDGER AND LOUIS VASQUEZ. THEY ARE TRAPPERS. THEY TRAP AND SELL BEAVER PELTS.
THEY RUN FORT BRIDGER, A TRADING POST THE DONNER PARTY WILL SOON VISIT.
HAD A MISSIONARY FELLA CUT IT OUT OF ME.
HE HAD TO DIG DEEP.
SEE, IT WAS STUCK RIGHT IN THE BONE. THE BONE HAD GROWN RIGHT AROUND IT.
MUST'A HURT.
SURE DID.
AND NOW YOU PICK YOUR TEETH WITH IT.
AIN'T MUCH ELSE TO DO 'ROUND HERE.
NOBODY COMES THIS WAY.
WE SHOULD'A BUILT CLOSER TO THE MAIN ROUTE.
HERE COMES SOMEBODY!

31

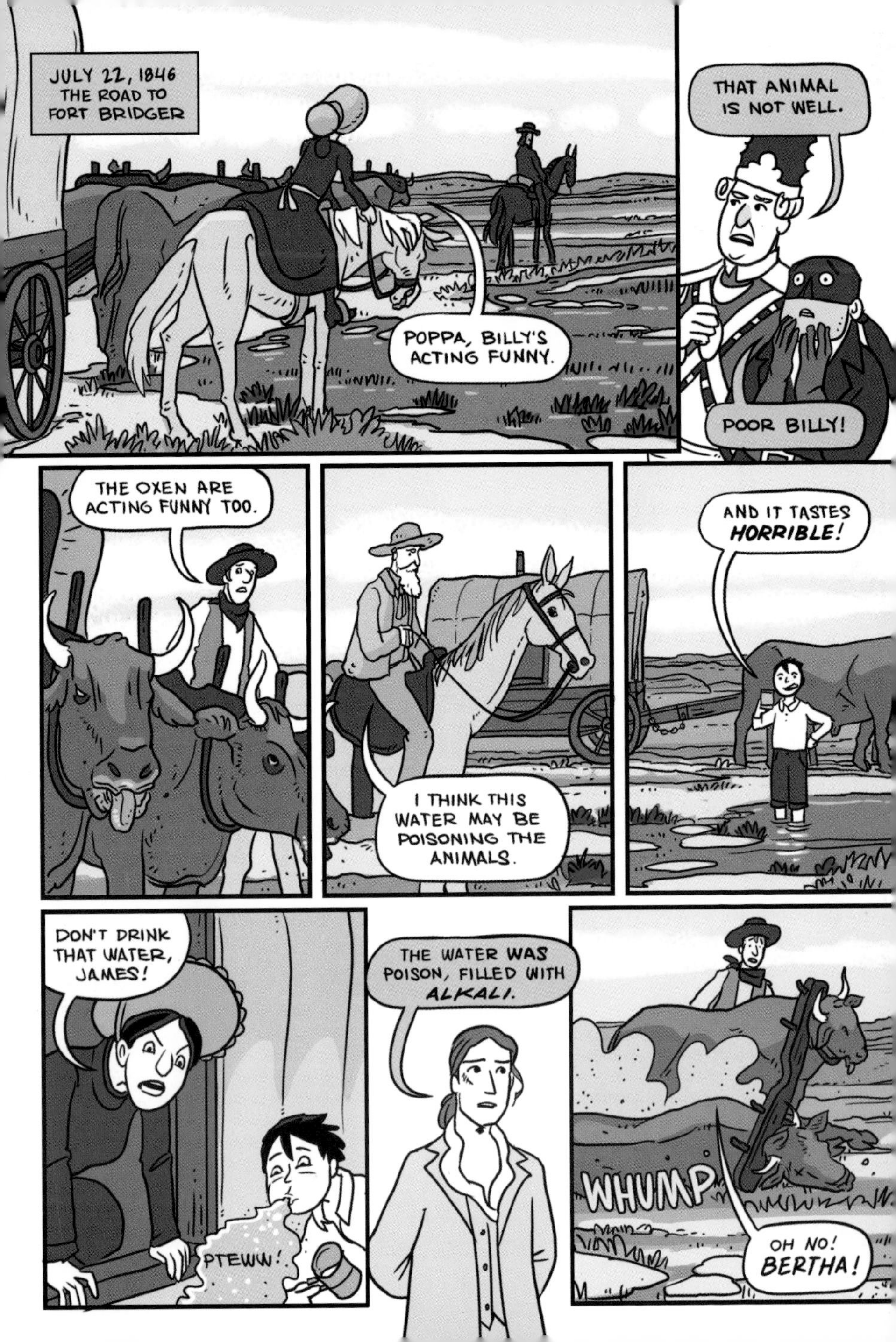
JULY 22, 1846 THE ROAD TO FORT BRIDGER
POPPA, BILLY'S ACTING FUNNY.
THAT ANIMAL IS NOT WELL.
POOR BILLY!
THE OXEN ARE ACTING FUNNY TOO.
I THINK THIS WATER MAY BE POISONING THE ANIMALS.
AND IT TASTES *HORRIBLE*!
DON'T DRINK THAT WATER, JAMES!
PTEWW!
THE WATER WAS POISON, FILLED WITH *ALKALI*.
WHUMP
OH NO! BERTHA!

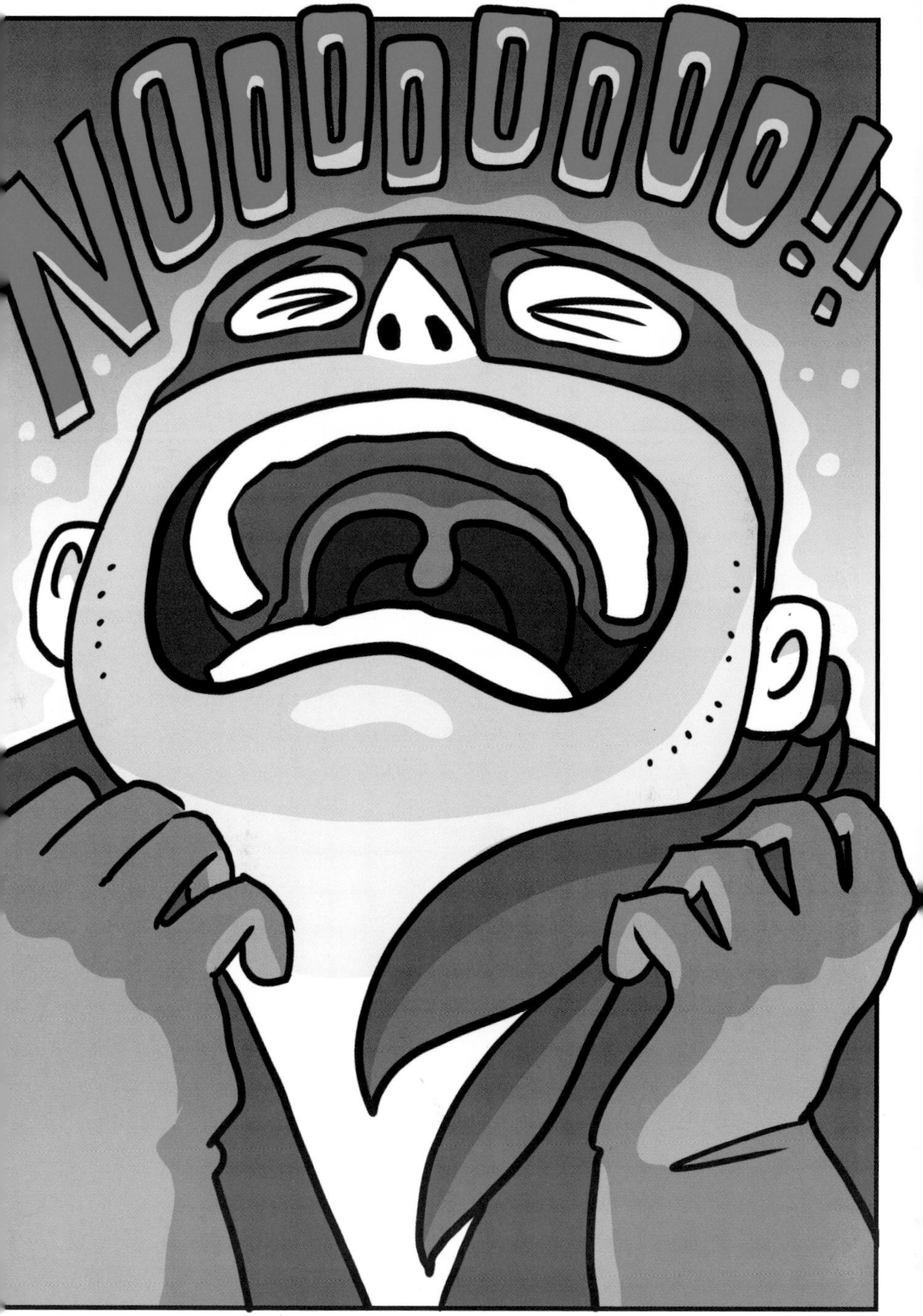
NOOOOOOOOO!!!

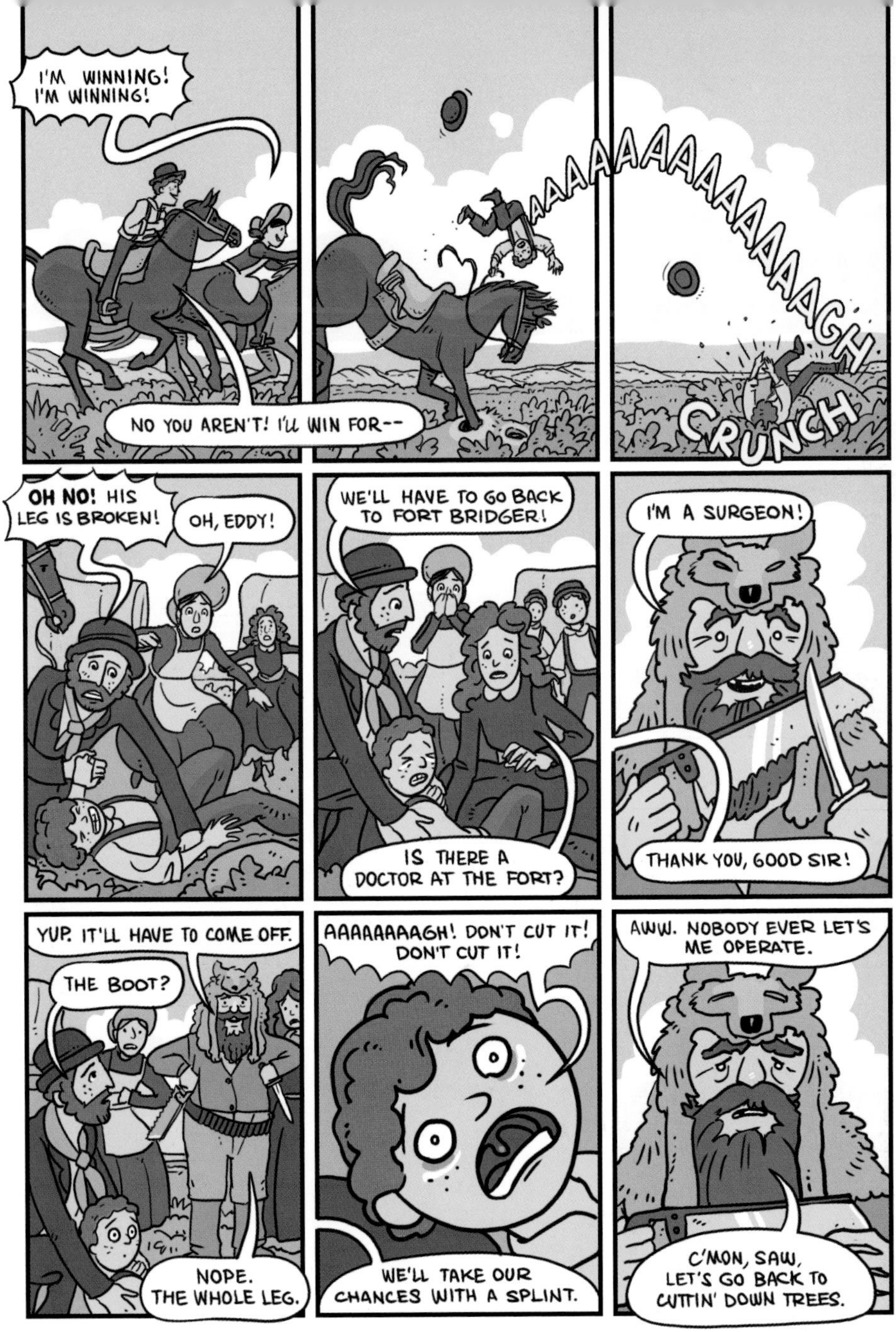
I'M WINNING! I'M WINNING!
NO YOU AREN'T! I'LL WIN FOR--
AAAAAAAAAAAAAAAAAAGH
CRUNCH
OH NO! HIS LEG IS BROKEN!
OH, EDDY!
WE'LL HAVE TO GO BACK TO FORT BRIDGER!
IS THERE A DOCTOR AT THE FORT?
I'M A SURGEON!
THANK YOU, GOOD SIR!
YUP. IT'LL HAVE TO COME OFF.
THE BOOT?
NOPE. THE WHOLE LEG.
AAAAAAAAGH! DON'T CUT IT! DON'T CUT IT!
WE'LL TAKE OUR CHANCES WITH A SPLINT.
AWW. NOBODY EVER LET'S ME OPERATE.
C'MON, SAW, LET'S GO BACK TO CUTTIN' DOWN TREES.

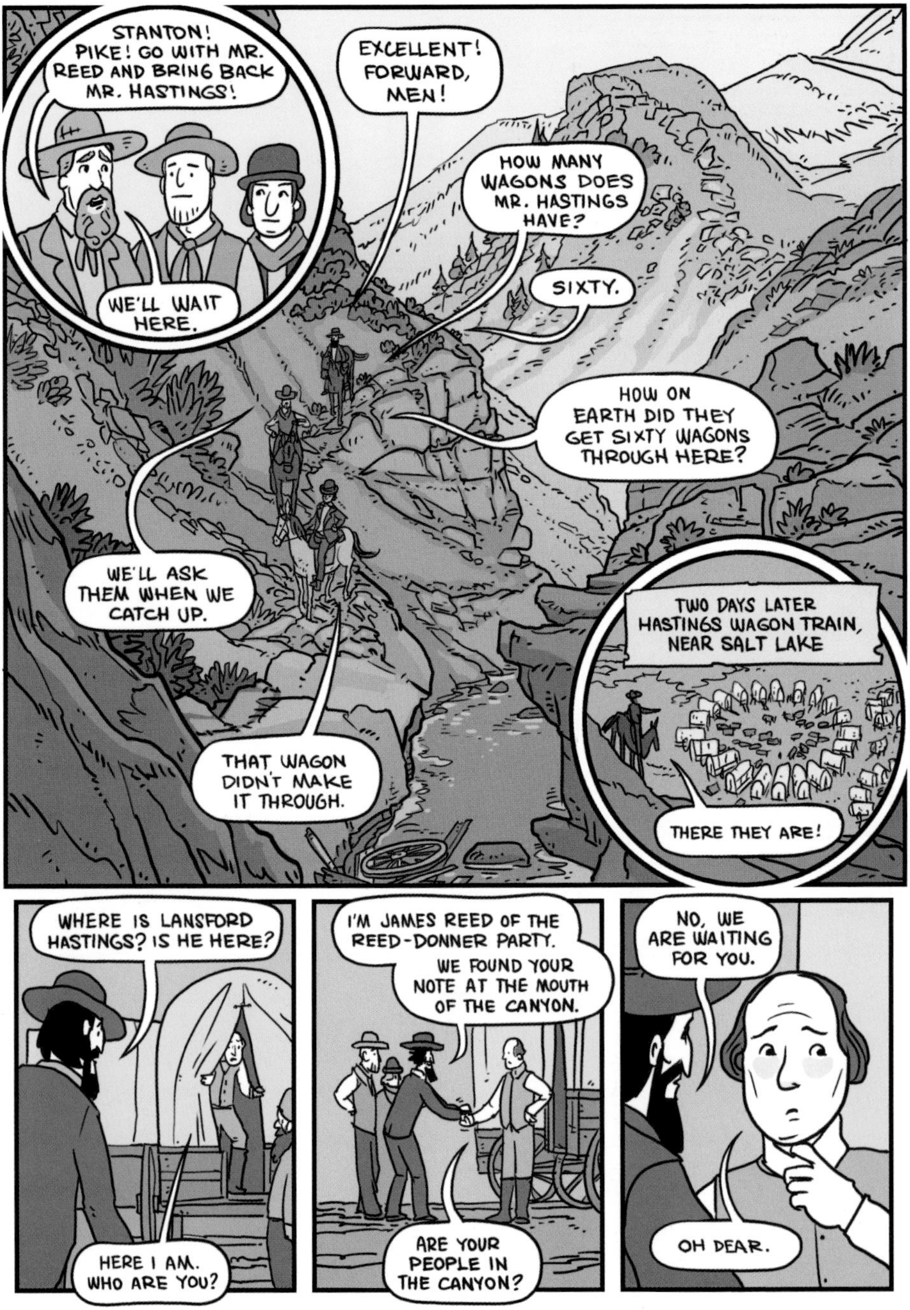
STANTON! PIKE! GO WITH MR. REED AND BRING BACK MR. HASTINGS!
WE'LL WAIT HERE.
EXCELLENT! FORWARD, MEN!
HOW MANY WAGONS DOES MR. HASTINGS HAVE?
SIXTY.
HOW ON EARTH DID THEY GET SIXTY WAGONS THROUGH HERE?
WE'LL ASK THEM WHEN WE CATCH UP.
THAT WAGON DIDN'T MAKE IT THROUGH.
TWO DAYS LATER HASTINGS WAGON TRAIN, NEAR SALT LAKE
THERE THEY ARE!
WHERE IS LANSFORD HASTINGS? IS HE HERE?
HERE I AM. WHO ARE YOU?
I'M JAMES REED OF THE REED-DONNER PARTY.
WE FOUND YOUR NOTE AT THE MOUTH OF THE CANYON.
ARE YOUR PEOPLE IN THE CANYON?
NO, WE ARE WAITING FOR YOU.
OH DEAR.

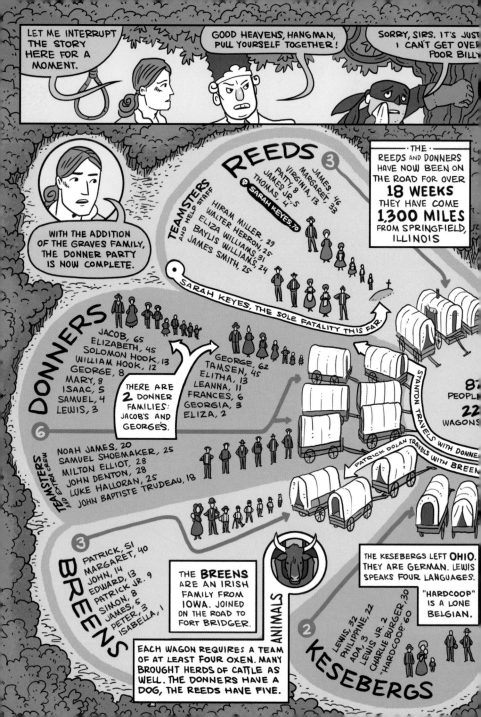

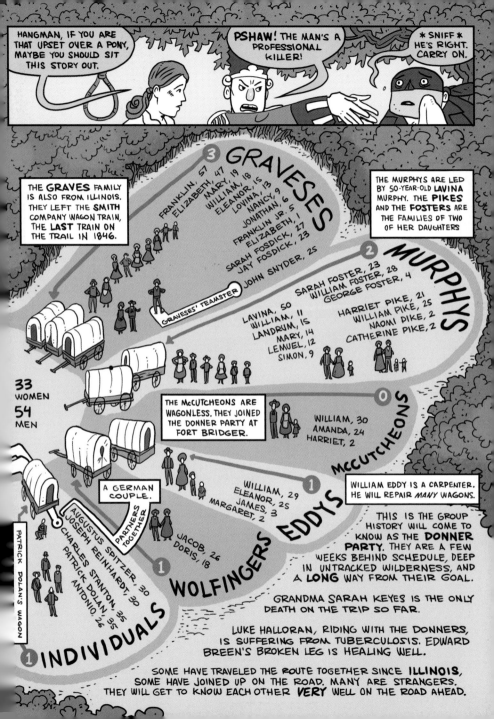

44

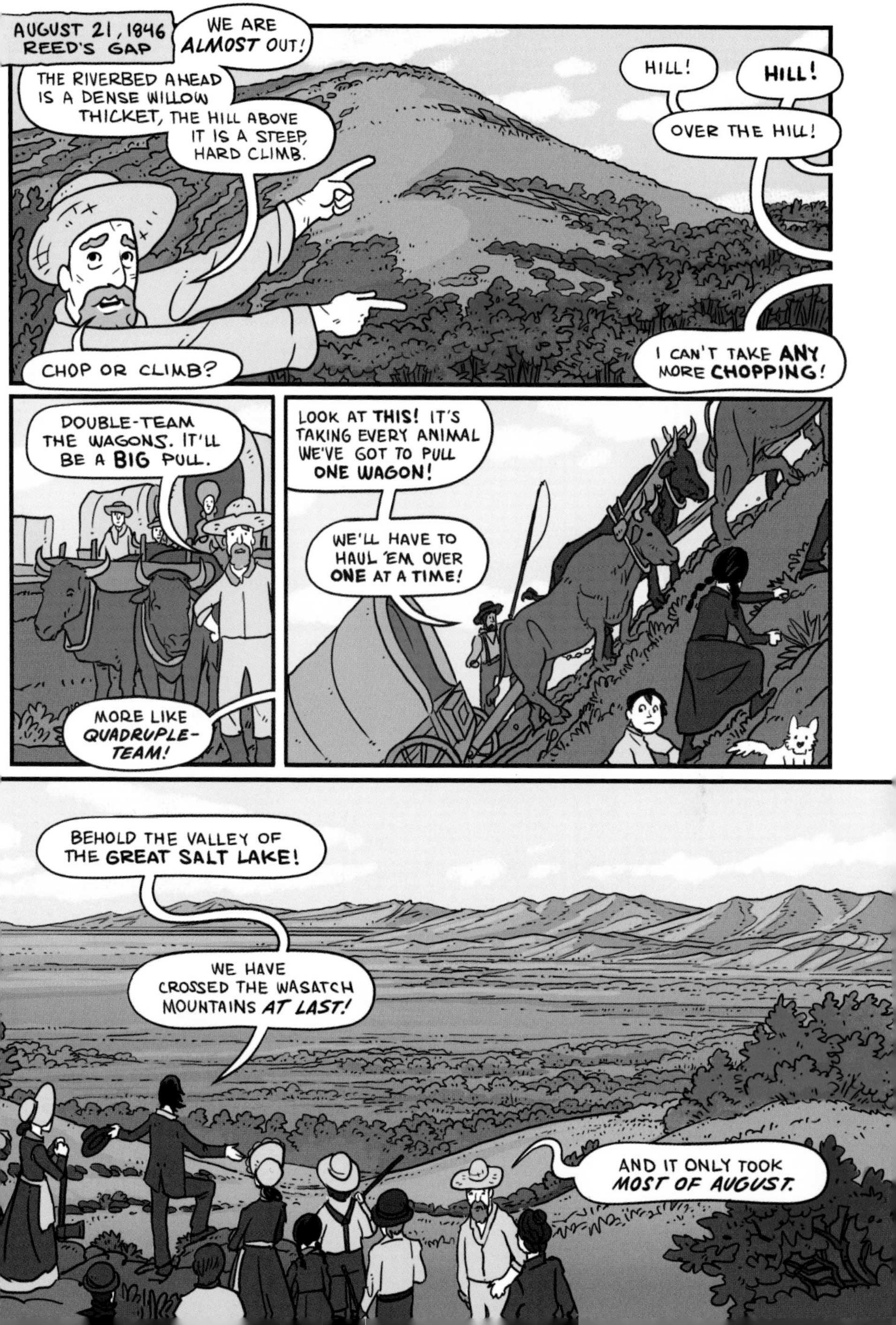
AUGUST 21, 1846
REED'S GAP
WE ARE *ALMOST* OUT!
THE RIVERBED AHEAD IS A DENSE WILLOW THICKET, THE HILL ABOVE IT IS A STEEP, HARD CLIMB.
CHOP OR CLIMB?
HILL!
HILL!
OVER THE HILL!
I CAN'T TAKE **ANY** MORE **CHOPPING**!
DOUBLE-TEAM THE WAGONS. IT'LL BE A **BIG** PULL.
MORE LIKE *QUADRUPLE-TEAM!*
LOOK AT **THIS!** IT'S TAKING EVERY ANIMAL WE'VE GOT TO PULL **ONE WAGON!**
WE'LL HAVE TO HAUL 'EM OVER **ONE** AT A TIME!
BEHOLD THE VALLEY OF THE **GREAT SALT LAKE!**
WE HAVE CROSSED THE WASATCH MOUNTAINS *AT LAST!*
AND IT ONLY TOOK *MOST OF AUGUST.*

47

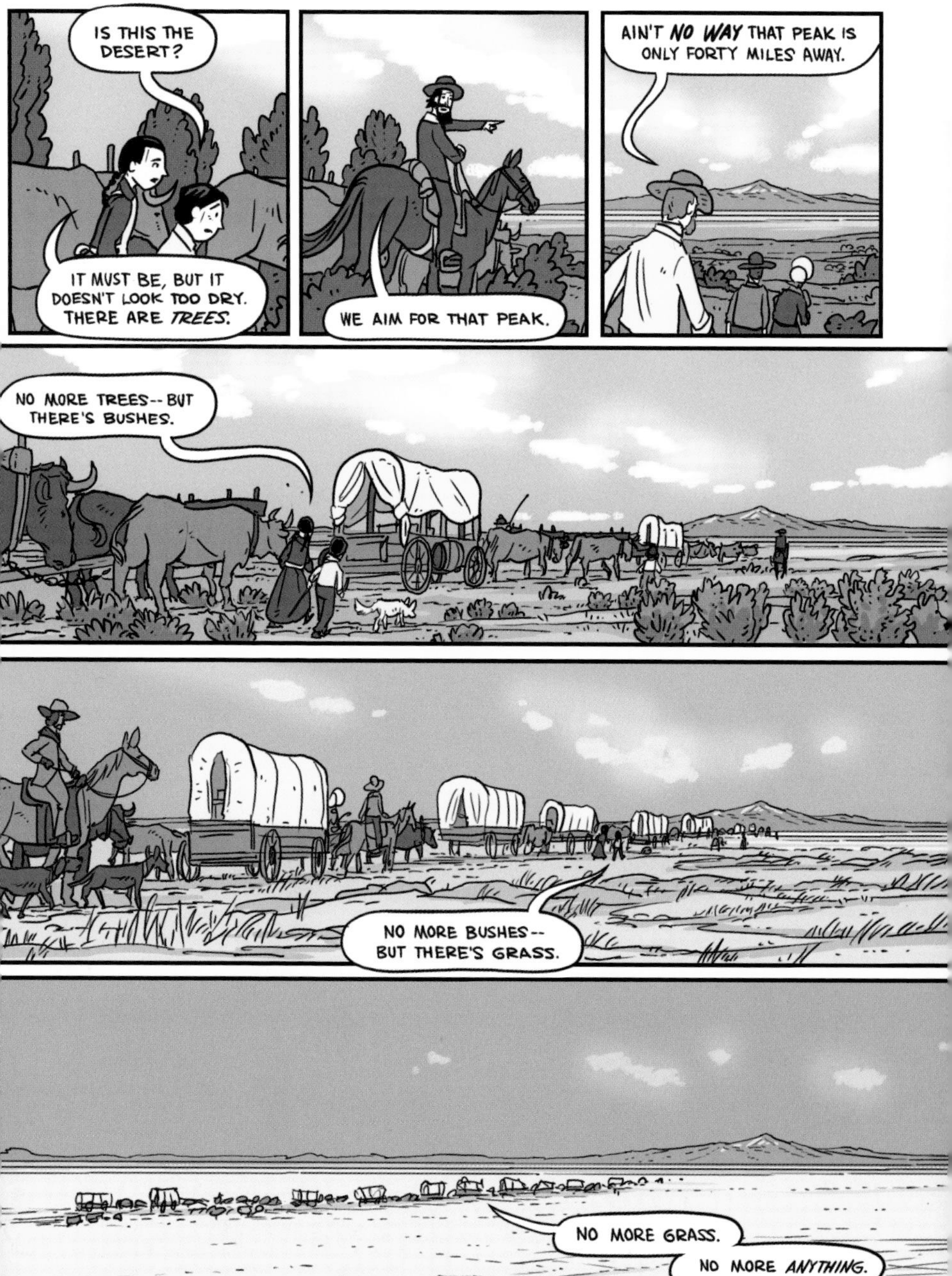
IS THIS THE DESERT?
IT MUST BE, BUT IT DOESN'T LOOK TOO DRY. THERE ARE *TREES.*
WE AIM FOR THAT PEAK.
AIN'T ***NO WAY*** THAT PEAK IS ONLY FORTY MILES AWAY.
NO MORE TREES-- BUT THERE'S BUSHES.
NO MORE BUSHES-- BUT THERE'S GRASS.
NO MORE GRASS.
NO MORE *ANYTHING.*

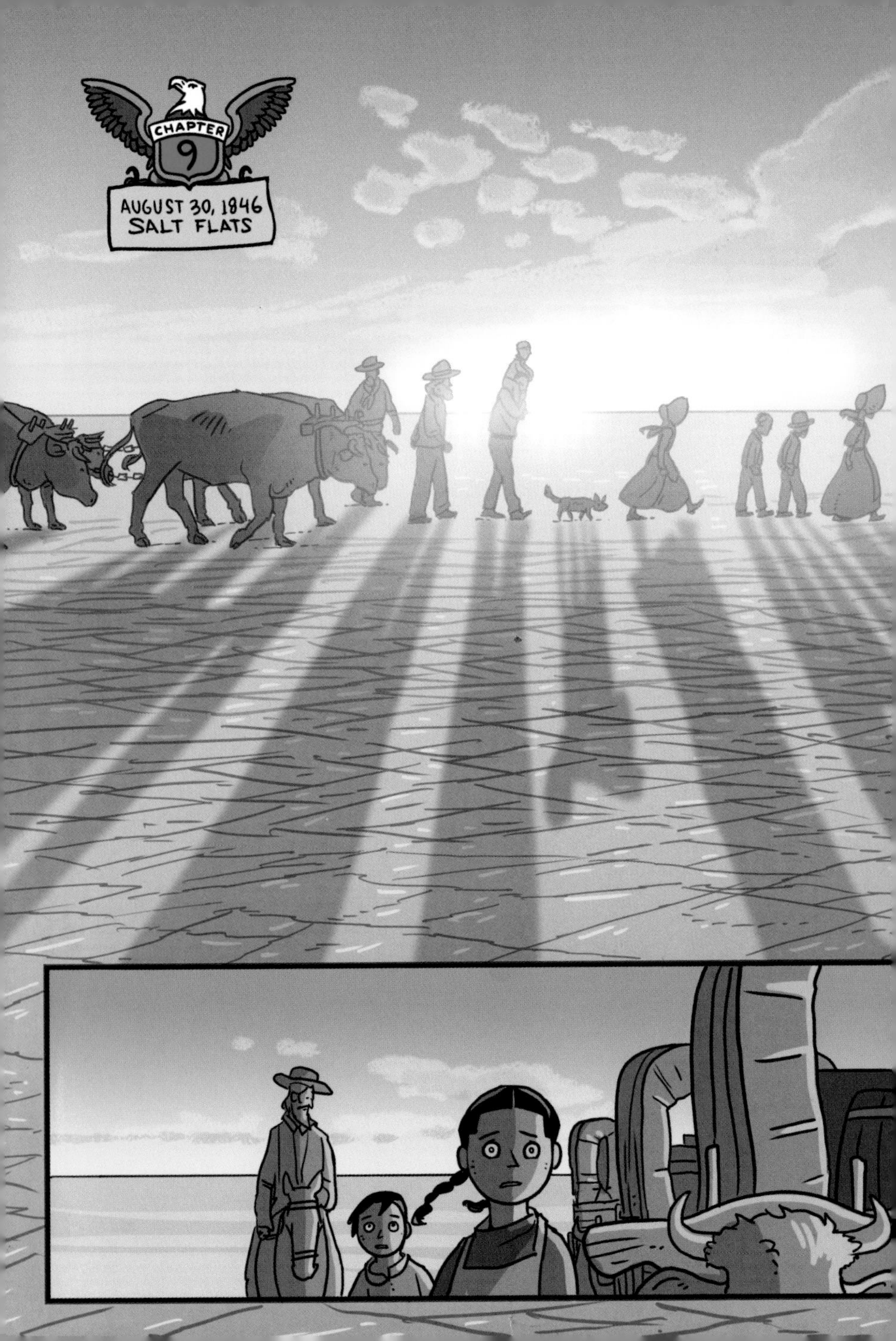
CHAPTER
9
AUGUST 30, 1846
SALT FLATS

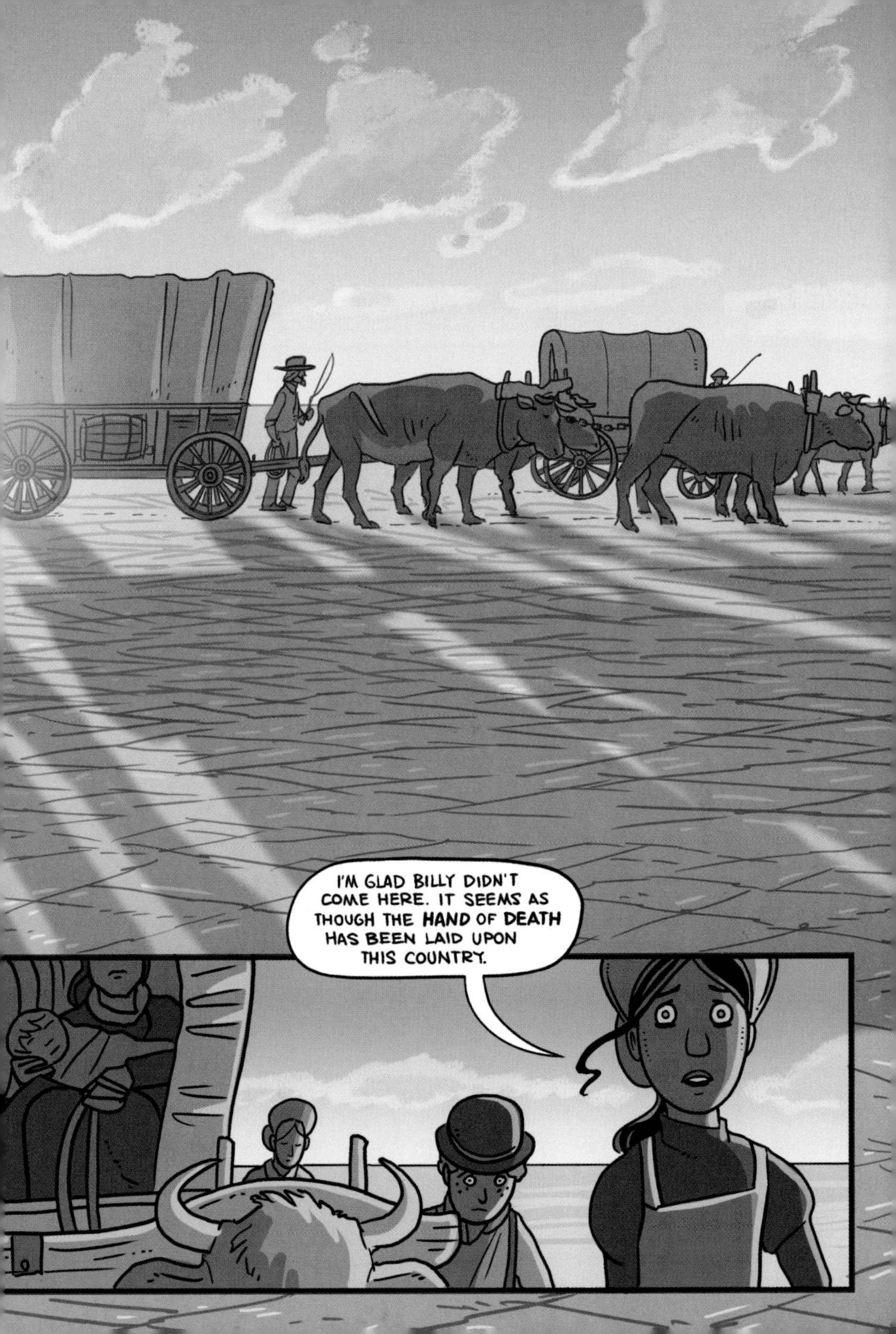
I'M GLAD BILLY DIDN'T COME HERE. IT SEEMS AS THOUGH THE HAND OF DEATH HAS BEEN LAID UPON THIS COUNTRY.

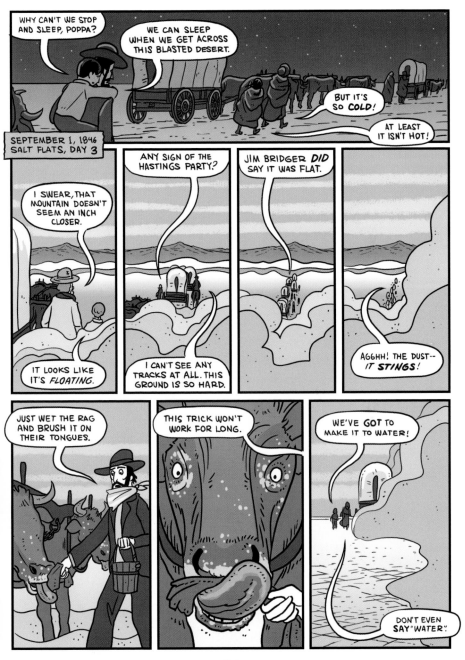

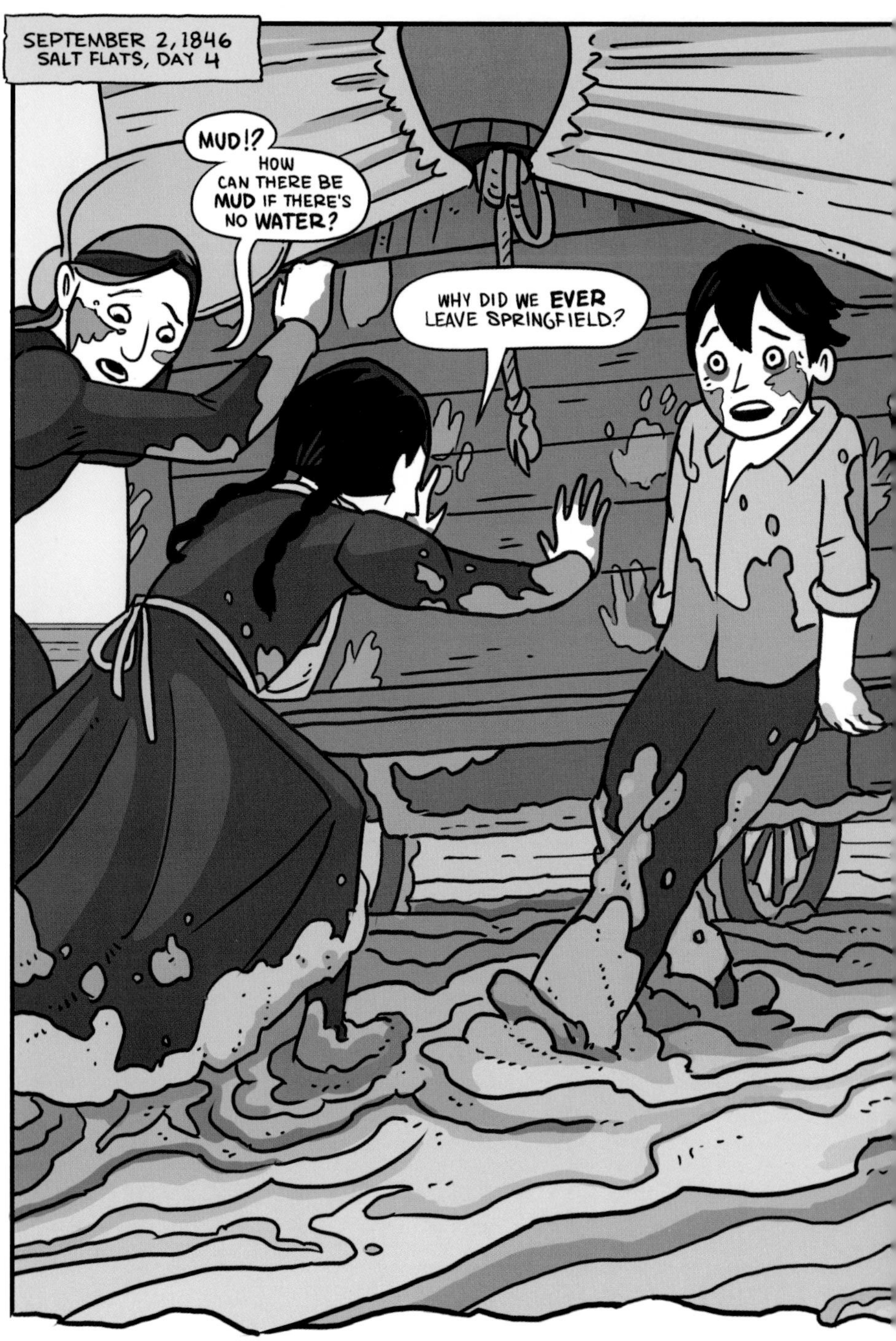
SEPTEMBER 2, 1846
SALT FLATS, DAY 4
MUD!? HOW CAN THERE BE MUD IF THERE'S NO WATER?
WHY DID WE EVER LEAVE SPRINGFIELD?

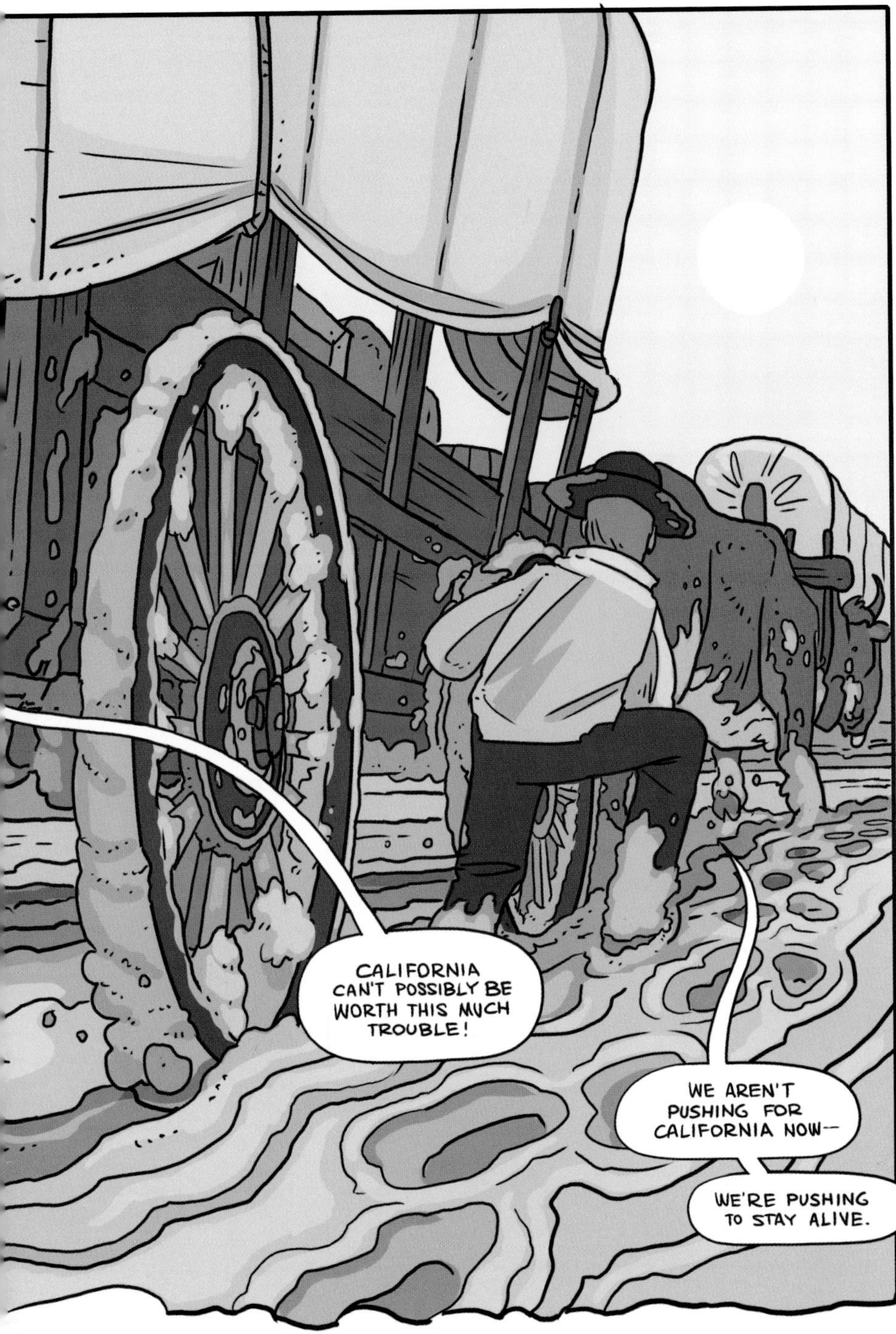
CALIFORNIA CAN'T POSSIBLY BE WORTH THIS MUCH TROUBLE!
WE AREN'T PUSHING FOR CALIFORNIA NOW--
WE'RE PUSHING TO STAY ALIVE.

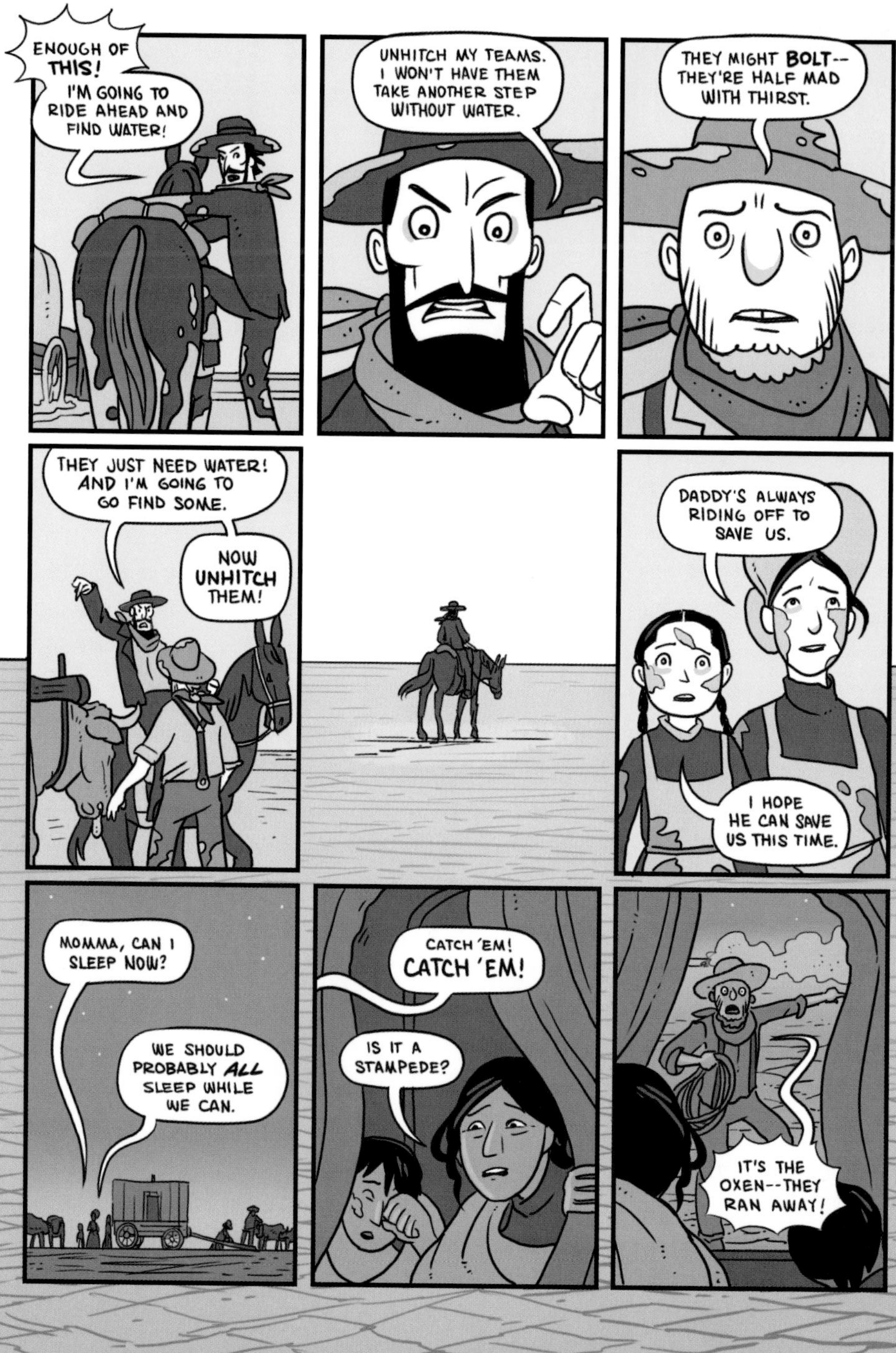
ENOUGH OF THIS!
I'M GOING TO RIDE AHEAD AND FIND WATER!
UNHITCH MY TEAMS. I WON'T HAVE THEM TAKE ANOTHER STEP WITHOUT WATER.
THEY MIGHT BOLT-- THEY'RE HALF MAD WITH THIRST.
THEY JUST NEED WATER! AND I'M GOING TO GO FIND SOME.
NOW UNHITCH THEM!
DADDY'S ALWAYS RIDING OFF TO SAVE US.
I HOPE HE CAN SAVE US THIS TIME.
MOMMA, CAN I SLEEP NOW?
WE SHOULD PROBABLY ALL SLEEP WHILE WE CAN.
CATCH 'EM! CATCH 'EM!
IS IT A STAMPEDE?
IT'S THE OXEN--THEY RAN AWAY!

57

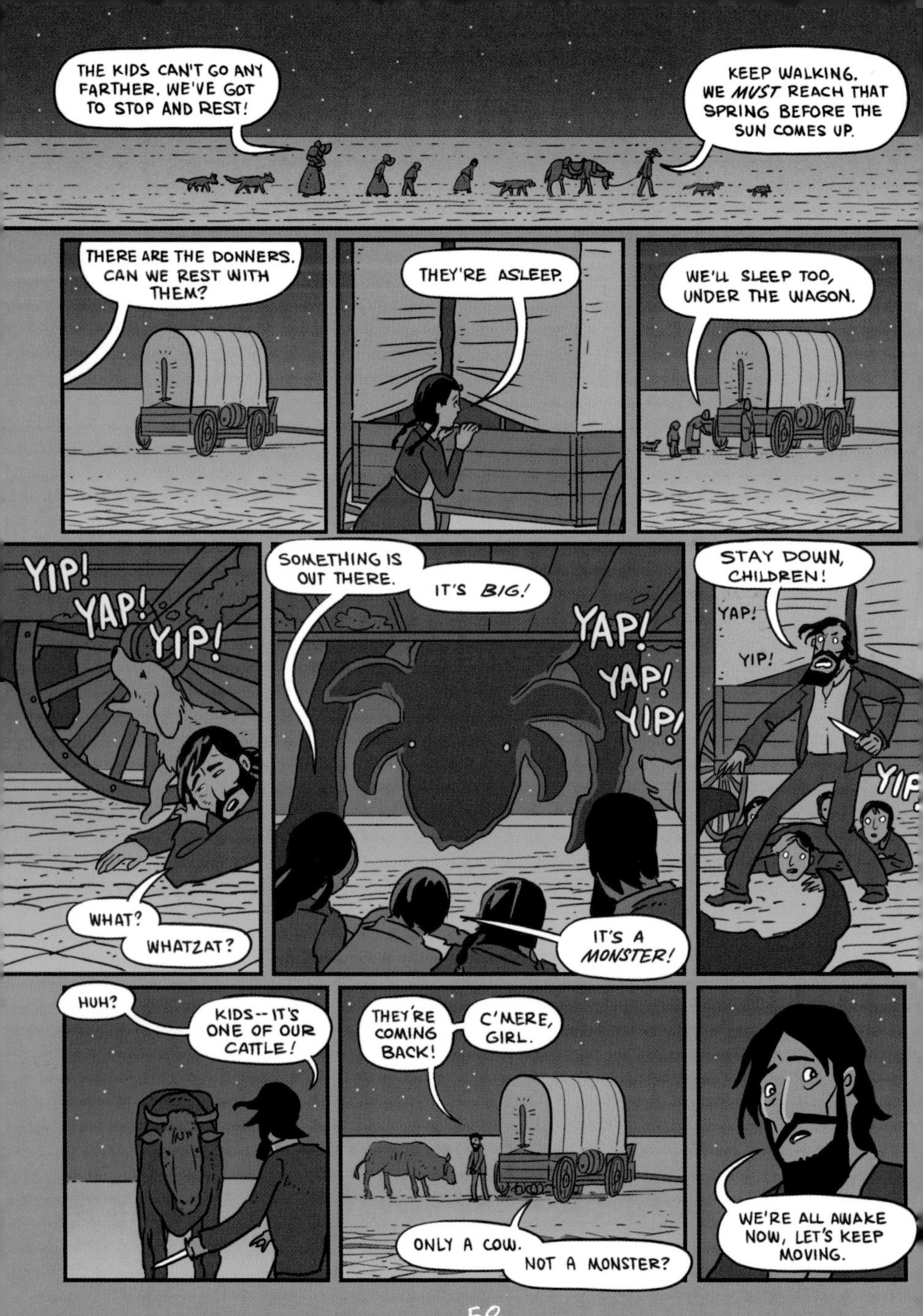
THE KIDS CAN'T GO ANY FARTHER. WE'VE GOT TO STOP AND REST!
KEEP WALKING. WE MUST REACH THAT SPRING BEFORE THE SUN COMES UP.
THERE ARE THE DONNERS. CAN WE REST WITH THEM?
THEY'RE ASLEEP.
WE'LL SLEEP TOO, UNDER THE WAGON.
YIP!
YAP!
YIP!
WHAT?
WHATZAT?
SOMETHING IS OUT THERE.
IT'S BIG!
YAP!
YAP!
YIP!
IT'S A MONSTER!
STAY DOWN, CHILDREN!
YAP!
YIP!
YIP!
HUH?
KIDS-- IT'S ONE OF OUR CATTLE!
THEY'RE COMING BACK!
C'MERE, GIRL.
ONLY A COW.
NOT A MONSTER?
WE'RE ALL AWAKE NOW, LET'S KEEP MOVING.

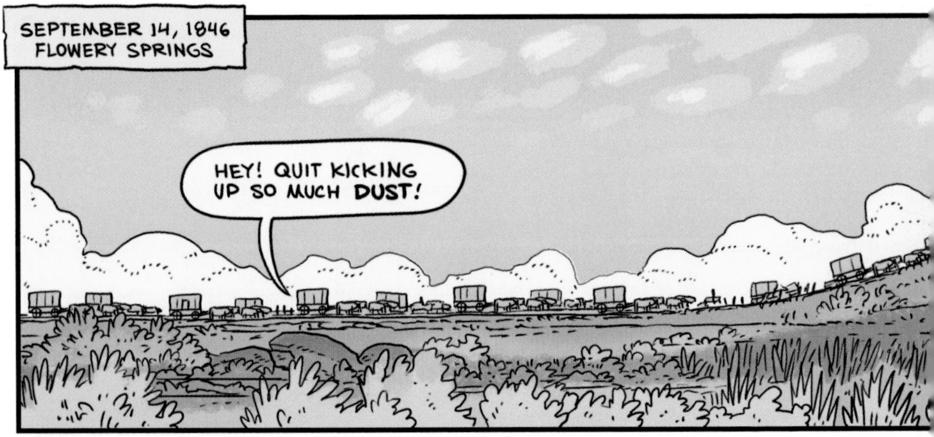
SEPTEMBER 14, 1846
FLOWERY SPRINGS
HEY! QUIT KICKING UP SO MUCH DUST!

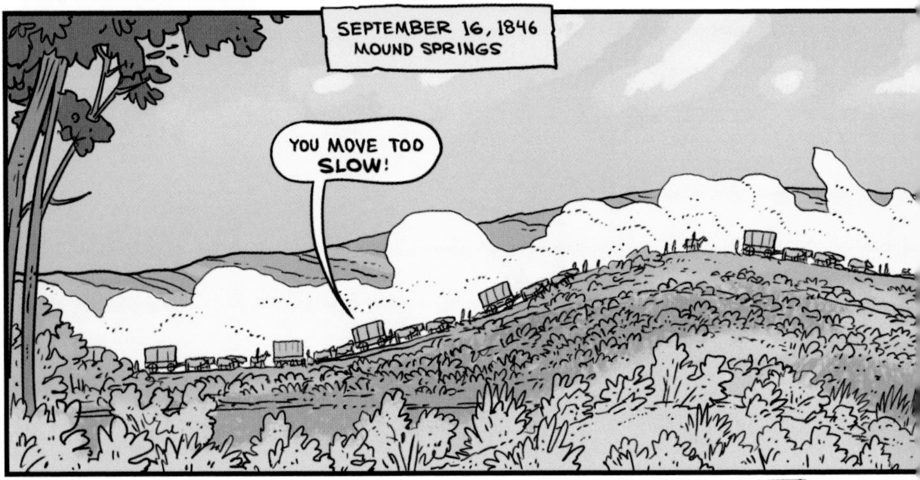
SEPTEMBER 16, 1846
MOUND SPRINGS
YOU MOVE TOO SLOW!

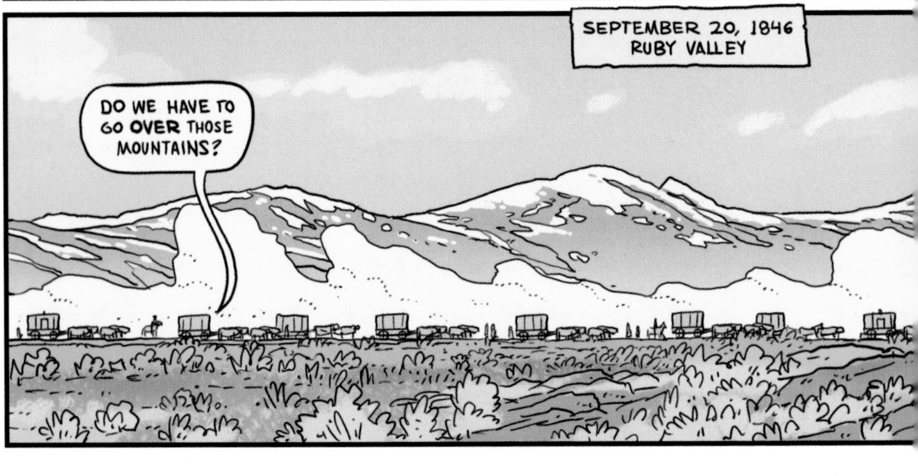
SEPTEMBER 20, 1846
RUBY VALLEY
DO WE HAVE TO GO OVER THOSE MOUNTAINS?

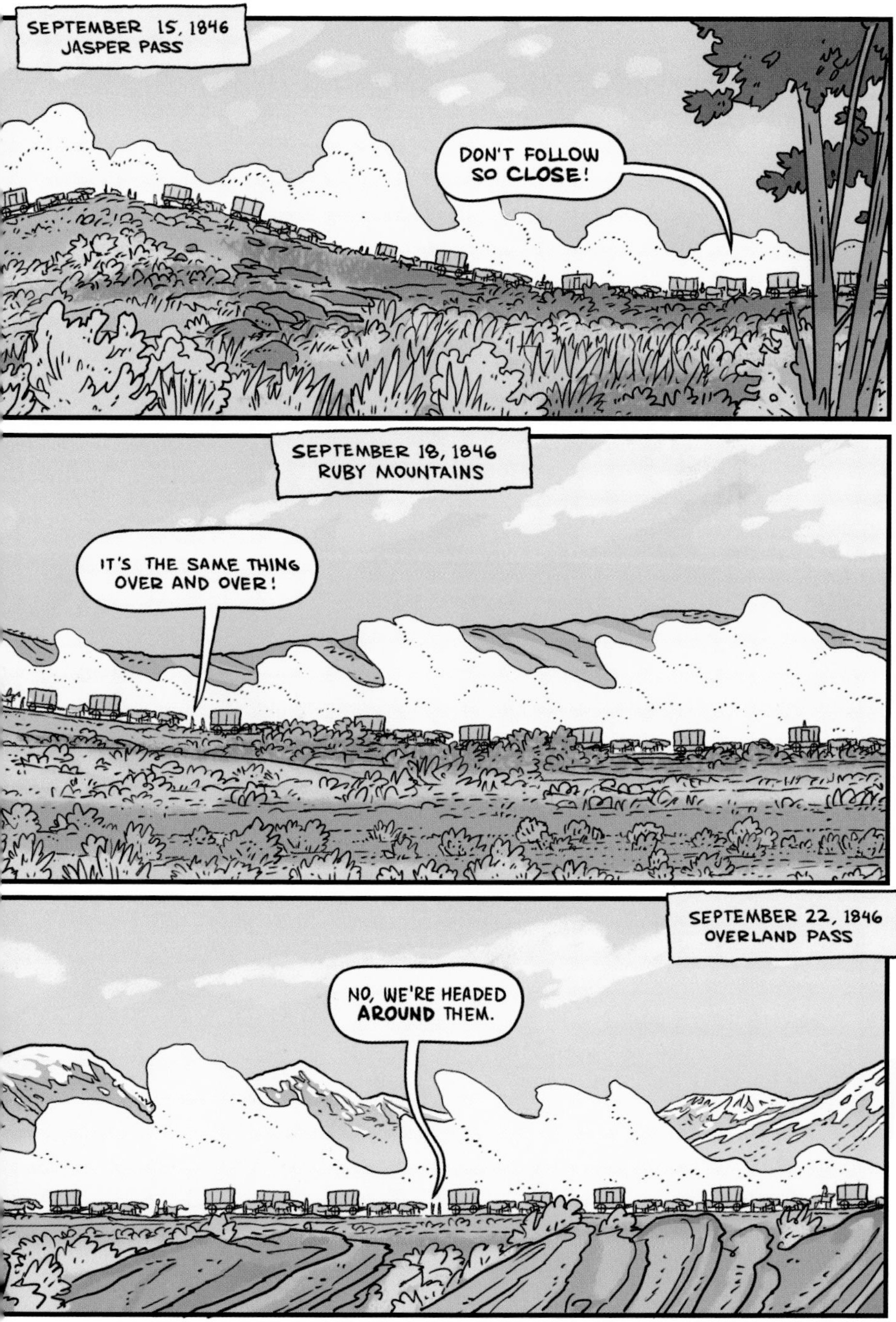
SEPTEMBER 15, 1846
JASPER PASS
DON'T FOLLOW SO CLOSE!
SEPTEMBER 18, 1846
RUBY MOUNTAINS
IT'S THE SAME THING OVER AND OVER!
SEPTEMBER 22, 1846
OVERLAND PASS
NO, WE'RE HEADED AROUND THEM.

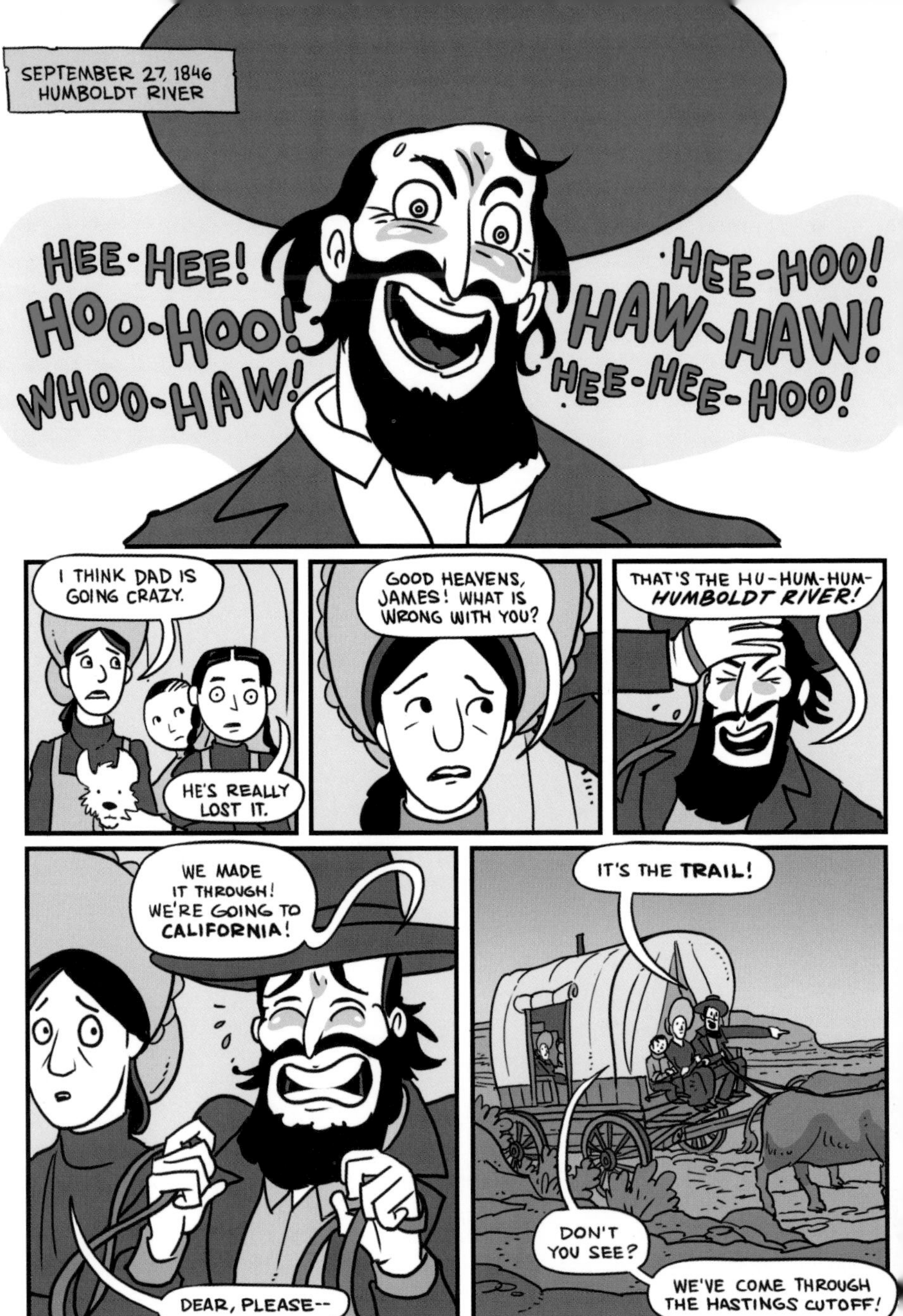
SEPTEMBER 27, 1846
HUMBOLDT RIVER
HEE-HEE! HOO-HOO! WHOO-HAW!
HEE-HOO! HAW-HAW! HEE-HEE-HOO!
I THINK DAD IS GOING CRAZY.
HE'S REALLY LOST IT.
GOOD HEAVENS, JAMES! WHAT IS WRONG WITH YOU?
THAT'S THE HU-HUM-HUM-HUMBOLDT RIVER!
WE MADE IT THROUGH! WE'RE GOING TO CALIFORNIA!
DEAR, PLEASE--
IT'S THE TRAIL!
DON'T YOU SEE?
WE'VE COME THROUGH THE HASTINGS CUTOFF!

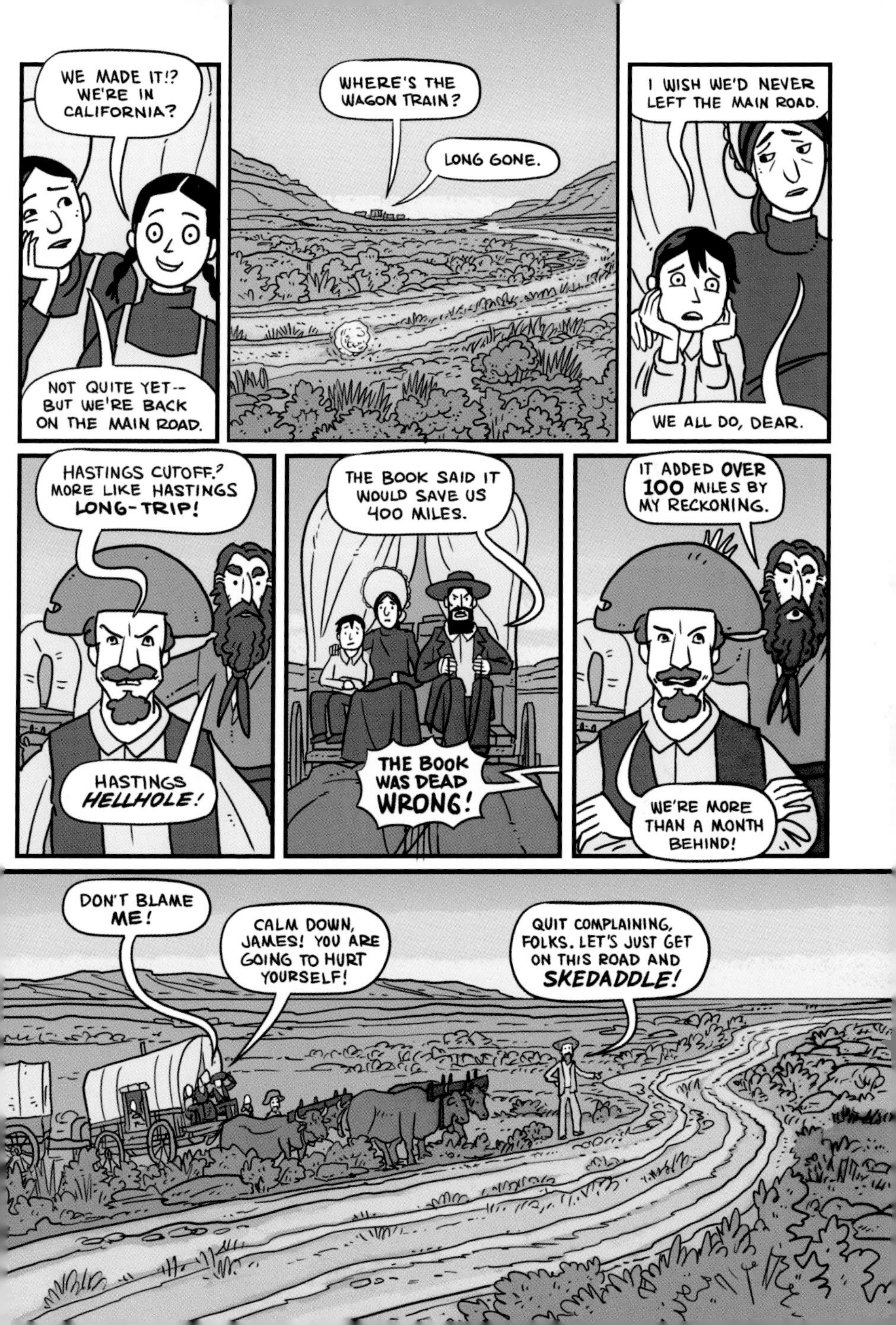
WE MADE IT!? WE'RE IN CALIFORNIA?
NOT QUITE YET-- BUT WE'RE BACK ON THE MAIN ROAD.
WHERE'S THE WAGON TRAIN?
LONG GONE.
I WISH WE'D NEVER LEFT THE MAIN ROAD.
WE ALL DO, DEAR.
HASTINGS CUTOFF? MORE LIKE HASTINGS LONG-TRIP!
HASTINGS HELLHOLE!
THE BOOK SAID IT WOULD SAVE US 400 MILES.
THE BOOK WAS DEAD WRONG!
IT ADDED OVER 100 MILES BY MY RECKONING.
WE'RE MORE THAN A MONTH BEHIND!
DON'T BLAME ME!
CALM DOWN, JAMES! YOU ARE GOING TO HURT YOURSELF!
QUIT COMPLAINING, FOLKS. LET'S JUST GET ON THIS ROAD AND SKEDADDLE!

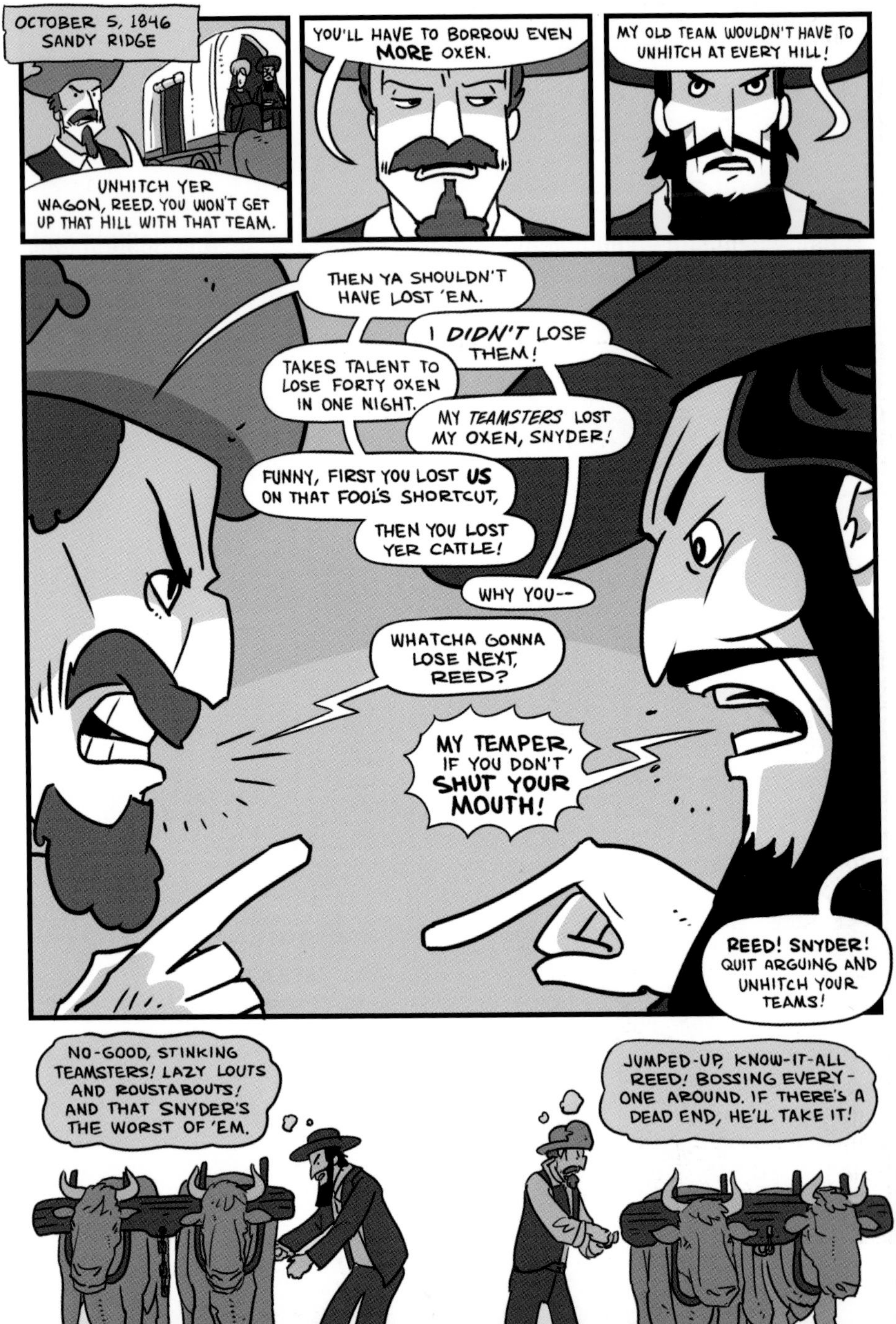
OCTOBER 5, 1846
SANDY RIDGE
UNHITCH YER WAGON, REED. YOU WON'T GET UP THAT HILL WITH THAT TEAM.
YOU'LL HAVE TO BORROW EVEN MORE OXEN.
MY OLD TEAM WOULDN'T HAVE TO UNHITCH AT EVERY HILL!
THEN YA SHOULDN'T HAVE LOST 'EM.
I DIDN'T LOSE THEM!
TAKES TALENT TO LOSE FORTY OXEN IN ONE NIGHT.
MY TEAMSTERS LOST MY OXEN, SNYDER!
FUNNY, FIRST YOU LOST US ON THAT FOOL'S SHORTCUT,
THEN YOU LOST YER CATTLE!
WHY YOU--
WHATCHA GONNA LOSE NEXT, REED?
MY TEMPER, IF YOU DON'T SHUT YOUR MOUTH!
REED! SNYDER! QUIT ARGUING AND UNHITCH YOUR TEAMS!
NO-GOOD, STINKING TEAMSTERS! LAZY LOUTS AND ROUSTABOUTS! AND THAT SNYDER'S THE WORST OF 'EM.
JUMPED-UP, KNOW-IT-ALL REED! BOSSING EVERY-ONE AROUND. IF THERE'S A DEAD END, HE'LL TAKE IT!

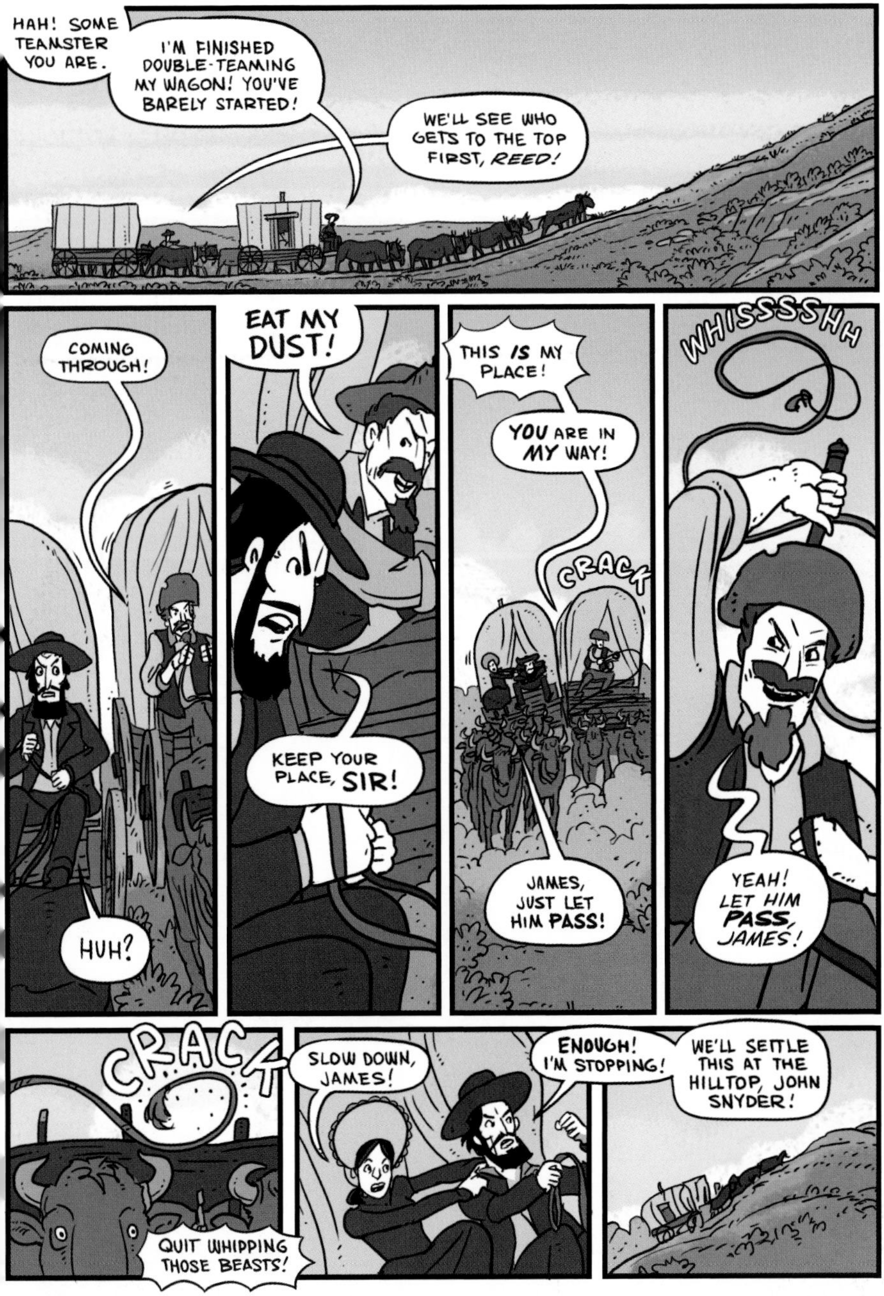
HAH! SOME TEAMSTER YOU ARE.
I'M FINISHED DOUBLE-TEAMING MY WAGON! YOU'VE BARELY STARTED!
WE'LL SEE WHO GETS TO THE TOP FIRST, REED!
COMING THROUGH!
HUH?
EAT MY DUST!
KEEP YOUR PLACE, SIR!
THIS IS MY PLACE!
YOU ARE IN MY WAY!
CRACK
JAMES, JUST LET HIM PASS!
WHISSSSSHH
YEAH! LET HIM PASS, JAMES!
CRACK
QUIT WHIPPING THOSE BEASTS!
SLOW DOWN, JAMES!
ENOUGH! I'M STOPPING!
WE'LL SETTLE THIS AT THE HILLTOP, JOHN SNYDER!

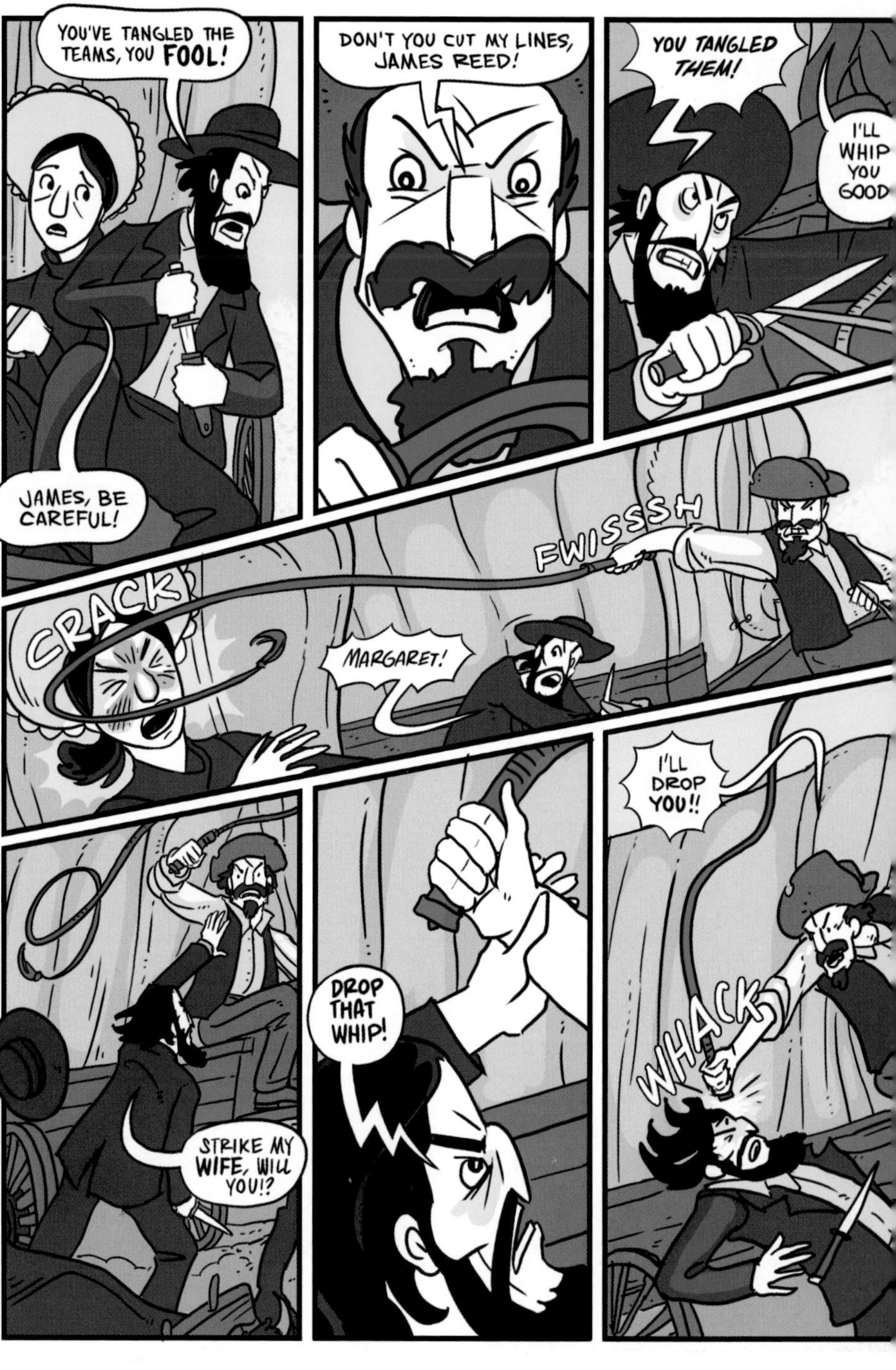
YOU'VE TANGLED THE TEAMS, YOU FOOL!
JAMES, BE CAREFUL!
DON'T YOU CUT MY LINES, JAMES REED!
YOU TANGLED THEM!
I'LL WHIP YOU GOOD
FWISSSSH
CRACK
MARGARET!
STRIKE MY WIFE, WILL YOU!?
DROP THAT WHIP!
I'LL DROP YOU!!
WHACK

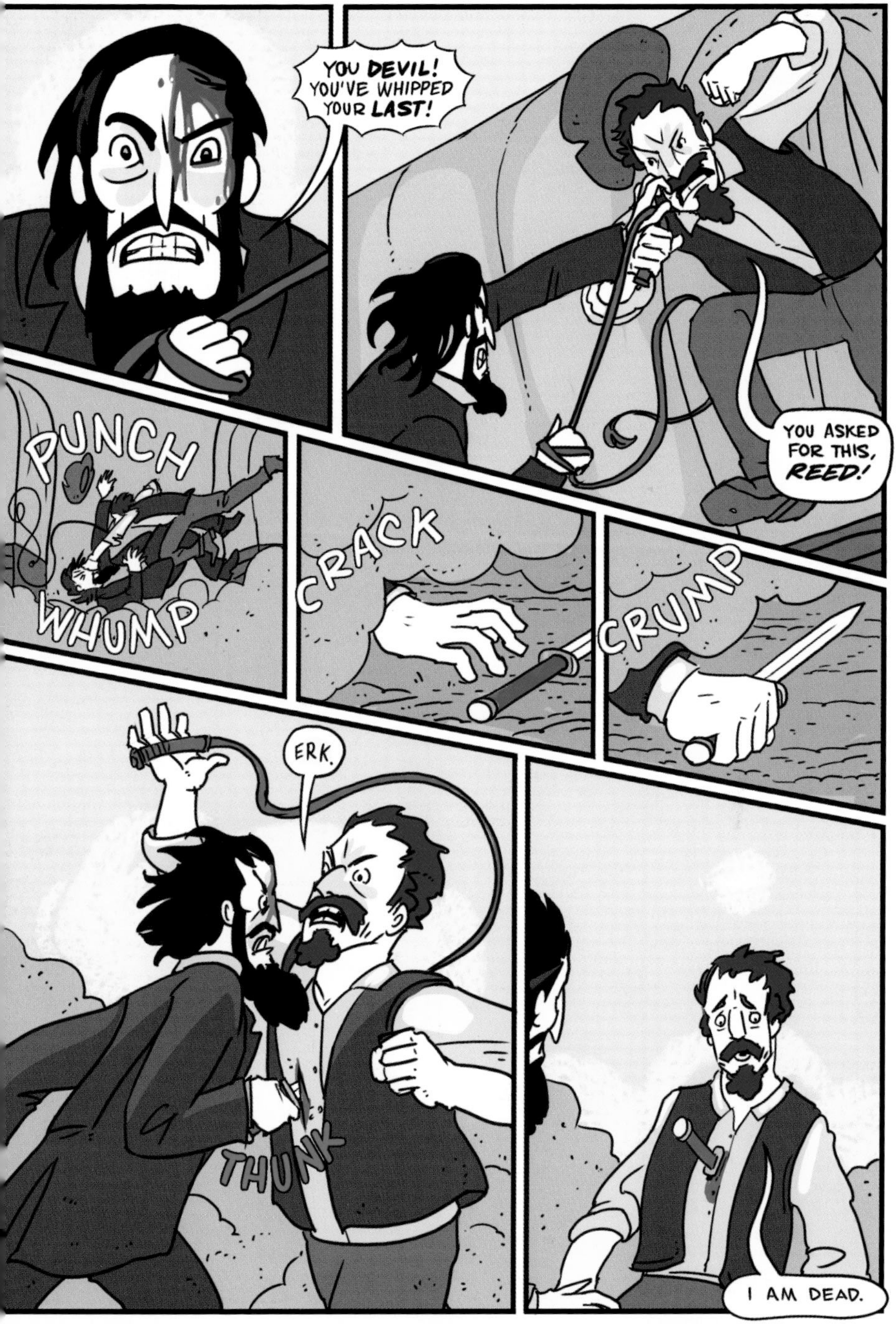
YOU DEVIL! YOU'VE WHIPPED YOUR LAST!
YOU ASKED FOR THIS, REED!
PUNCH
WHUMP
CRACK
CRUMP
ERK.
THUNK
I AM DEAD.

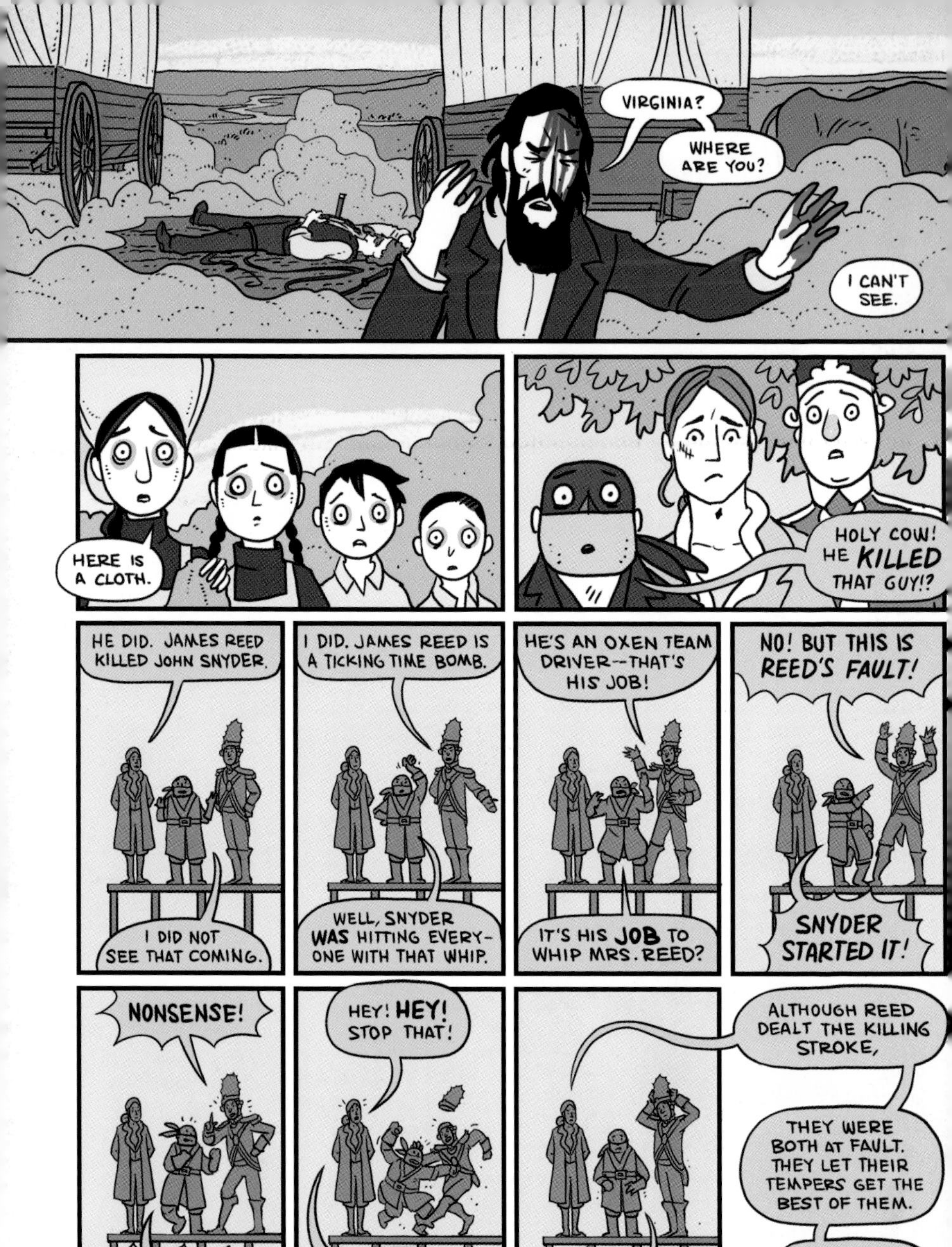
VIRGINIA?
WHERE ARE YOU?
I CAN'T SEE.
HERE IS A CLOTH.
HOLY COW! HE KILLED THAT GUY!?
HE DID. JAMES REED KILLED JOHN SNYDER.
I DID NOT SEE THAT COMING.
I DID. JAMES REED IS A TICKING TIME BOMB.
WELL, SNYDER WAS HITTING EVERY-ONE WITH THAT WHIP.
HE'S AN OXEN TEAM DRIVER--THAT'S HIS JOB!
IT'S HIS JOB TO WHIP MRS. REED?
NO! BUT THIS IS REED'S FAULT!
SNYDER STARTED IT!
NONSENSE!
WE'LL SETTLE THIS NOW!
HEY! HEY! STOP THAT!
SEE WHERE FIGHTING GETS YOU?
SORRY.
ALTHOUGH REED DEALT THE KILLING STROKE,
THEY WERE BOTH AT FAULT. THEY LET THEIR TEMPERS GET THE BEST OF THEM.
NOW ANOTHER MEMBER OF THE DONNER PARTY LIES DEAD.

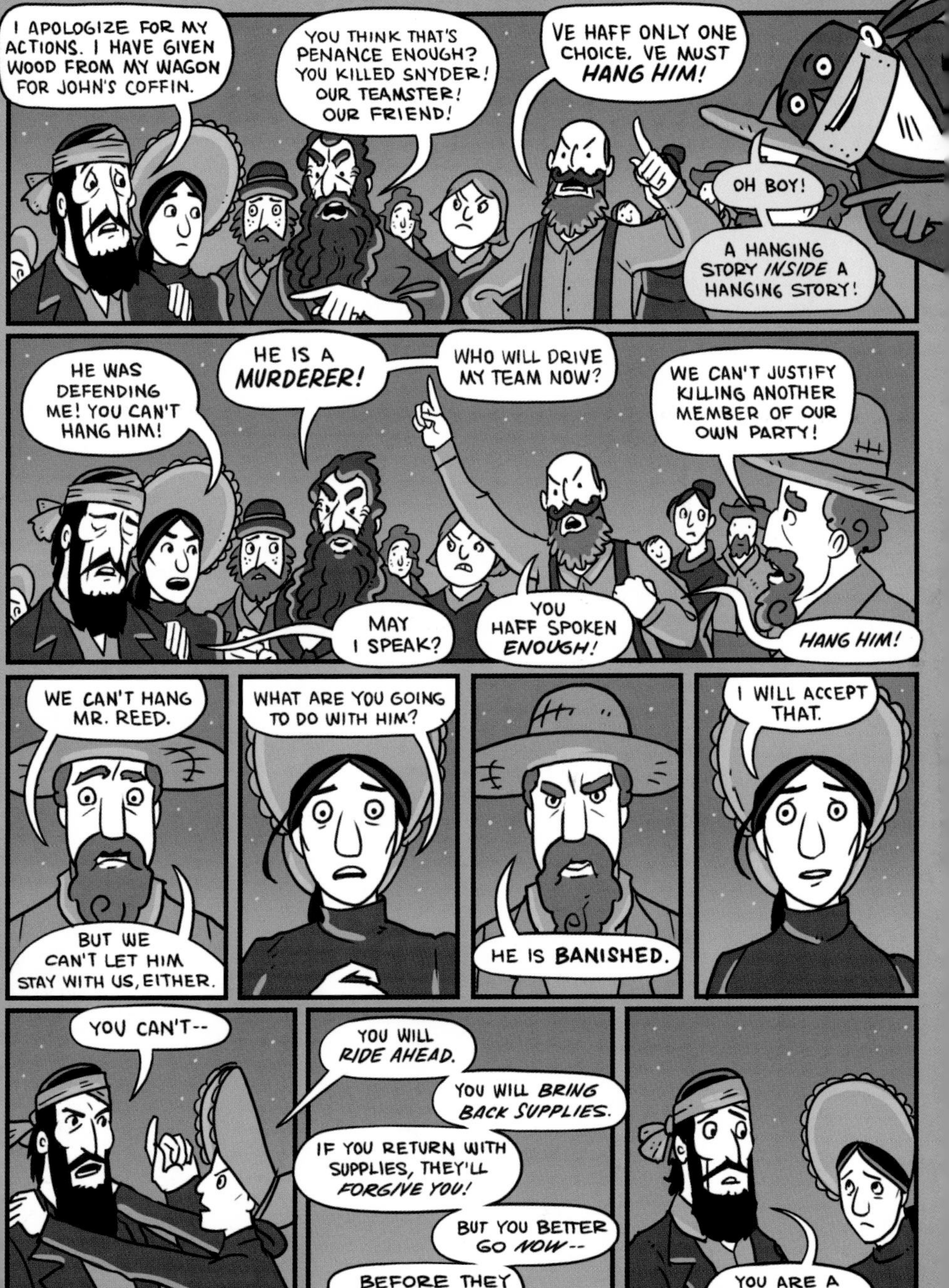
I APOLOGIZE FOR MY ACTIONS. I HAVE GIVEN WOOD FROM MY WAGON FOR JOHN'S COFFIN.
YOU THINK THAT'S PENANCE ENOUGH? YOU KILLED SNYDER! OUR TEAMSTER! OUR FRIEND!
VE HAFF ONLY ONE CHOICE. VE MUST *HANG HIM!*
OH BOY!
A HANGING STORY *INSIDE* A HANGING STORY!
HE WAS DEFENDING ME! YOU CAN'T HANG HIM!
HE IS A *MURDERER!*
WHO WILL DRIVE MY TEAM NOW?
WE CAN'T JUSTIFY KILLING ANOTHER MEMBER OF OUR OWN PARTY!
MAY I SPEAK?
YOU HAFF SPOKEN *ENOUGH!*
HANG HIM!
WE CAN'T HANG MR. REED.
BUT WE CAN'T LET HIM STAY WITH US, EITHER.
WHAT ARE YOU GOING TO DO WITH HIM?
HE IS **BANISHED.**
I WILL ACCEPT THAT.
YOU CAN'T--
YOU WILL *RIDE AHEAD.*
YOU WILL *BRING BACK SUPPLIES.*
IF YOU RETURN WITH SUPPLIES, THEY'LL *FORGIVE YOU!*
BUT YOU BETTER GO *NOW*--
BEFORE THEY *HANG YOU!*
YOU ARE A WISE WOMAN.

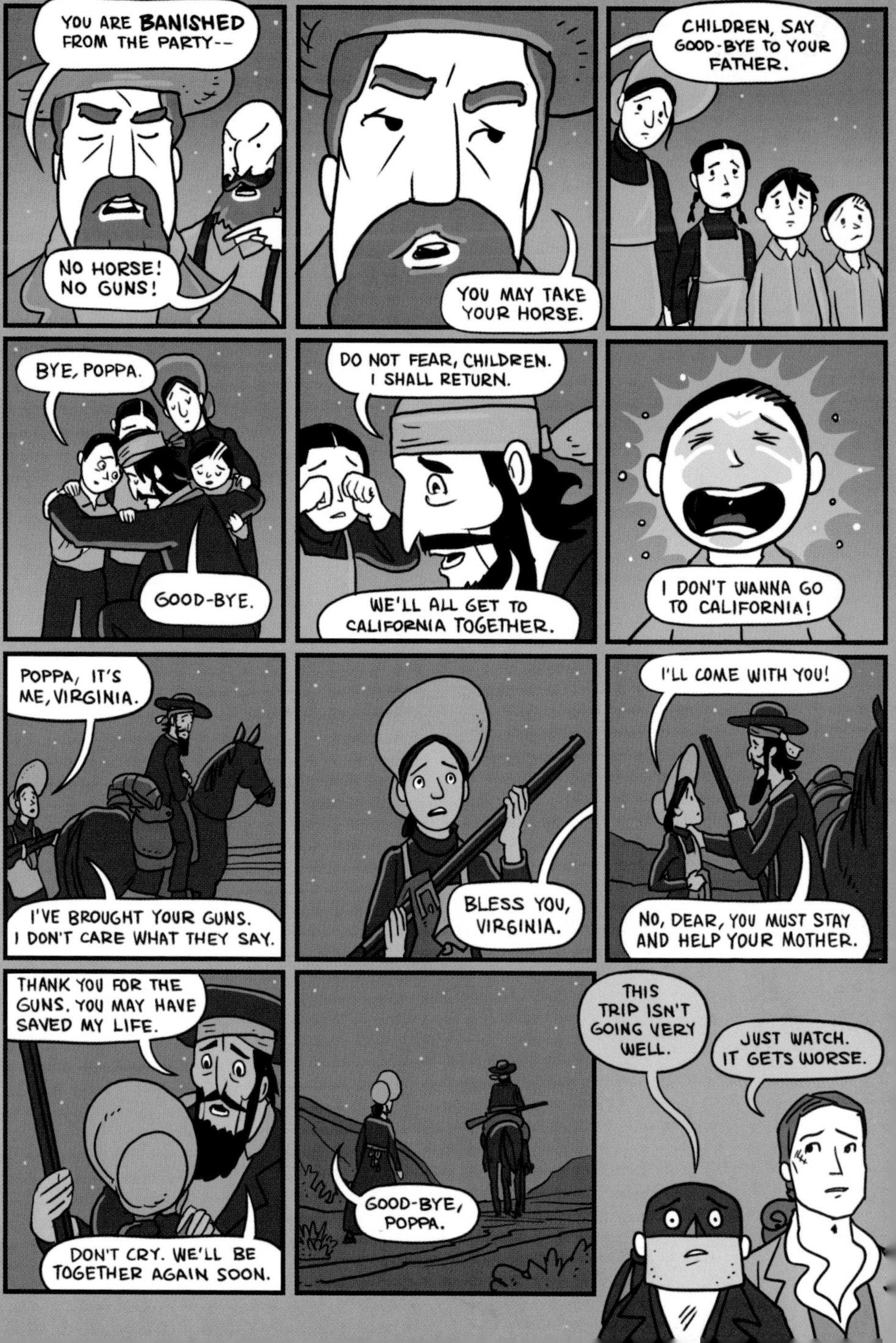

YOU ARE BANISHED FROM THE PARTY--
NO HORSE! NO GUNS!
YOU MAY TAKE YOUR HORSE.
CHILDREN, SAY GOOD-BYE TO YOUR FATHER.
BYE, POPPA.
GOOD-BYE.
DO NOT FEAR, CHILDREN. I SHALL RETURN.
WE'LL ALL GET TO CALIFORNIA TOGETHER.
I DON'T WANNA GO TO CALIFORNIA!
POPPA, IT'S ME, VIRGINIA.
I'VE BROUGHT YOUR GUNS. I DON'T CARE WHAT THEY SAY.
BLESS YOU, VIRGINIA.
I'LL COME WITH YOU!
NO, DEAR, YOU MUST STAY AND HELP YOUR MOTHER.
THANK YOU FOR THE GUNS. YOU MAY HAVE SAVED MY LIFE.
DON'T CRY. WE'LL BE TOGETHER AGAIN SOON.
GOOD-BYE, POPPA.
THIS TRIP ISN'T GOING VERY WELL.
JUST WATCH. IT GETS WORSE.

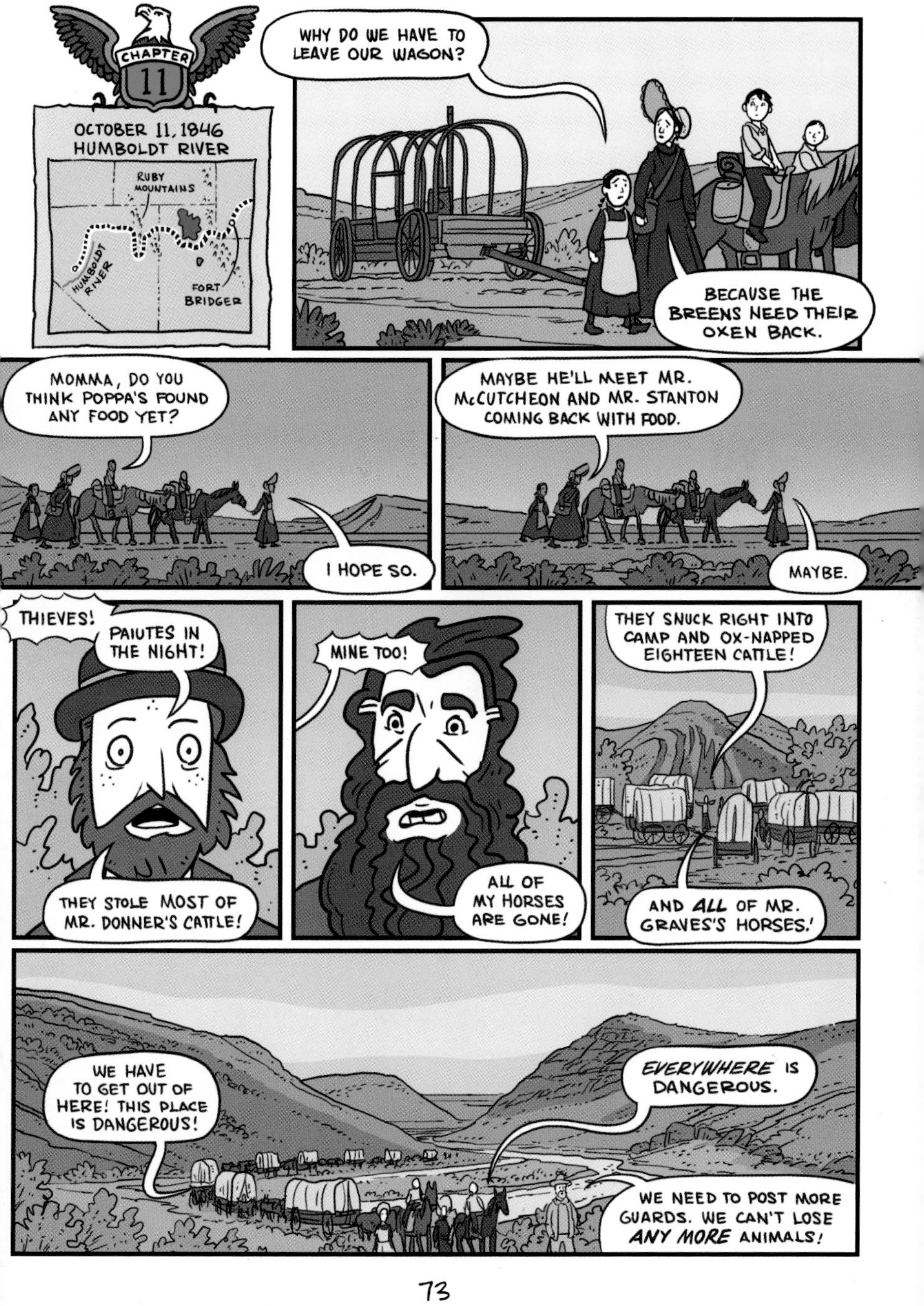
CHAPTER 11
OCTOBER 11, 1846
HUMBOLDT RIVER
RUBY MOUNTAINS
HUMBOLDT RIVER
FORT BRIDGER
WHY DO WE HAVE TO LEAVE OUR WAGON?
BECAUSE THE BREENS NEED THEIR OXEN BACK.
MOMMA, DO YOU THINK POPPA'S FOUND ANY FOOD YET?
I HOPE SO.
MAYBE HE'LL MEET MR. McCUTCHEON AND MR. STANTON COMING BACK WITH FOOD.
MAYBE.
THIEVES!
PAIUTES IN THE NIGHT!
THEY STOLE MOST OF MR. DONNER'S CATTLE!
MINE TOO!
ALL OF MY HORSES ARE GONE!
THEY SNUCK RIGHT INTO CAMP AND OX-NAPPED EIGHTEEN CATTLE!
AND ALL OF MR. GRAVES'S HORSES!
WE HAVE TO GET OUT OF HERE! THIS PLACE IS DANGEROUS!
EVERYWHERE IS DANGEROUS.
WE NEED TO POST MORE GUARDS. WE CAN'T LOSE ANY MORE ANIMALS!

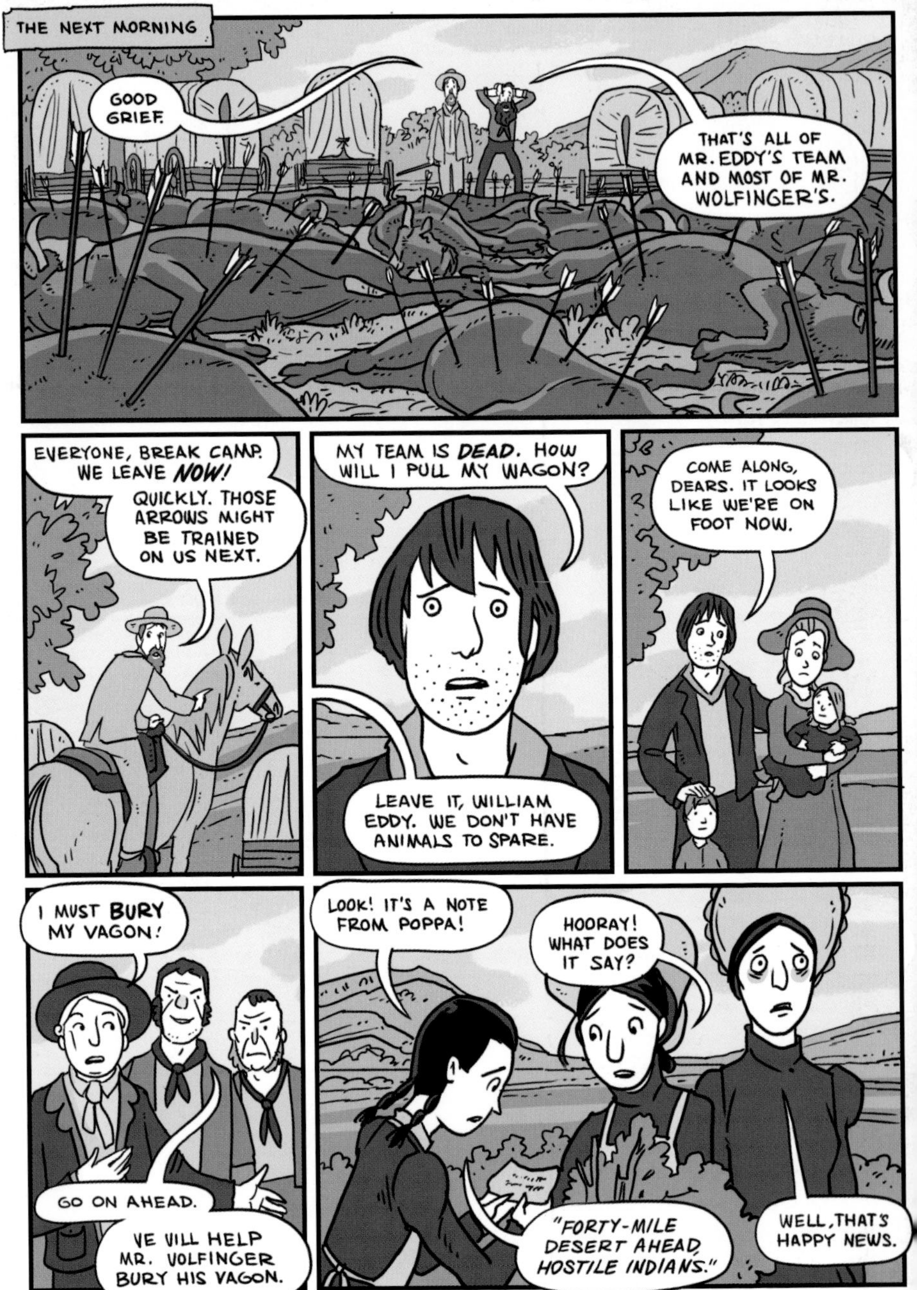
THE NEXT MORNING
GOOD GRIEF.
THAT'S ALL OF MR. EDDY'S TEAM AND MOST OF MR. WOLFINGER'S.
EVERYONE, BREAK CAMP. WE LEAVE *NOW!*
QUICKLY. THOSE ARROWS MIGHT BE TRAINED ON US NEXT.
MY TEAM IS ***DEAD***. HOW WILL I PULL MY WAGON?
LEAVE IT, WILLIAM EDDY. WE DON'T HAVE ANIMALS TO SPARE.
COME ALONG, DEARS. IT LOOKS LIKE WE'RE ON FOOT NOW.
I MUST **BURY** MY VAGON!
GO ON AHEAD.
VE VILL HELP MR. VOLFINGER BURY HIS VAGON.
LOOK! IT'S A NOTE FROM POPPA!
HOORAY! WHAT DOES IT SAY?
"FORTY-MILE DESERT AHEAD, HOSTILE INDIANS."
WELL, THAT'S HAPPY NEWS.

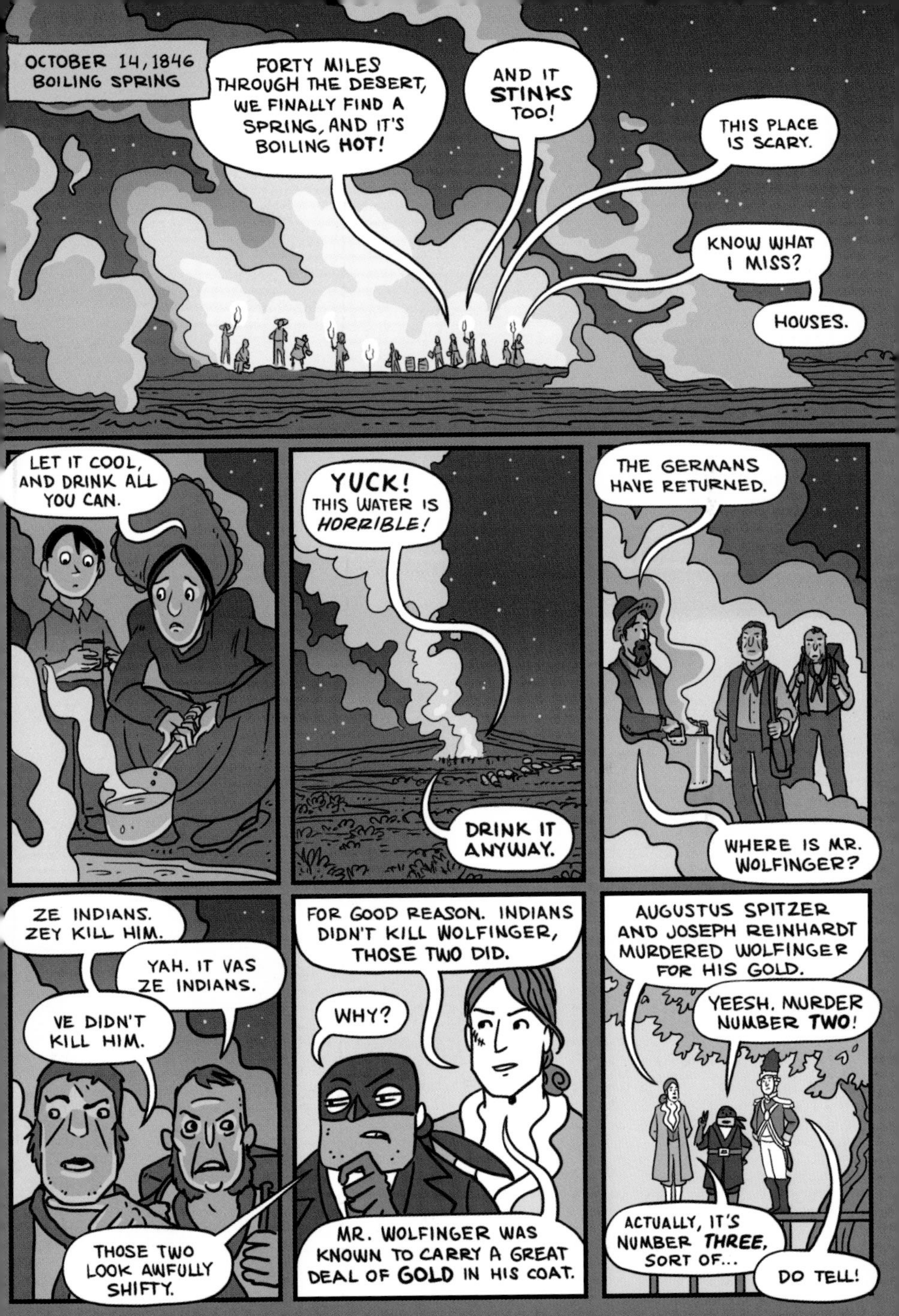
OCTOBER 14, 1846
BOILING SPRING
FORTY MILES THROUGH THE DESERT, WE FINALLY FIND A SPRING, AND IT'S BOILING **HOT**!
AND IT **STINKS** TOO!
THIS PLACE IS SCARY.
KNOW WHAT I MISS?
HOUSES.
LET IT COOL, AND DRINK ALL YOU CAN.
YUCK! THIS WATER IS *HORRIBLE!*
DRINK IT ANYWAY.
THE GERMANS HAVE RETURNED.
WHERE IS MR. WOLFINGER?
ZE INDIANS. ZEY KILL HIM.
YAH. IT VAS ZE INDIANS.
VE DIDN'T KILL HIM.
THOSE TWO LOOK AWFULLY SHIFTY.
FOR GOOD REASON. INDIANS DIDN'T KILL WOLFINGER, **THOSE TWO DID.**
WHY?
MR. WOLFINGER WAS KNOWN TO CARRY A GREAT DEAL OF **GOLD** IN HIS COAT.
AUGUSTUS SPITZER AND JOSEPH REINHARDT MURDERED WOLFINGER FOR HIS GOLD.
YEESH. MURDER NUMBER **TWO**!
ACTUALLY, IT'S NUMBER ***THREE,*** SORT OF...
DO TELL!

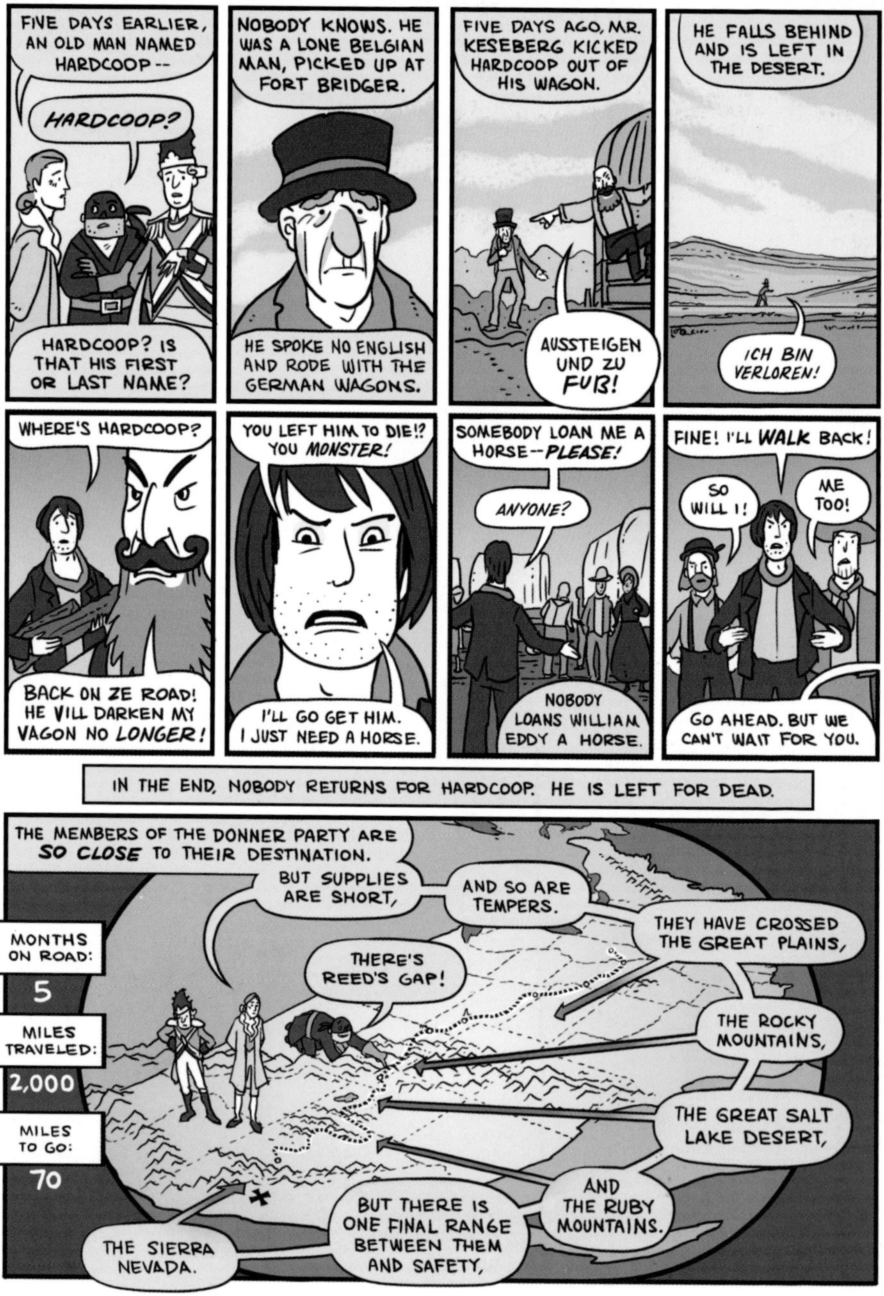
FIVE DAYS EARLIER, AN OLD MAN NAMED HARDCOOP--
HARDCOOP?
HARDCOOP? IS THAT HIS FIRST OR LAST NAME?
NOBODY KNOWS. HE WAS A LONE BELGIAN MAN, PICKED UP AT FORT BRIDGER.
HE SPOKE NO ENGLISH AND RODE WITH THE GERMAN WAGONS.
FIVE DAYS AGO, MR. KESEBERG KICKED HARDCOOP OUT OF HIS WAGON.
AUSSTEIGEN UND ZU FUß!
HE FALLS BEHIND AND IS LEFT IN THE DESERT.
ICH BIN VERLOREN!
WHERE'S HARDCOOP?
BACK ON ZE ROAD! HE VILL DARKEN MY VAGON NO LONGER!
YOU LEFT HIM TO DIE!? YOU MONSTER!
I'LL GO GET HIM. I JUST NEED A HORSE.
SOMEBODY LOAN ME A HORSE--PLEASE!
ANYONE?
NOBODY LOANS WILLIAM EDDY A HORSE.
FINE! I'LL WALK BACK!
SO WILL I!
ME TOO!
GO AHEAD. BUT WE CAN'T WAIT FOR YOU.
IN THE END, NOBODY RETURNS FOR HARDCOOP. HE IS LEFT FOR DEAD.
THE MEMBERS OF THE DONNER PARTY ARE SO CLOSE TO THEIR DESTINATION.
BUT SUPPLIES ARE SHORT,
AND SO ARE TEMPERS.
MONTHS ON ROAD:
5
MILES TRAVELED:
2,000
MILES TO GO:
70
THERE'S REED'S GAP!
THEY HAVE CROSSED THE GREAT PLAINS,
THE ROCKY MOUNTAINS,
THE GREAT SALT LAKE DESERT,
AND THE RUBY MOUNTAINS.
BUT THERE IS ONE FINAL RANGE BETWEEN THEM AND SAFETY,
THE SIERRA NEVADA.

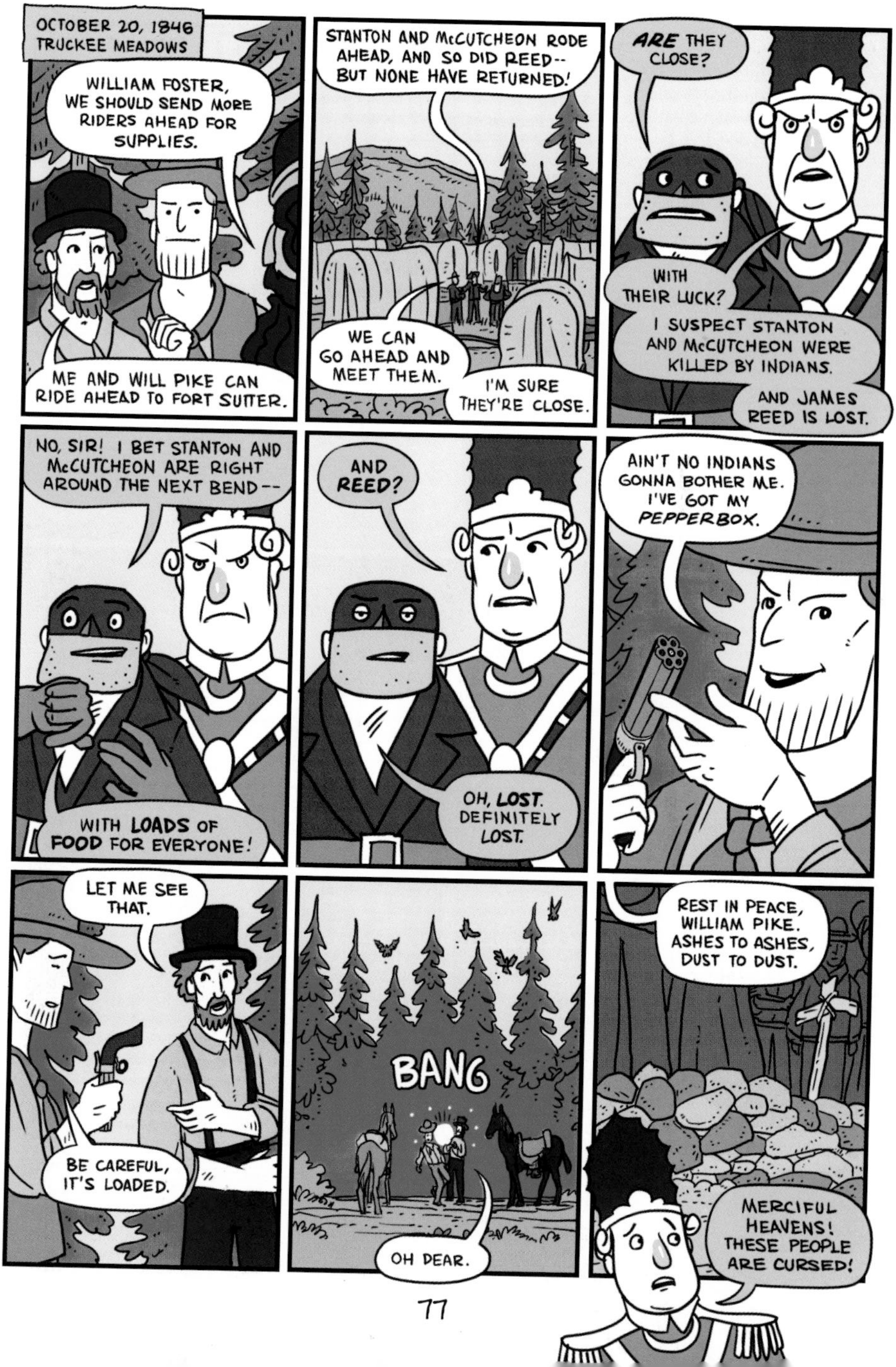
OCTOBER 20, 1846
TRUCKEE MEADOWS
WILLIAM FOSTER, WE SHOULD SEND MORE RIDERS AHEAD FOR SUPPLIES.
ME AND WILL PIKE CAN RIDE AHEAD TO FORT SUTTER.
STANTON AND McCUTCHEON RODE AHEAD, AND SO DID REED-- BUT NONE HAVE RETURNED!
WE CAN GO AHEAD AND MEET THEM.
I'M SURE THEY'RE CLOSE.
ARE THEY CLOSE?
WITH THEIR LUCK?
I SUSPECT STANTON AND McCUTCHEON WERE KILLED BY INDIANS.
AND JAMES REED IS LOST.
NO, SIR! I BET STANTON AND McCUTCHEON ARE RIGHT AROUND THE NEXT BEND--
WITH LOADS OF FOOD FOR EVERYONE!
AND REED?
OH, LOST. DEFINITELY LOST.
AIN'T NO INDIANS GONNA BOTHER ME. I'VE GOT MY PEPPERBOX.
LET ME SEE THAT.
BE CAREFUL, IT'S LOADED.
BANG
OH DEAR.
REST IN PEACE, WILLIAM PIKE. ASHES TO ASHES, DUST TO DUST.
MERCIFUL HEAVENS! THESE PEOPLE ARE CURSED!

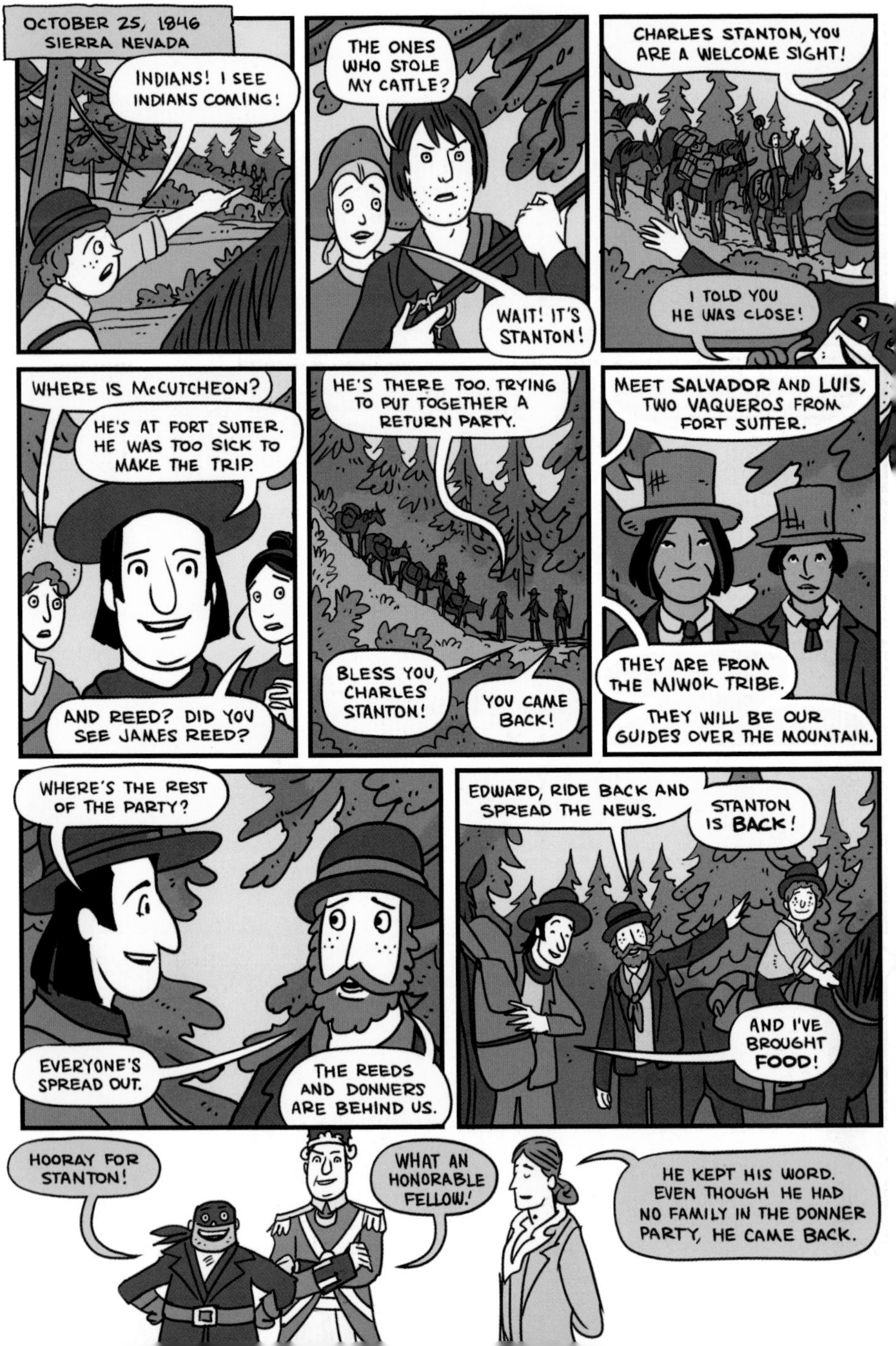
OCTOBER 25, 1846
SIERRA NEVADA
INDIANS! I SEE INDIANS COMING!
THE ONES WHO STOLE MY CATTLE?
WAIT! IT'S STANTON!
CHARLES STANTON, YOU ARE A WELCOME SIGHT!
I TOLD YOU HE WAS CLOSE!
WHERE IS McCUTCHEON?
HE'S AT FORT SUTTER. HE WAS TOO SICK TO MAKE THE TRIP.
AND REED? DID YOU SEE JAMES REED?
HE'S THERE TOO. TRYING TO PUT TOGETHER A RETURN PARTY.
BLESS YOU, CHARLES STANTON!
YOU CAME BACK!
MEET SALVADOR AND LUIS, TWO VAQUEROS FROM FORT SUTTER.
THEY ARE FROM THE MIWOK TRIBE.
THEY WILL BE OUR GUIDES OVER THE MOUNTAIN.
WHERE'S THE REST OF THE PARTY?
EVERYONE'S SPREAD OUT.
THE REEDS AND DONNERS ARE BEHIND US.
EDWARD, RIDE BACK AND SPREAD THE NEWS.
STANTON IS BACK!
AND I'VE BROUGHT FOOD!
HOORAY FOR STANTON!
WHAT AN HONORABLE FELLOW!
HE KEPT HIS WORD. EVEN THOUGH HE HAD NO FAMILY IN THE DONNER PARTY, HE CAME BACK.

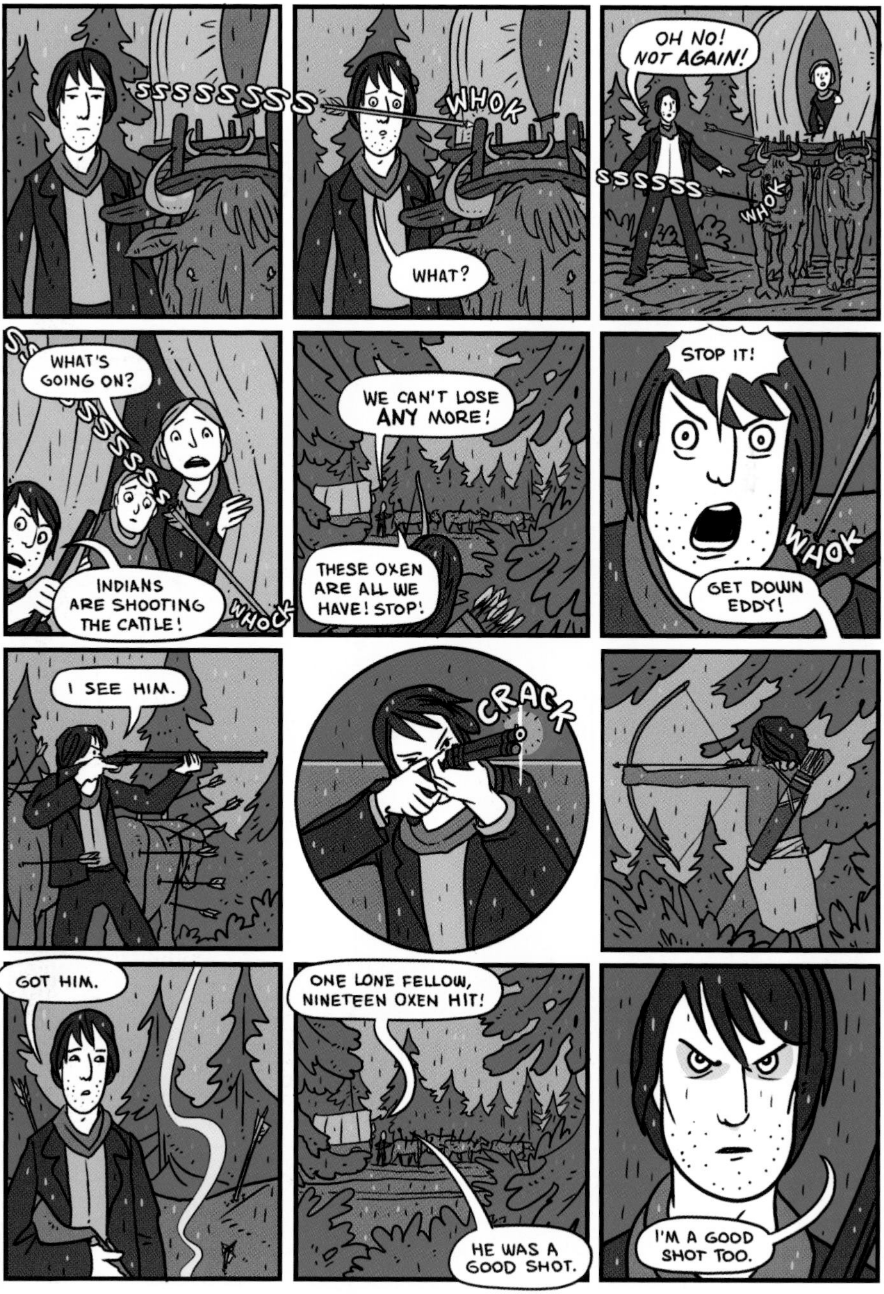
SSSSSSSS
WHOK
WHAT?
OH NO! NOT AGAIN!
SSSSSS
WHOK
WHAT'S GOING ON?
INDIANS ARE SHOOTING THE CATTLE!
WHOCK
WE CAN'T LOSE ANY MORE!
THESE OXEN ARE ALL WE HAVE! STOP!
STOP IT!
WHOK
GET DOWN EDDY!
I SEE HIM.
CRACK
GOT HIM.
ONE LONE FELLOW, NINETEEN OXEN HIT!
HE WAS A GOOD SHOT.
I'M A GOOD SHOT TOO.

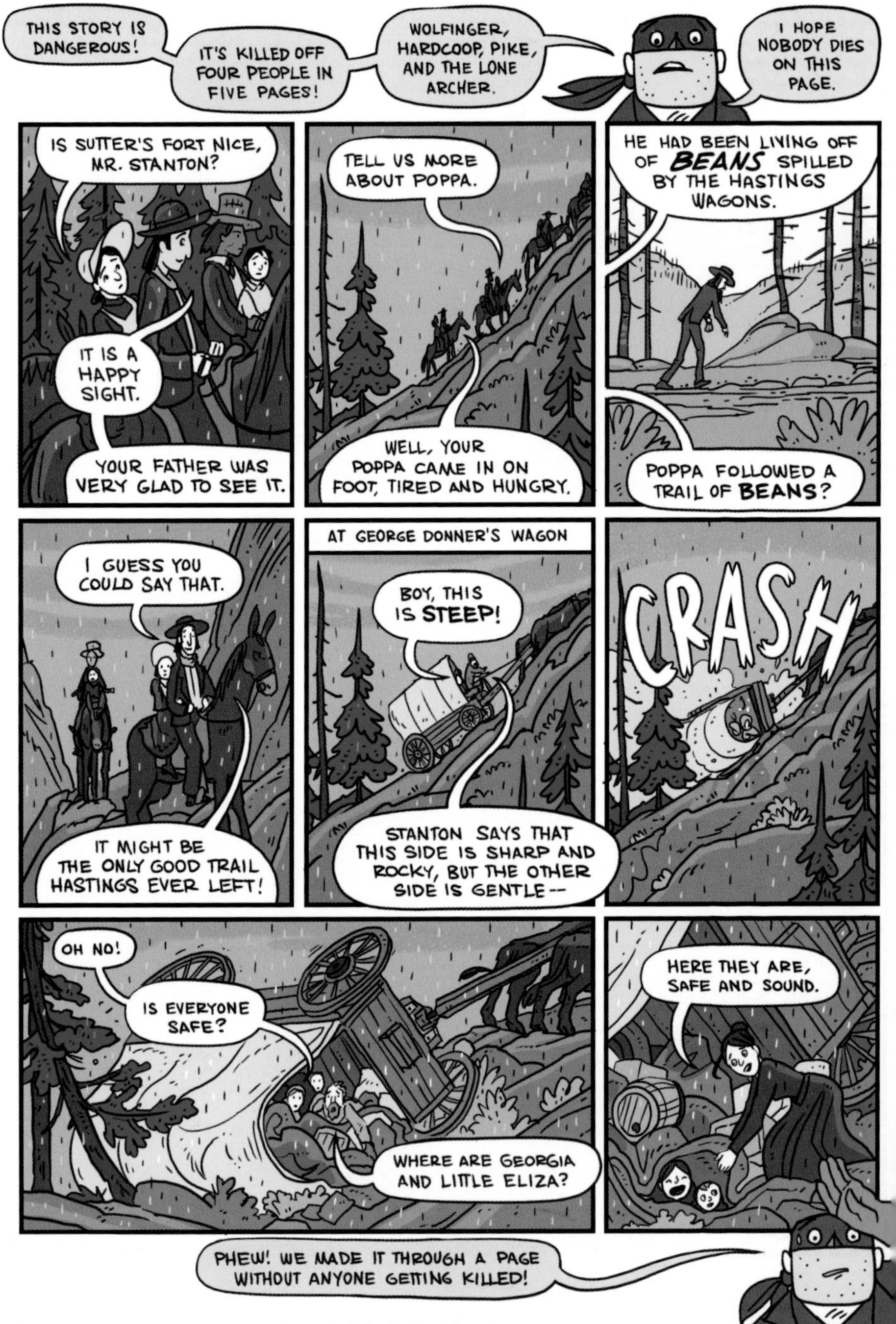
THIS STORY IS DANGEROUS!
IT'S KILLED OFF FOUR PEOPLE IN FIVE PAGES!
WOLFINGER, HARDCOOP, PIKE, AND THE LONE ARCHER.
I HOPE NOBODY DIES ON THIS PAGE.
IS SUTTER'S FORT NICE, MR. STANTON?
IT IS A HAPPY SIGHT.
YOUR FATHER WAS VERY GLAD TO SEE IT.
TELL US MORE ABOUT POPPA.
WELL, YOUR POPPA CAME IN ON FOOT, TIRED AND HUNGRY.
HE HAD BEEN LIVING OFF OF BEANS SPILLED BY THE HASTINGS WAGONS.
POPPA FOLLOWED A TRAIL OF BEANS?
I GUESS YOU COULD SAY THAT.
IT MIGHT BE THE ONLY GOOD TRAIL HASTINGS EVER LEFT!
AT GEORGE DONNER'S WAGON
BOY, THIS IS STEEP!
STANTON SAYS THAT THIS SIDE IS SHARP AND ROCKY, BUT THE OTHER SIDE IS GENTLE--
CRASH
OH NO!
IS EVERYONE SAFE?
WHERE ARE GEORGIA AND LITTLE ELIZA?
HERE THEY ARE, SAFE AND SOUND.
PHEW! WE MADE IT THROUGH A PAGE WITHOUT ANYONE GETTING KILLED!

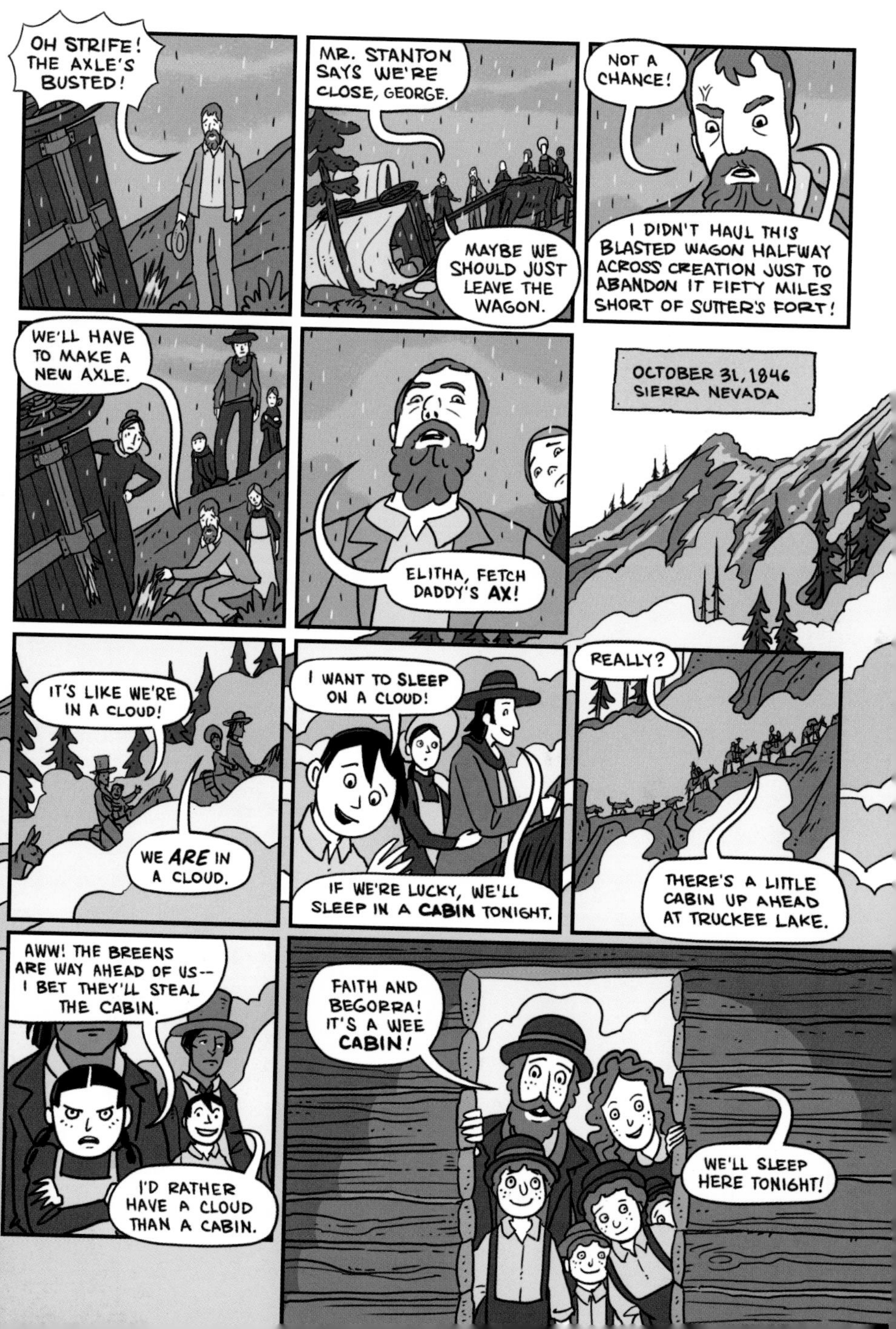
OH STRIFE! THE AXLE'S BUSTED!
MR. STANTON SAYS WE'RE CLOSE, GEORGE.
MAYBE WE SHOULD JUST LEAVE THE WAGON.
NOT A CHANCE!
I DIDN'T HAUL THIS BLASTED WAGON HALFWAY ACROSS CREATION JUST TO ABANDON IT FIFTY MILES SHORT OF SUTTER'S FORT!
WE'LL HAVE TO MAKE A NEW AXLE.
ELITHA, FETCH DADDY'S AX!
OCTOBER 31, 1846 SIERRA NEVADA
IT'S LIKE WE'RE IN A CLOUD!
WE ARE IN A CLOUD.
I WANT TO SLEEP ON A CLOUD!
IF WE'RE LUCKY, WE'LL SLEEP IN A CABIN TONIGHT.
REALLY?
THERE'S A LITTLE CABIN UP AHEAD AT TRUCKEE LAKE.
AWW! THE BREENS ARE WAY AHEAD OF US-- I BET THEY'LL STEAL THE CABIN.
I'D RATHER HAVE A CLOUD THAN A CABIN.
FAITH AND BEGORRA! IT'S A WEE CABIN!
WE'LL SLEEP HERE TONIGHT!

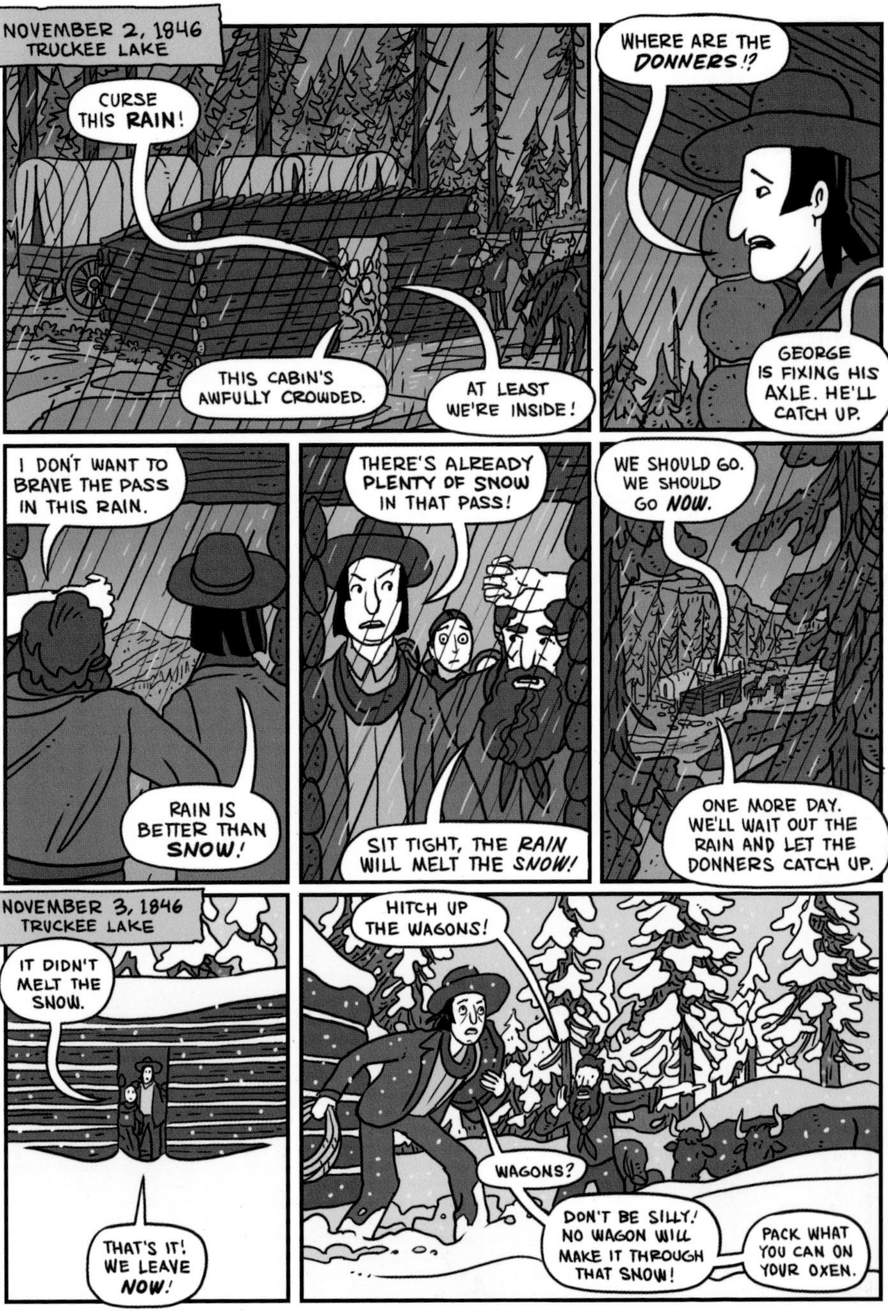

NOVEMBER 2, 1846
TRUCKEE LAKE
CURSE THIS RAIN!
THIS CABIN'S AWFULLY CROWDED.
AT LEAST WE'RE INSIDE!
WHERE ARE THE DONNERS!?
GEORGE IS FIXING HIS AXLE. HE'LL CATCH UP.
I DON'T WANT TO BRAVE THE PASS IN THIS RAIN.
RAIN IS BETTER THAN SNOW!
THERE'S ALREADY PLENTY OF SNOW IN THAT PASS!
SIT TIGHT, THE RAIN WILL MELT THE SNOW!
WE SHOULD GO. WE SHOULD GO NOW.
ONE MORE DAY. WE'LL WAIT OUT THE RAIN AND LET THE DONNERS CATCH UP.
NOVEMBER 3, 1846
TRUCKEE LAKE
IT DIDN'T MELT THE SNOW.
THAT'S IT! WE LEAVE NOW!
HITCH UP THE WAGONS!
WAGONS?
DON'T BE SILLY! NO WAGON WILL MAKE IT THROUGH THAT SNOW!
PACK WHAT YOU CAN ON YOUR OXEN.

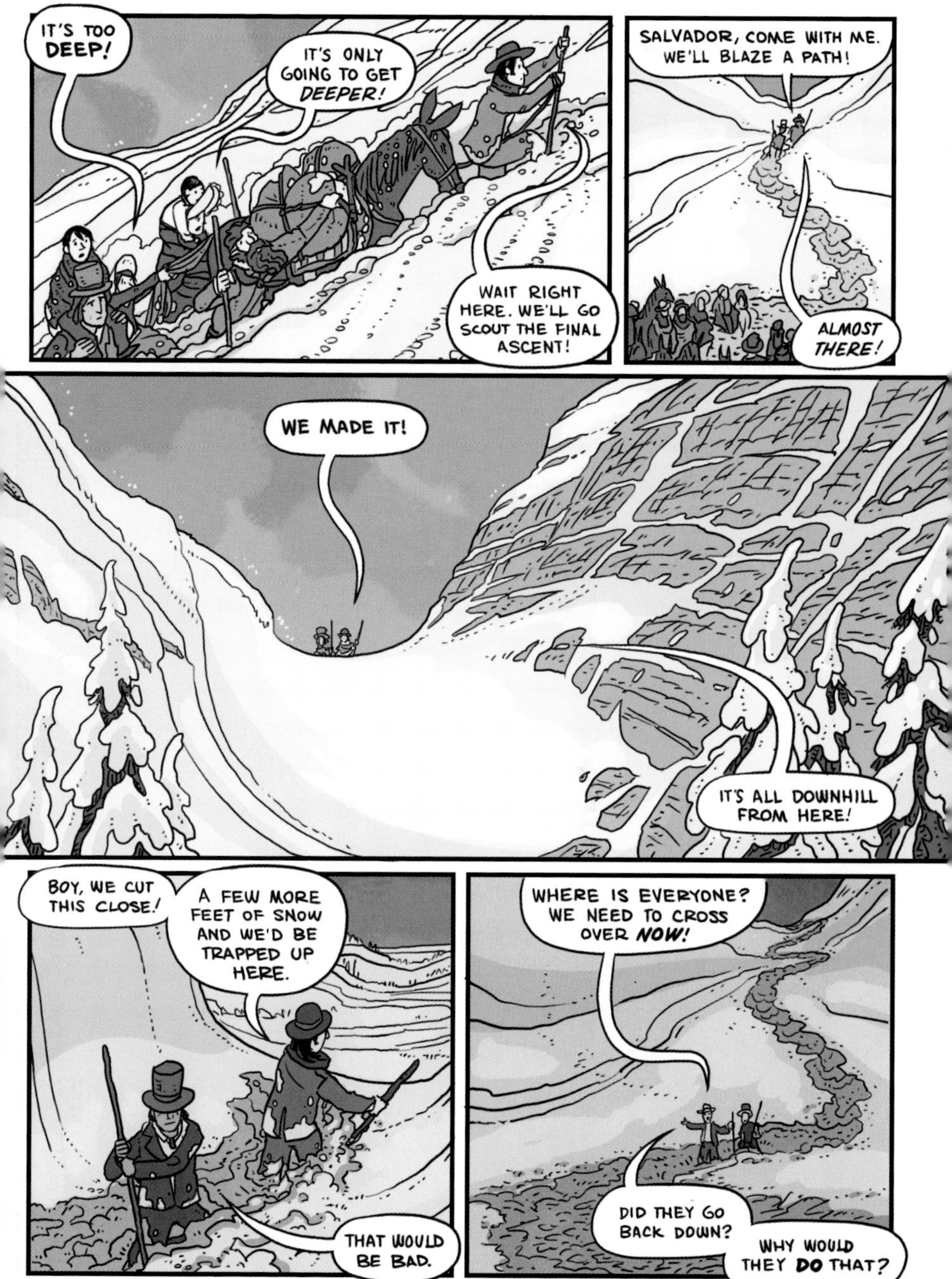
IT'S TOO DEEP!
IT'S ONLY GOING TO GET DEEPER!
WAIT RIGHT HERE. WE'LL GO SCOUT THE FINAL ASCENT!
SALVADOR, COME WITH ME. WE'LL BLAZE A PATH!
ALMOST THERE!
WE MADE IT!
IT'S ALL DOWNHILL FROM HERE!
BOY, WE CUT THIS CLOSE!
A FEW MORE FEET OF SNOW AND WE'D BE TRAPPED UP HERE.
THAT WOULD BE BAD.
WHERE IS EVERYONE? WE NEED TO CROSS OVER NOW!
DID THEY GO BACK DOWN?
WHY WOULD THEY DO THAT?

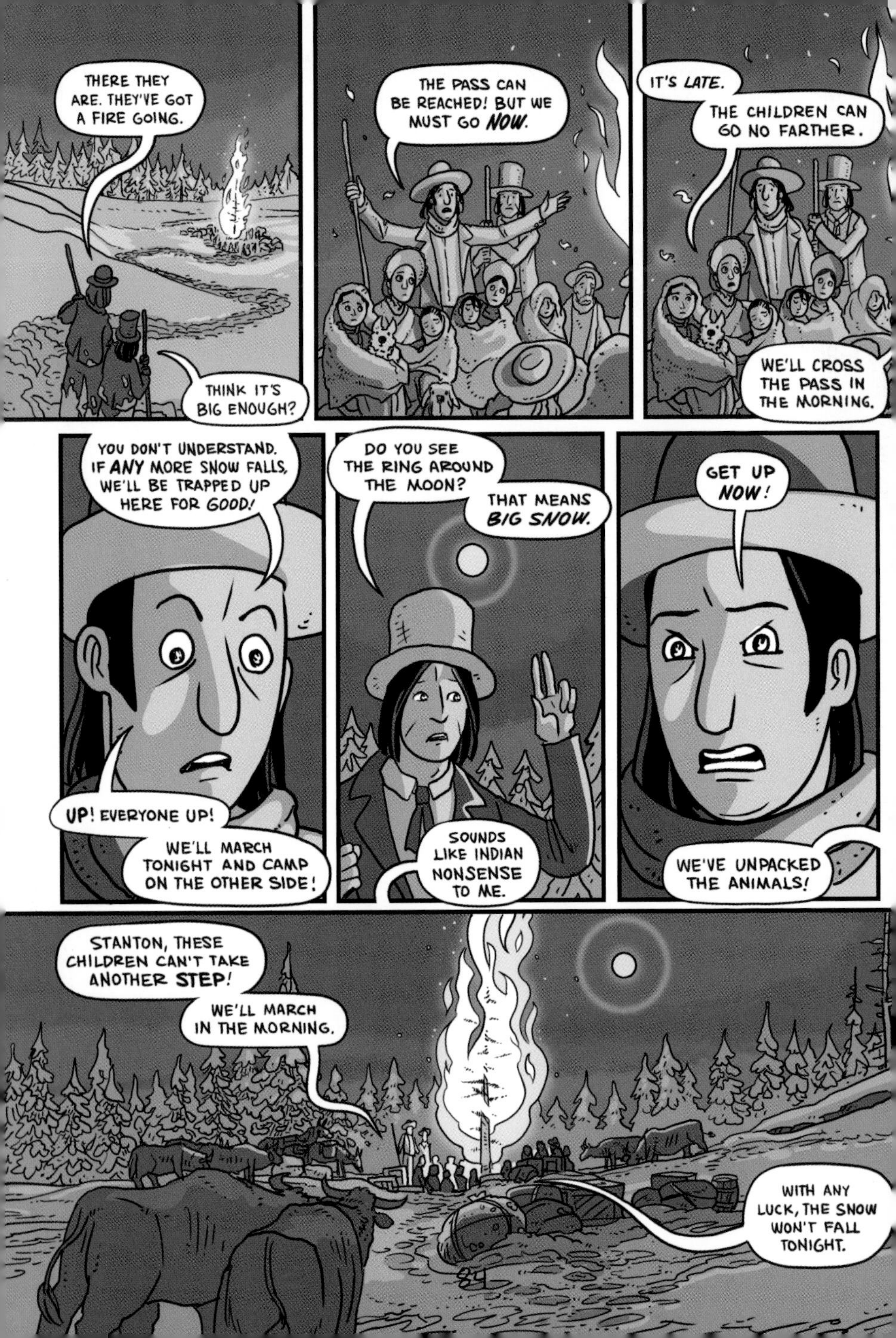
THERE THEY ARE. THEY'VE GOT A FIRE GOING.
THINK IT'S BIG ENOUGH?
THE PASS CAN BE REACHED! BUT WE MUST GO NOW.
IT'S LATE.
THE CHILDREN CAN GO NO FARTHER.
WE'LL CROSS THE PASS IN THE MORNING.
YOU DON'T UNDERSTAND. IF ANY MORE SNOW FALLS, WE'LL BE TRAPPED UP HERE FOR GOOD!
UP! EVERYONE UP!
WE'LL MARCH TONIGHT AND CAMP ON THE OTHER SIDE!
DO YOU SEE THE RING AROUND THE MOON?
THAT MEANS BIG SNOW.
SOUNDS LIKE INDIAN NONSENSE TO ME.
GET UP NOW!
WE'VE UNPACKED THE ANIMALS!
STANTON, THESE CHILDREN CAN'T TAKE ANOTHER STEP!
WE'LL MARCH IN THE MORNING.
WITH ANY LUCK, THE SNOW WON'T FALL TONIGHT.

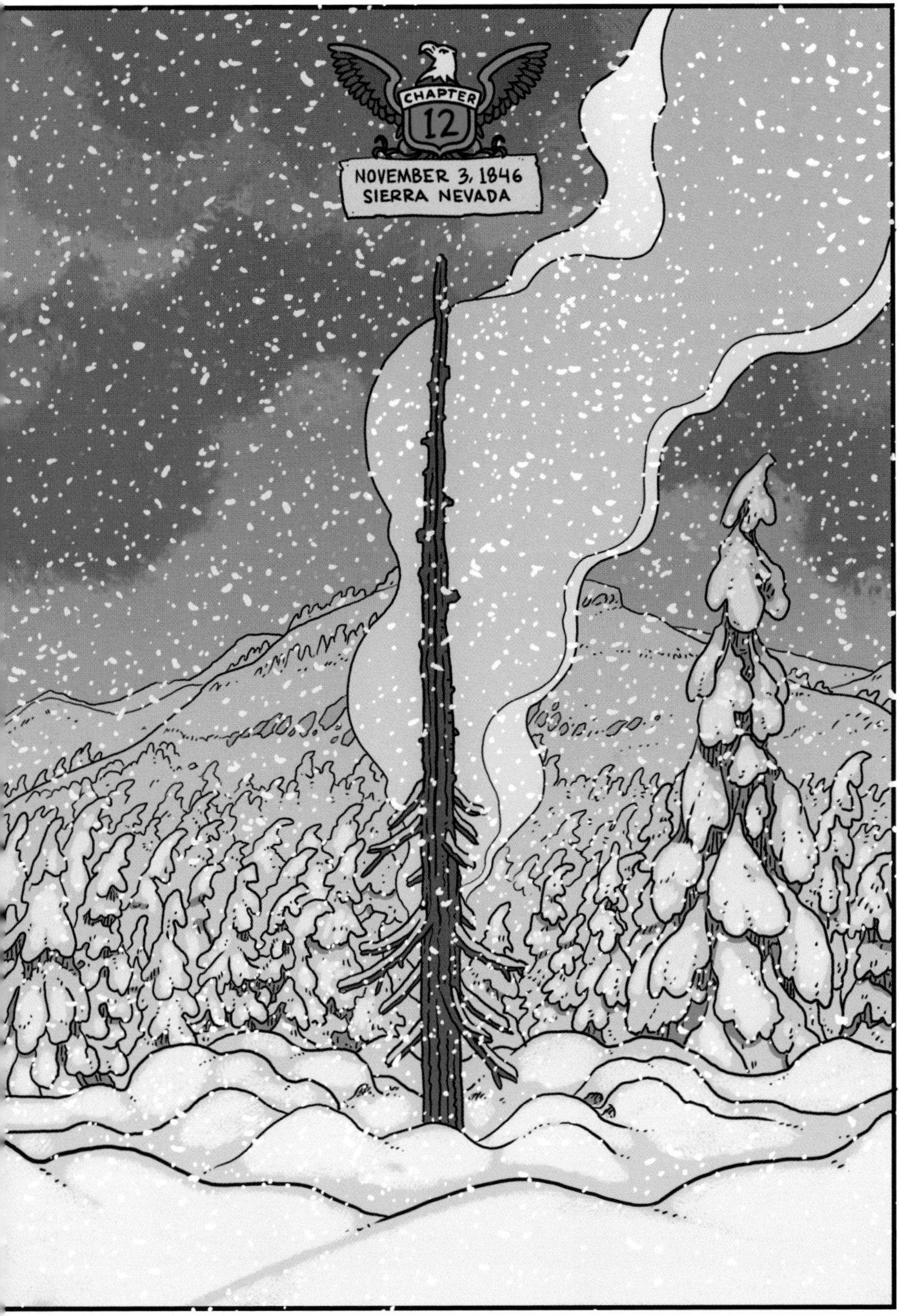
CHAPTER
12
NOVEMBER 3, 1846
SIERRA NEVADA

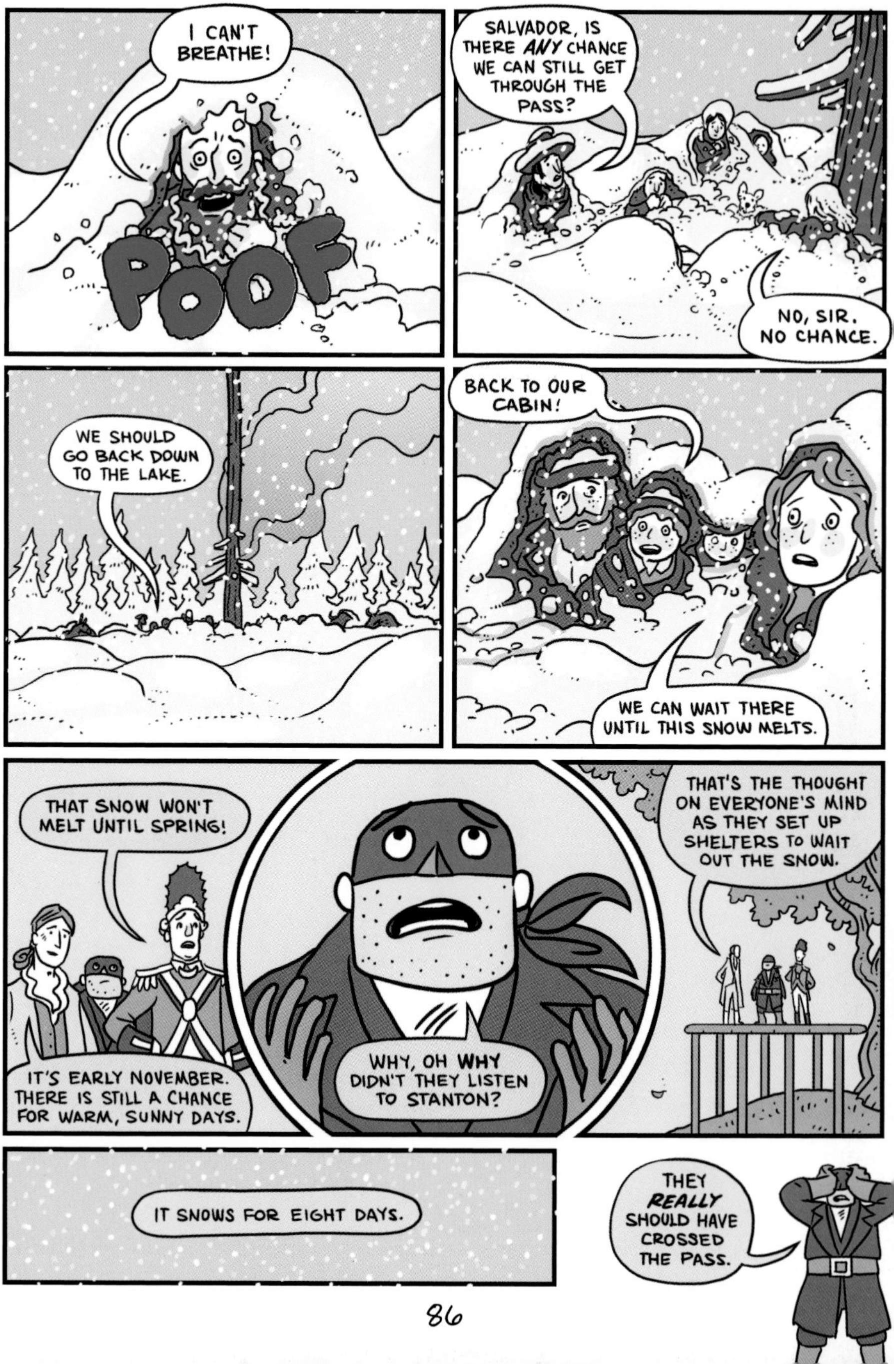
I CAN'T BREATHE!
POOF
SALVADOR, IS THERE ANY CHANCE WE CAN STILL GET THROUGH THE PASS?
NO, SIR. NO CHANCE.
WE SHOULD GO BACK DOWN TO THE LAKE.
BACK TO OUR CABIN!
WE CAN WAIT THERE UNTIL THIS SNOW MELTS.
THAT SNOW WON'T MELT UNTIL SPRING!
IT'S EARLY NOVEMBER. THERE IS STILL A CHANCE FOR WARM, SUNNY DAYS.
WHY, OH WHY DIDN'T THEY LISTEN TO STANTON?
THAT'S THE THOUGHT ON EVERYONE'S MIND AS THEY SET UP SHELTERS TO WAIT OUT THE SNOW.
IT SNOWS FOR EIGHT DAYS.
THEY REALLY SHOULD HAVE CROSSED THE PASS.

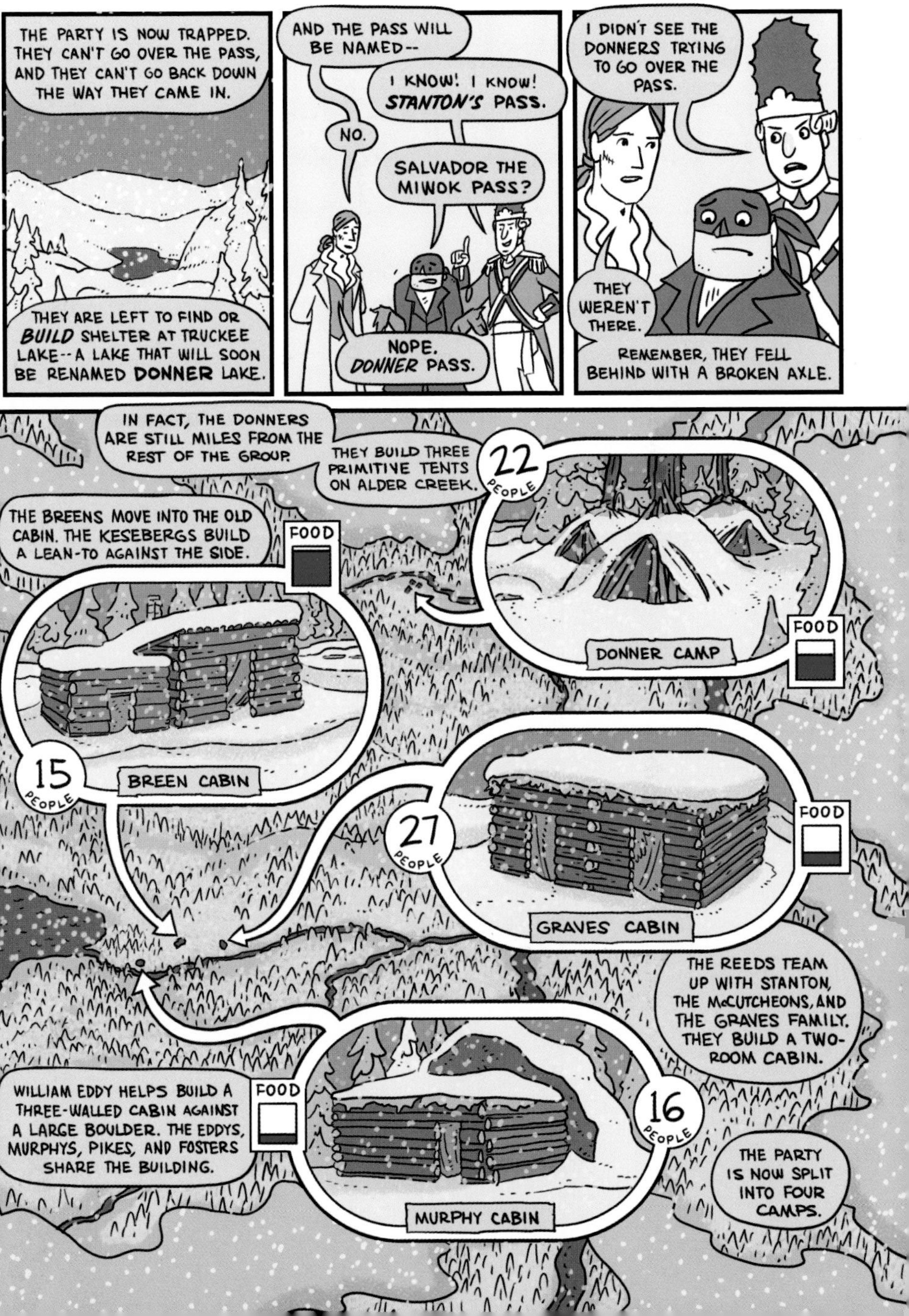
THE PARTY IS NOW TRAPPED. THEY CAN'T GO OVER THE PASS, AND THEY CAN'T GO BACK DOWN THE WAY THEY CAME IN.
THEY ARE LEFT TO FIND OR BUILD SHELTER AT TRUCKEE LAKE--A LAKE THAT WILL SOON BE RENAMED DONNER LAKE.
AND THE PASS WILL BE NAMED--
I KNOW! I KNOW! STANTON'S PASS.
NO.
SALVADOR THE MIWOK PASS?
NOPE. DONNER PASS.
I DIDN'T SEE THE DONNERS TRYING TO GO OVER THE PASS.
THEY WEREN'T THERE.
REMEMBER, THEY FELL BEHIND WITH A BROKEN AXLE.
IN FACT, THE DONNERS ARE STILL MILES FROM THE REST OF THE GROUP.
THEY BUILD THREE PRIMITIVE TENTS ON ALDER CREEK.
22 PEOPLE
DONNER CAMP
FOOD
THE BREENS MOVE INTO THE OLD CABIN. THE KESEBERGS BUILD A LEAN-TO AGAINST THE SIDE.
FOOD
15 PEOPLE
BREEN CABIN
27 PEOPLE
GRAVES CABIN
FOOD
THE REEDS TEAM UP WITH STANTON, THE McCUTCHEONS, AND THE GRAVES FAMILY. THEY BUILD A TWO-ROOM CABIN.
WILLIAM EDDY HELPS BUILD A THREE-WALLED CABIN AGAINST A LARGE BOULDER. THE EDDYS, MURPHYS, PIKES, AND FOSTERS SHARE THE BUILDING.
FOOD
16 PEOPLE
MURPHY CABIN
THE PARTY IS NOW SPLIT INTO FOUR CAMPS.

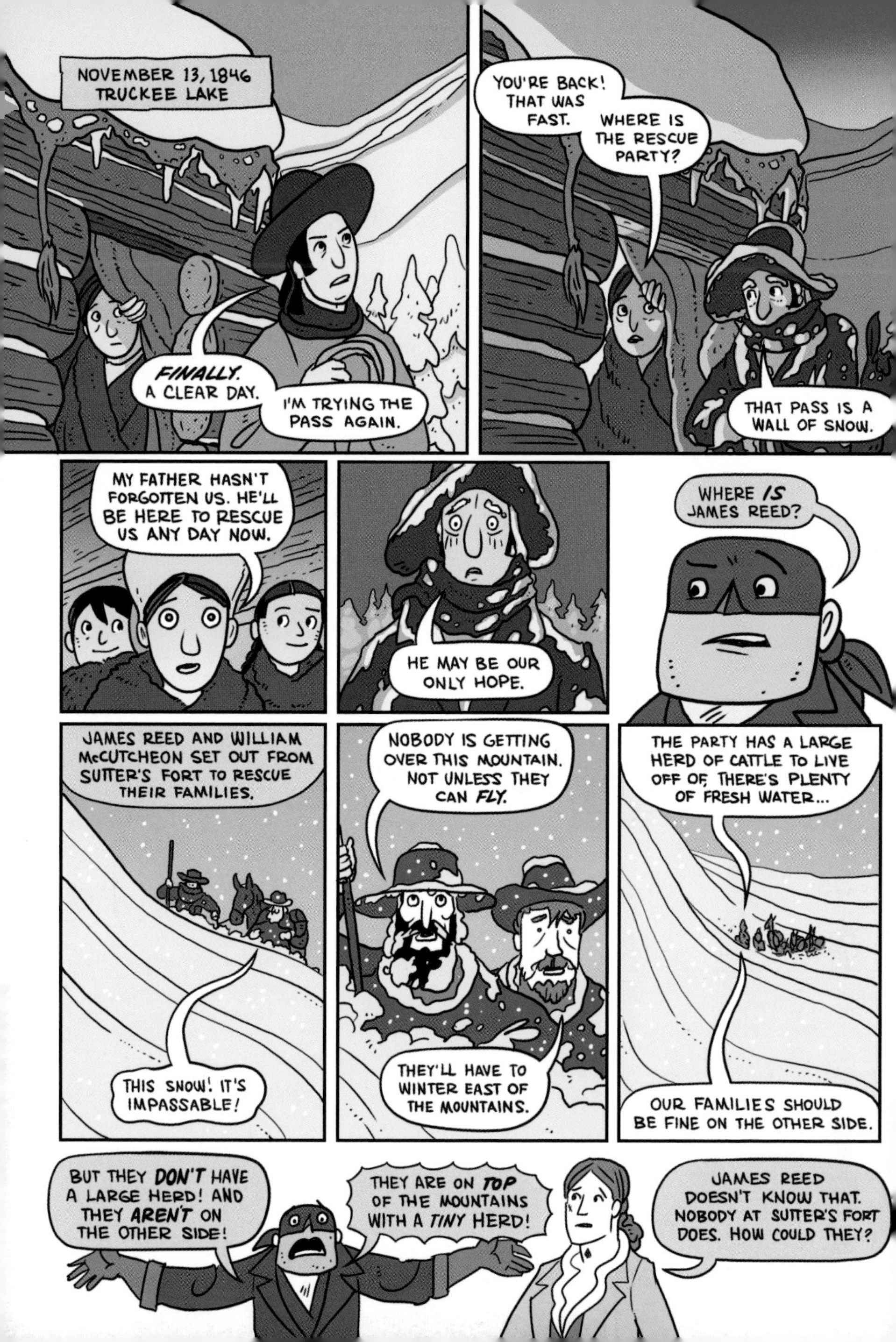
NOVEMBER 13, 1846
TRUCKEE LAKE
FINALLY. A CLEAR DAY.
I'M TRYING THE PASS AGAIN.
YOU'RE BACK! THAT WAS FAST.
WHERE IS THE RESCUE PARTY?
THAT PASS IS A WALL OF SNOW.
MY FATHER HASN'T FORGOTTEN US. HE'LL BE HERE TO RESCUE US ANY DAY NOW.
HE MAY BE OUR ONLY HOPE.
WHERE *IS* JAMES REED?
JAMES REED AND WILLIAM McCUTCHEON SET OUT FROM SUTTER'S FORT TO RESCUE THEIR FAMILIES.
THIS SNOW! IT'S IMPASSABLE!
NOBODY IS GETTING OVER THIS MOUNTAIN. NOT UNLESS THEY CAN *FLY.*
THEY'LL HAVE TO WINTER EAST OF THE MOUNTAINS.
THE PARTY HAS A LARGE HERD OF CATTLE TO LIVE OFF OF, THERE'S PLENTY OF FRESH WATER...
OUR FAMILIES SHOULD BE FINE ON THE OTHER SIDE.
BUT THEY **DON'T** HAVE A LARGE HERD! AND THEY ***AREN'T*** ON THE OTHER SIDE!
THEY ARE ON ***TOP*** OF THE MOUNTAINS WITH A *TINY* HERD!
JAMES REED DOESN'T KNOW THAT. NOBODY AT SUTTER'S FORT DOES. HOW COULD THEY?

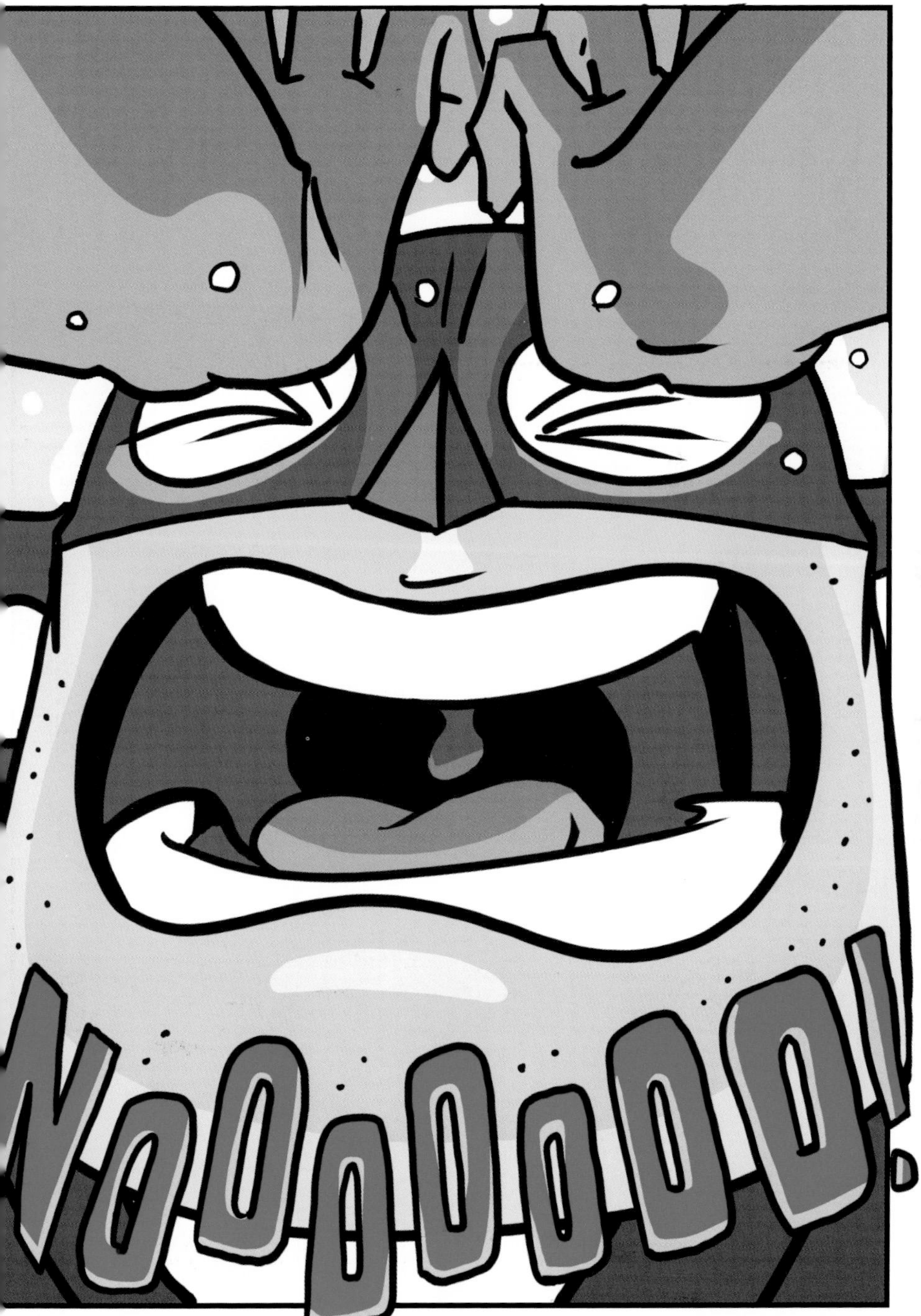
NOOOOOOOO!!

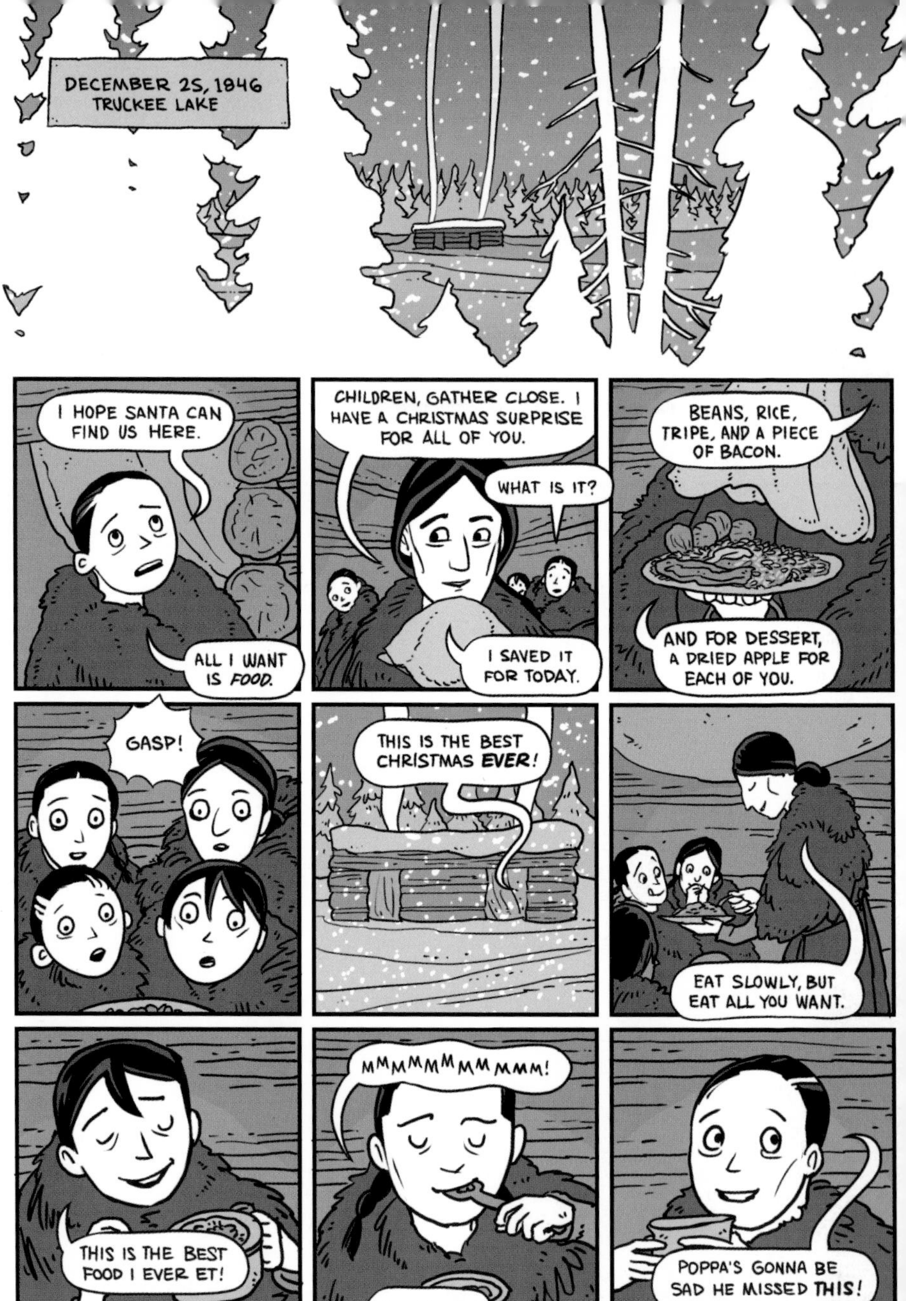

DECEMBER 25, 1846
TRUCKEE LAKE
I HOPE SANTA CAN FIND US HERE.
ALL I WANT IS FOOD.
CHILDREN, GATHER CLOSE. I HAVE A CHRISTMAS SURPRISE FOR ALL OF YOU.
WHAT IS IT?
I SAVED IT FOR TODAY.
BEANS, RICE, TRIPE, AND A PIECE OF BACON.
AND FOR DESSERT, A DRIED APPLE FOR EACH OF YOU.
GASP!
THIS IS THE BEST CHRISTMAS EVER!
EAT SLOWLY, BUT EAT ALL YOU WANT.
THIS IS THE BEST FOOD I EVER ET!
MMMMMMMMMMM!
EAT SLOWLY.
POPPA'S GONNA BE SAD HE MISSED THIS!

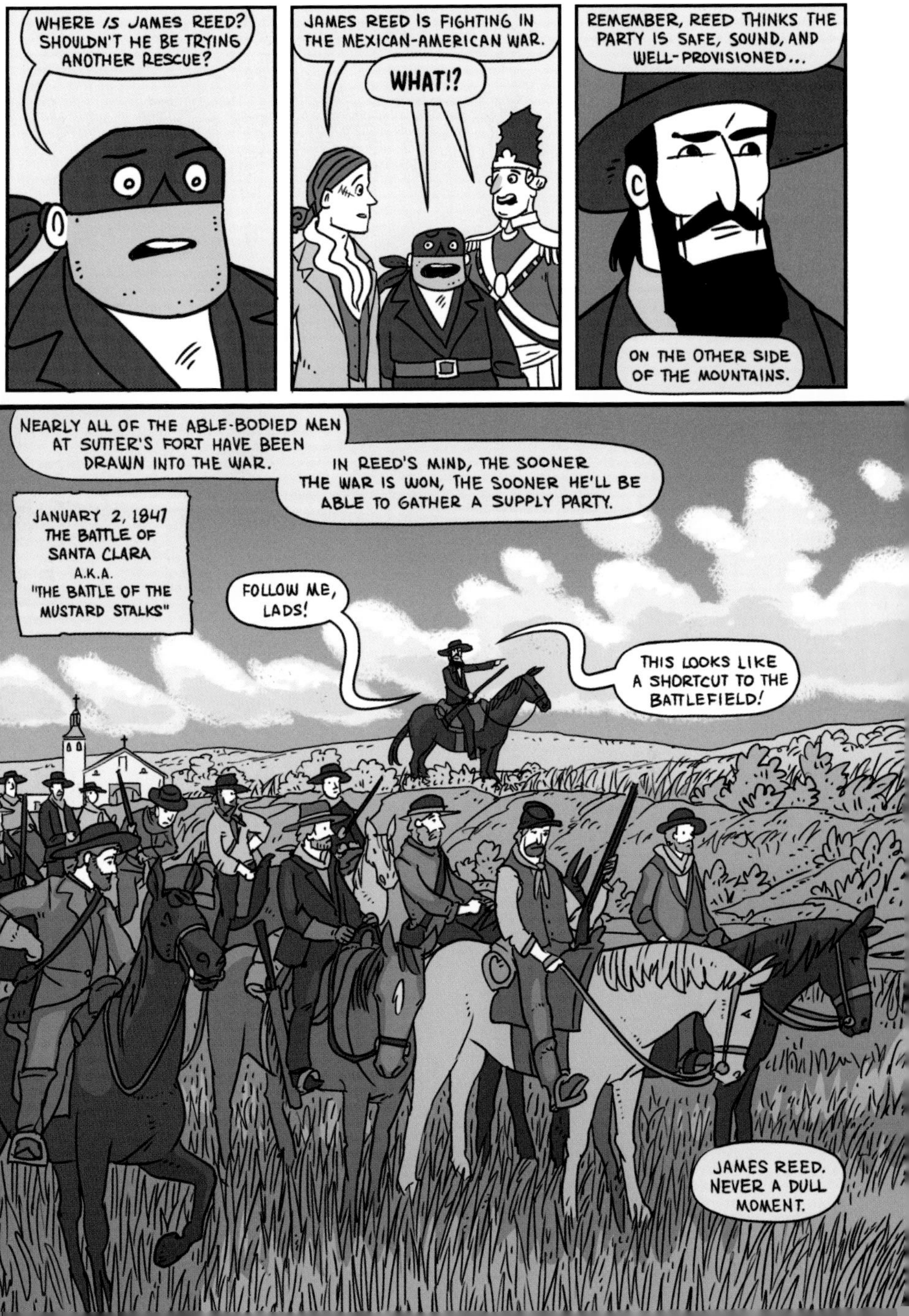
WHERE IS JAMES REED? SHOULDN'T HE BE TRYING ANOTHER RESCUE?
JAMES REED IS FIGHTING IN THE MEXICAN-AMERICAN WAR.
WHAT!?
REMEMBER, REED THINKS THE PARTY IS SAFE, SOUND, AND WELL-PROVISIONED...
ON THE OTHER SIDE OF THE MOUNTAINS.
NEARLY ALL OF THE ABLE-BODIED MEN AT SUTTER'S FORT HAVE BEEN DRAWN INTO THE WAR.
IN REED'S MIND, THE SOONER THE WAR IS WON, THE SOONER HE'LL BE ABLE TO GATHER A SUPPLY PARTY.
JANUARY 2, 1847 THE BATTLE OF SANTA CLARA A.K.A. "THE BATTLE OF THE MUSTARD STALKS"
FOLLOW ME, LADS!
THIS LOOKS LIKE A SHORTCUT TO THE BATTLEFIELD!
JAMES REED. NEVER A DULL MOMENT.

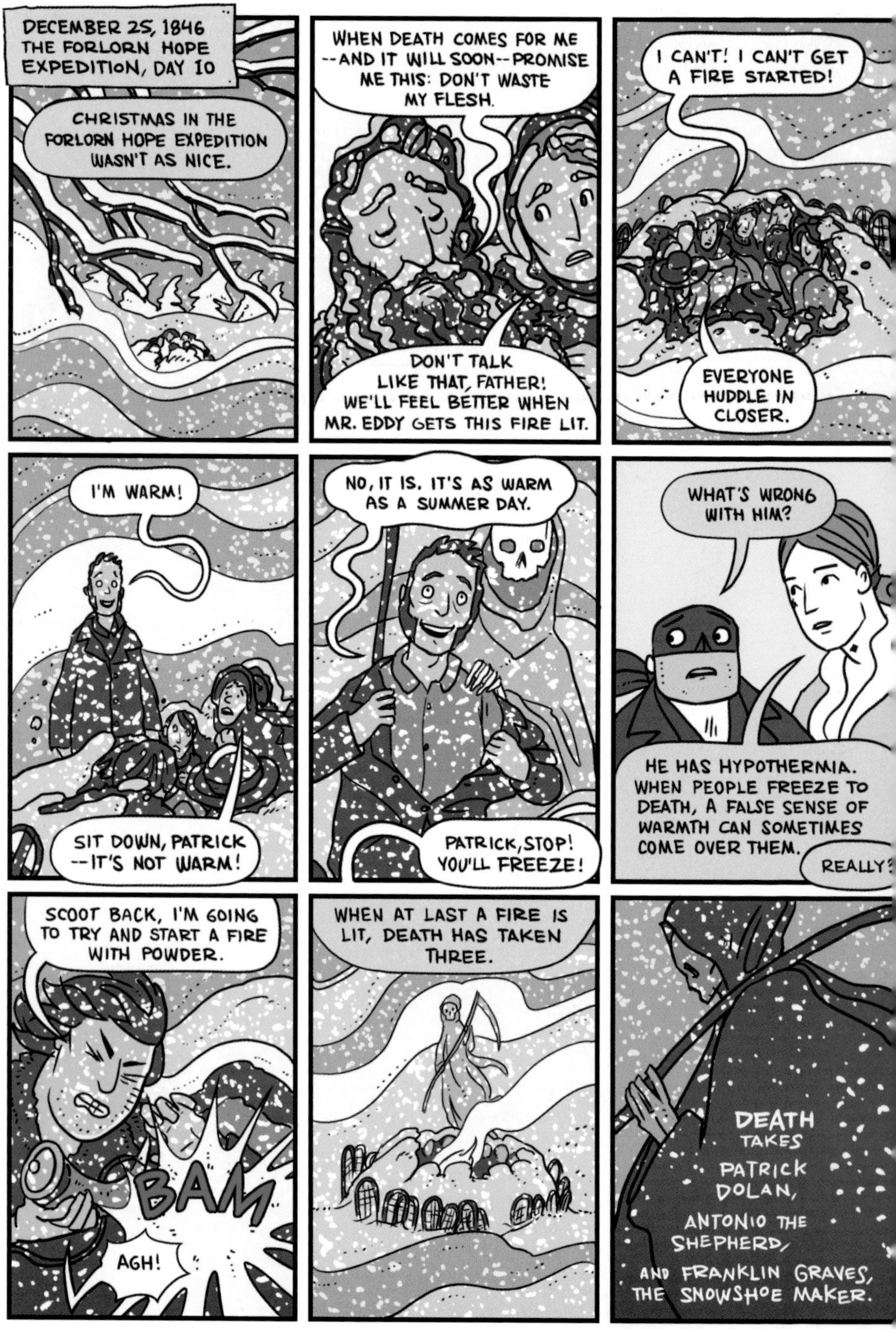
DECEMBER 25, 1846
THE FORLORN HOPE EXPEDITION, DAY 10
CHRISTMAS IN THE FORLORN HOPE EXPEDITION WASN'T AS NICE.
WHEN DEATH COMES FOR ME --AND IT WILL SOON-- PROMISE ME THIS: DON'T WASTE MY FLESH.
DON'T TALK LIKE THAT, FATHER! WE'LL FEEL BETTER WHEN MR. EDDY GETS THIS FIRE LIT.
I CAN'T! I CAN'T GET A FIRE STARTED!
EVERYONE HUDDLE IN CLOSER.
I'M WARM!
SIT DOWN, PATRICK --IT'S NOT WARM!
NO, IT IS. IT'S AS WARM AS A SUMMER DAY.
PATRICK, STOP! YOU'LL FREEZE!
WHAT'S WRONG WITH HIM?
HE HAS HYPOTHERMIA. WHEN PEOPLE FREEZE TO DEATH, A FALSE SENSE OF WARMTH CAN SOMETIMES COME OVER THEM.
REALLY?
SCOOT BACK, I'M GOING TO TRY AND START A FIRE WITH POWDER.
BAM
AGH!
WHEN AT LAST A FIRE IS LIT, DEATH HAS TAKEN THREE.
DEATH TAKES PATRICK DOLAN, ANTONIO THE SHEPHERD, AND FRANKLIN GRAVES, THE SNOWSHOE MAKER.

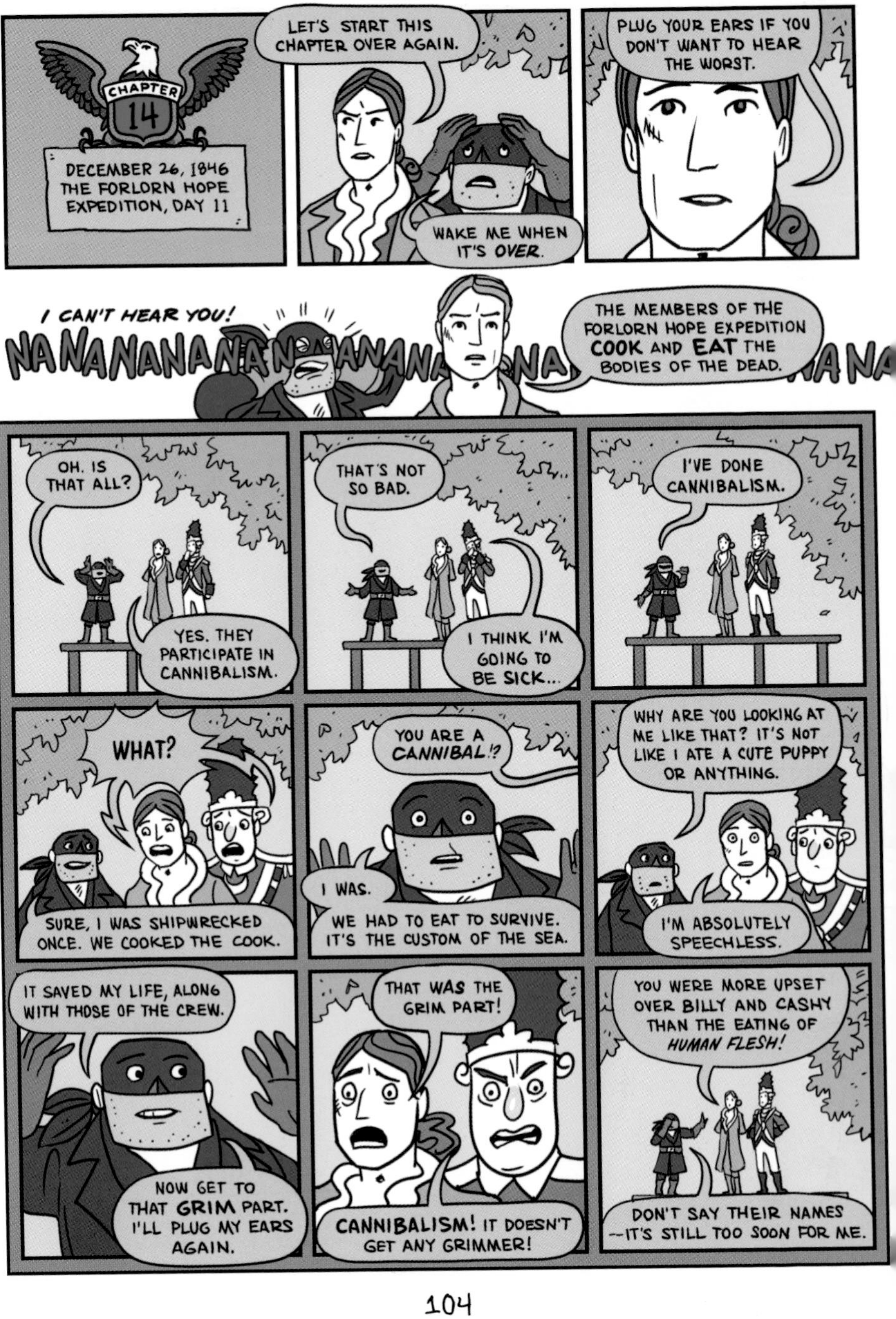
CHAPTER 14
DECEMBER 26, 1846 THE FORLORN HOPE EXPEDITION, DAY 11
LET'S START THIS CHAPTER OVER AGAIN.
WAKE ME WHEN IT'S *OVER*.
PLUG YOUR EARS IF YOU DON'T WANT TO HEAR THE WORST.
I CAN'T HEAR YOU!
NANANANANANANANANA
THE MEMBERS OF THE FORLORN HOPE EXPEDITION **COOK** AND **EAT** THE BODIES OF THE DEAD.
OH. IS THAT ALL?
YES. THEY PARTICIPATE IN CANNIBALISM.
THAT'S NOT SO BAD.
I THINK I'M GOING TO BE **SICK**...
I'VE DONE CANNIBALISM.
WHAT?
SURE, I WAS SHIPWRECKED ONCE. WE COOKED THE COOK.
YOU ARE A *CANNIBAL*!?
I WAS.
WE HAD TO EAT TO SURVIVE. IT'S THE CUSTOM OF THE SEA.
WHY ARE YOU LOOKING AT ME LIKE THAT? IT'S NOT LIKE I ATE A CUTE PUPPY OR ANYTHING.
I'M ABSOLUTELY SPEECHLESS.
IT SAVED MY LIFE, ALONG WITH THOSE OF THE CREW.
NOW GET TO THAT **GRIM** PART. I'LL PLUG MY EARS AGAIN.
THAT **WAS** THE GRIM PART!
CANNIBALISM! IT DOESN'T GET ANY GRIMMER!
YOU WERE MORE UPSET OVER BILLY AND CASHY THAN THE EATING OF *HUMAN FLESH*!
DON'T SAY THEIR NAMES --IT'S STILL TOO SOON FOR ME.

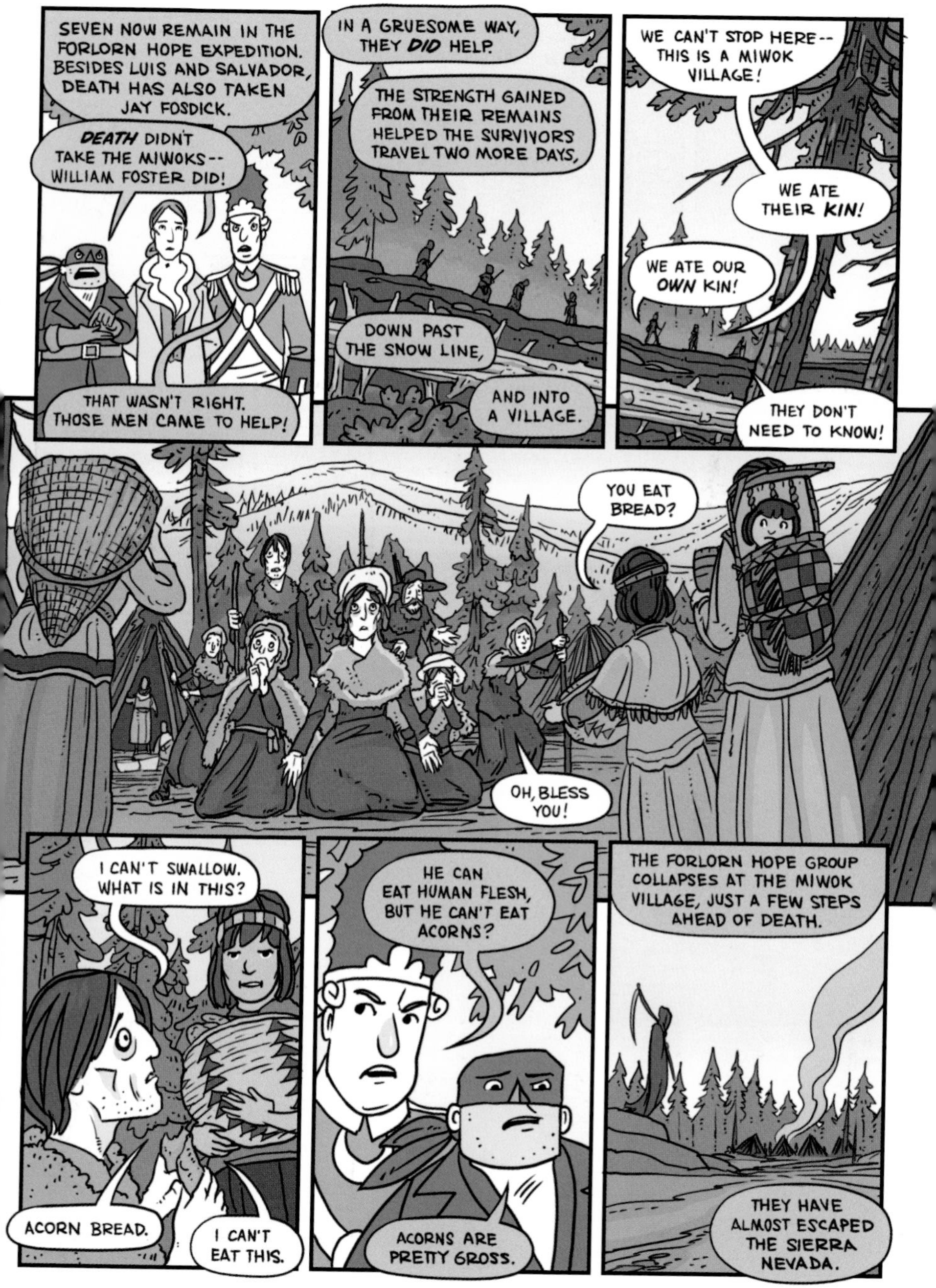

SEVEN NOW REMAIN IN THE FORLORN HOPE EXPEDITION. BESIDES LUIS AND SALVADOR, DEATH HAS ALSO TAKEN JAY FOSDICK.
DEATH DIDN'T TAKE THE MIWOKS-- WILLIAM FOSTER DID!
THAT WASN'T RIGHT. THOSE MEN CAME TO HELP!
IN A GRUESOME WAY, THEY DID HELP.
THE STRENGTH GAINED FROM THEIR REMAINS HELPED THE SURVIVORS TRAVEL TWO MORE DAYS,
DOWN PAST THE SNOW LINE,
AND INTO A VILLAGE.
WE CAN'T STOP HERE-- THIS IS A MIWOK VILLAGE!
WE ATE THEIR KIN!
WE ATE OUR OWN KIN!
THEY DON'T NEED TO KNOW!
YOU EAT BREAD?
OH, BLESS YOU!
I CAN'T SWALLOW. WHAT IS IN THIS?
ACORN BREAD.
I CAN'T EAT THIS.
HE CAN EAT HUMAN FLESH, BUT HE CAN'T EAT ACORNS?
ACORNS ARE PRETTY GROSS.
THE FORLORN HOPE GROUP COLLAPSES AT THE MIWOK VILLAGE, JUST A FEW STEPS AHEAD OF DEATH.
THEY HAVE ALMOST ESCAPED THE SIERRA NEVADA.

112

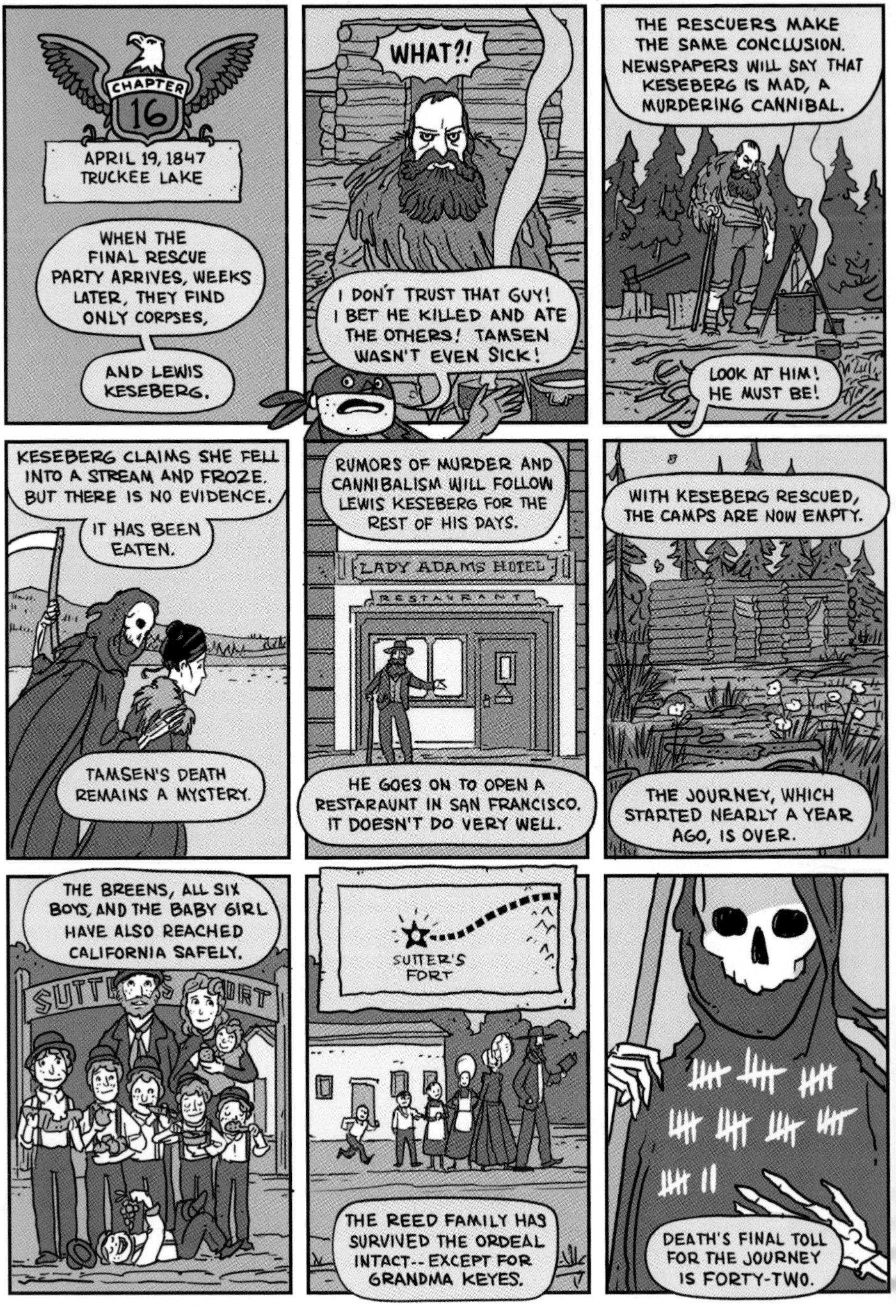
CHAPTER 16
APRIL 19, 1847 TRUCKEE LAKE
WHEN THE FINAL RESCUE PARTY ARRIVES, WEEKS LATER, THEY FIND ONLY CORPSES,
AND LEWIS KESEBERG.
WHAT?!
I DON'T TRUST THAT GUY! I BET HE KILLED AND ATE THE OTHERS! TAMSEN WASN'T EVEN SICK!
THE RESCUERS MAKE THE SAME CONCLUSION. NEWSPAPERS WILL SAY THAT KESEBERG IS MAD, A MURDERING CANNIBAL.
LOOK AT HIM! HE MUST BE!
KESEBERG CLAIMS SHE FELL INTO A STREAM AND FROZE. BUT THERE IS NO EVIDENCE.
IT HAS BEEN EATEN.
TAMSEN'S DEATH REMAINS A MYSTERY.
RUMORS OF MURDER AND CANNIBALISM WILL FOLLOW LEWIS KESEBERG FOR THE REST OF HIS DAYS.
LADY ADAMS HOTEL
RESTAURANT
HE GOES ON TO OPEN A RESTARAUNT IN SAN FRANCISCO. IT DOESN'T DO VERY WELL.
WITH KESEBERG RESCUED, THE CAMPS ARE NOW EMPTY.
THE JOURNEY, WHICH STARTED NEARLY A YEAR AGO, IS OVER.
THE BREENS, ALL SIX BOYS, AND THE BABY GIRL HAVE ALSO REACHED CALIFORNIA SAFELY.
SUTTER'S FORT
THE REED FAMILY HAS SURVIVED THE ORDEAL INTACT-- EXCEPT FOR GRANDMA KEYES.
DEATH'S FINAL TOLL FOR THE JOURNEY IS FORTY-TWO.

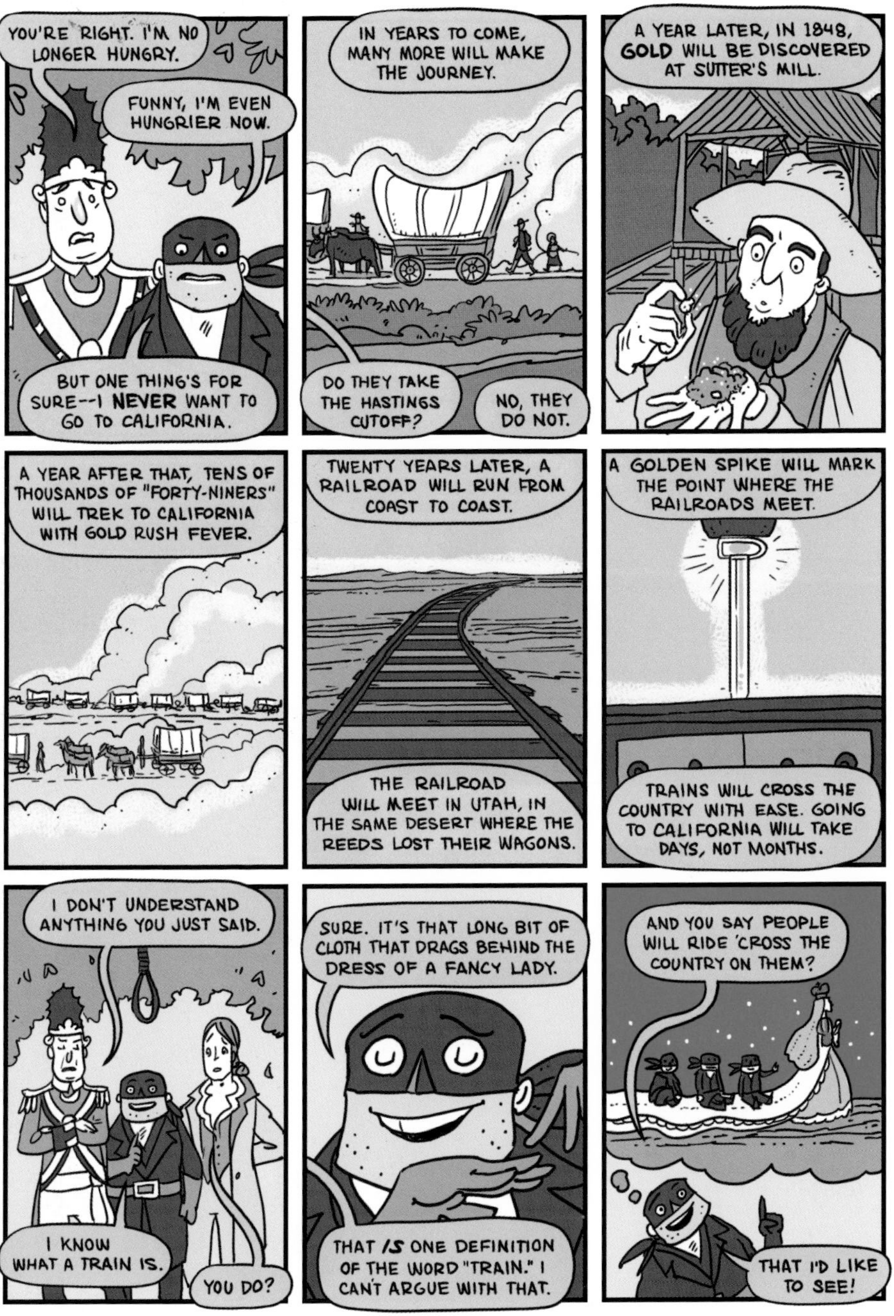
YOU'RE RIGHT. I'M NO LONGER HUNGRY.
FUNNY, I'M EVEN HUNGRIER NOW.
BUT ONE THING'S FOR SURE--I NEVER WANT TO GO TO CALIFORNIA.
IN YEARS TO COME, MANY MORE WILL MAKE THE JOURNEY.
DO THEY TAKE THE HASTINGS CUTOFF?
NO, THEY DO NOT.
A YEAR LATER, IN 1848, GOLD WILL BE DISCOVERED AT SUTTER'S MILL.
A YEAR AFTER THAT, TENS OF THOUSANDS OF "FORTY-NINERS" WILL TREK TO CALIFORNIA WITH GOLD RUSH FEVER.
TWENTY YEARS LATER, A RAILROAD WILL RUN FROM COAST TO COAST.
THE RAILROAD WILL MEET IN UTAH, IN THE SAME DESERT WHERE THE REEDS LOST THEIR WAGONS.
A GOLDEN SPIKE WILL MARK THE POINT WHERE THE RAILROADS MEET.
TRAINS WILL CROSS THE COUNTRY WITH EASE. GOING TO CALIFORNIA WILL TAKE DAYS, NOT MONTHS.
I DON'T UNDERSTAND ANYTHING YOU JUST SAID.
I KNOW WHAT A TRAIN IS.
YOU DO?
SURE. IT'S THAT LONG BIT OF CLOTH THAT DRAGS BEHIND THE DRESS OF A FANCY LADY.
THAT IS ONE DEFINITION OF THE WORD "TRAIN." I CAN'T ARGUE WITH THAT.
AND YOU SAY PEOPLE WILL RIDE 'CROSS THE COUNTRY ON THEM?
THAT I'D LIKE TO SEE!

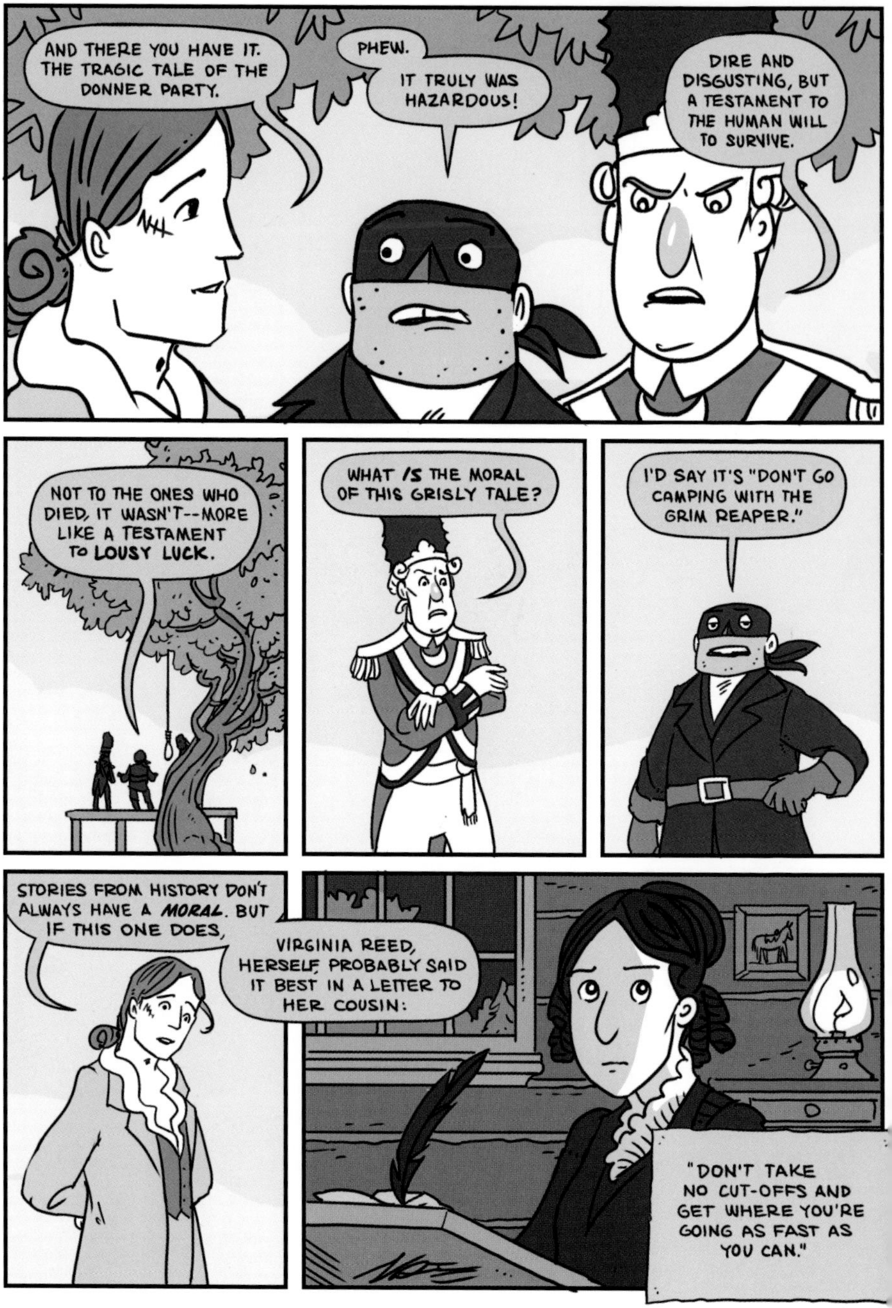

AND THERE YOU HAVE IT. THE TRAGIC TALE OF THE DONNER PARTY.
PHEW.
IT TRULY WAS HAZARDOUS!
DIRE AND DISGUSTING, BUT A TESTAMENT TO THE HUMAN WILL TO SURVIVE.
NOT TO THE ONES WHO DIED, IT WASN'T--MORE LIKE A TESTAMENT TO LOUSY LUCK.
WHAT IS THE MORAL OF THIS GRISLY TALE?
I'D SAY IT'S "DON'T GO CAMPING WITH THE GRIM REAPER."
STORIES FROM HISTORY DON'T ALWAYS HAVE A MORAL. BUT IF THIS ONE DOES,
VIRGINIA REED, HERSELF, PROBABLY SAID IT BEST IN A LETTER TO HER COUSIN:
"DON'T TAKE NO CUT-OFFS AND GET WHERE YOU'RE GOING AS FAST AS YOU CAN."

NH
HT

NATHAN HALE'S HAZARDOUS TALES

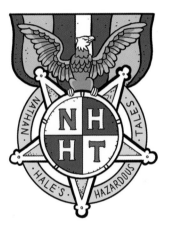

WHO DIED AND WHO SURVIVED

KEY: STARVATION/EXPOSURE ACCIDENTAL SHOOTING

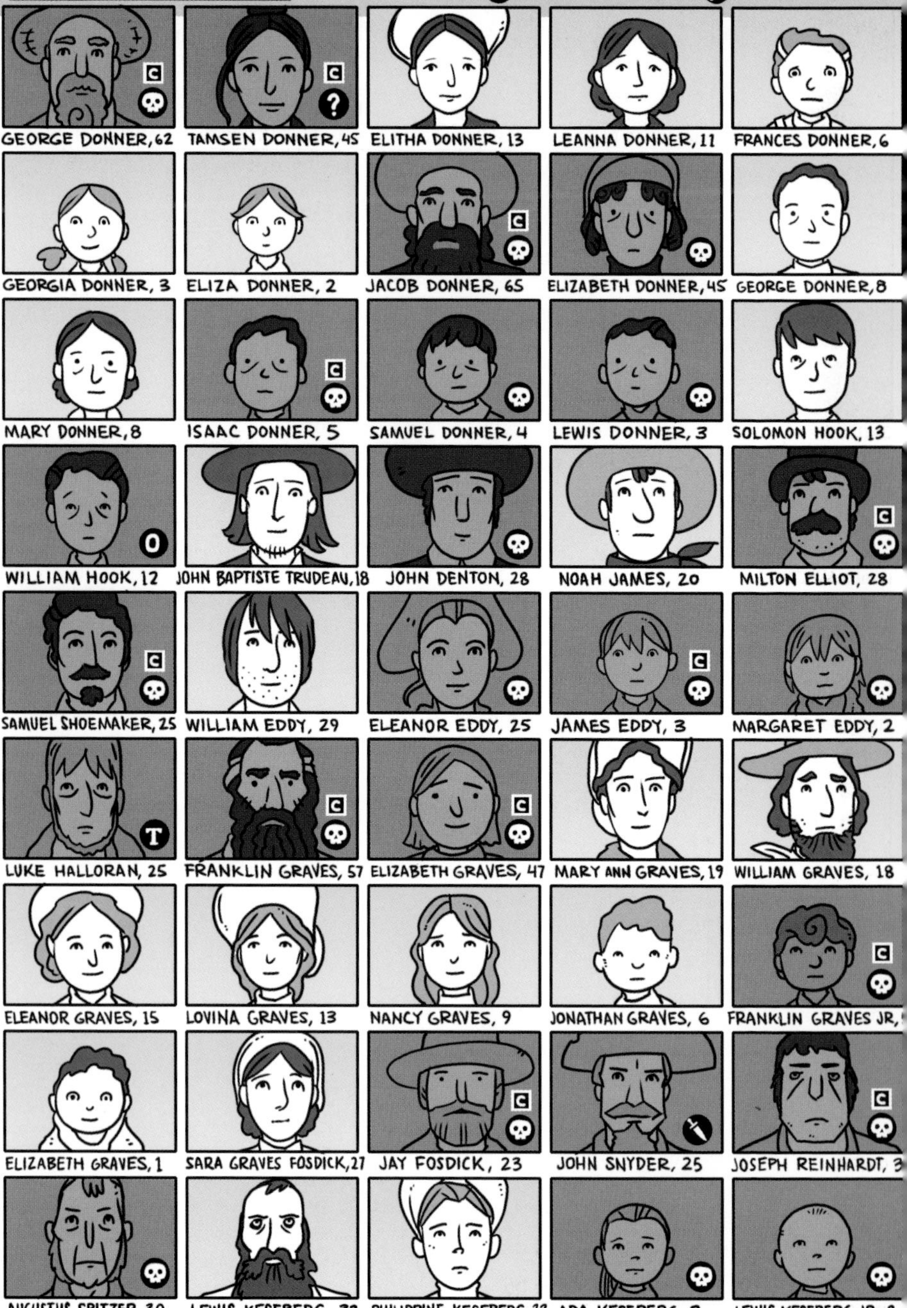

C
GEORGE DONNER, 62
C
?
TAMSEN DONNER, 45
ELITHA DONNER, 13
LEANNA DONNER, 11
FRANCES DONNER, 6
GEORGIA DONNER, 3
ELIZA DONNER, 2
C
JACOB DONNER, 65
ELIZABETH DONNER, 45
GEORGE DONNER, 8
MARY DONNER, 8
C
ISAAC DONNER, 5
SAMUEL DONNER, 4
LEWIS DONNER, 3
SOLOMON HOOK, 13
O
WILLIAM HOOK, 12
JOHN BAPTISTE TRUDEAU, 18
JOHN DENTON, 28
NOAH JAMES, 20
C
MILTON ELLIOT, 28
C
SAMUEL SHOEMAKER, 25
WILLIAM EDDY, 29
ELEANOR EDDY, 25
C
JAMES EDDY, 3
MARGARET EDDY, 2
T
LUKE HALLORAN, 25
C
FRANKLIN GRAVES, 57
C
ELIZABETH GRAVES, 47
MARY ANN GRAVES, 19
WILLIAM GRAVES, 18
ELEANOR GRAVES, 15
LOVINA GRAVES, 13
NANCY GRAVES, 9
JONATHAN GRAVES, 6
C
FRANKLIN GRAVES JR,
ELIZABETH GRAVES, 1
SARA GRAVES FOSDICK, 27
C
JAY FOSDICK, 23
JOHN SNYDER, 25
C
JOSEPH REINHARDT, 3
AUGUSTUS SPITZER, 30
LEWIS KESEBERG, 32
PHILIPPINE KESEBERG, 22
ADA KESEBERG, 3
LEWIS KESEBERG JR, 2

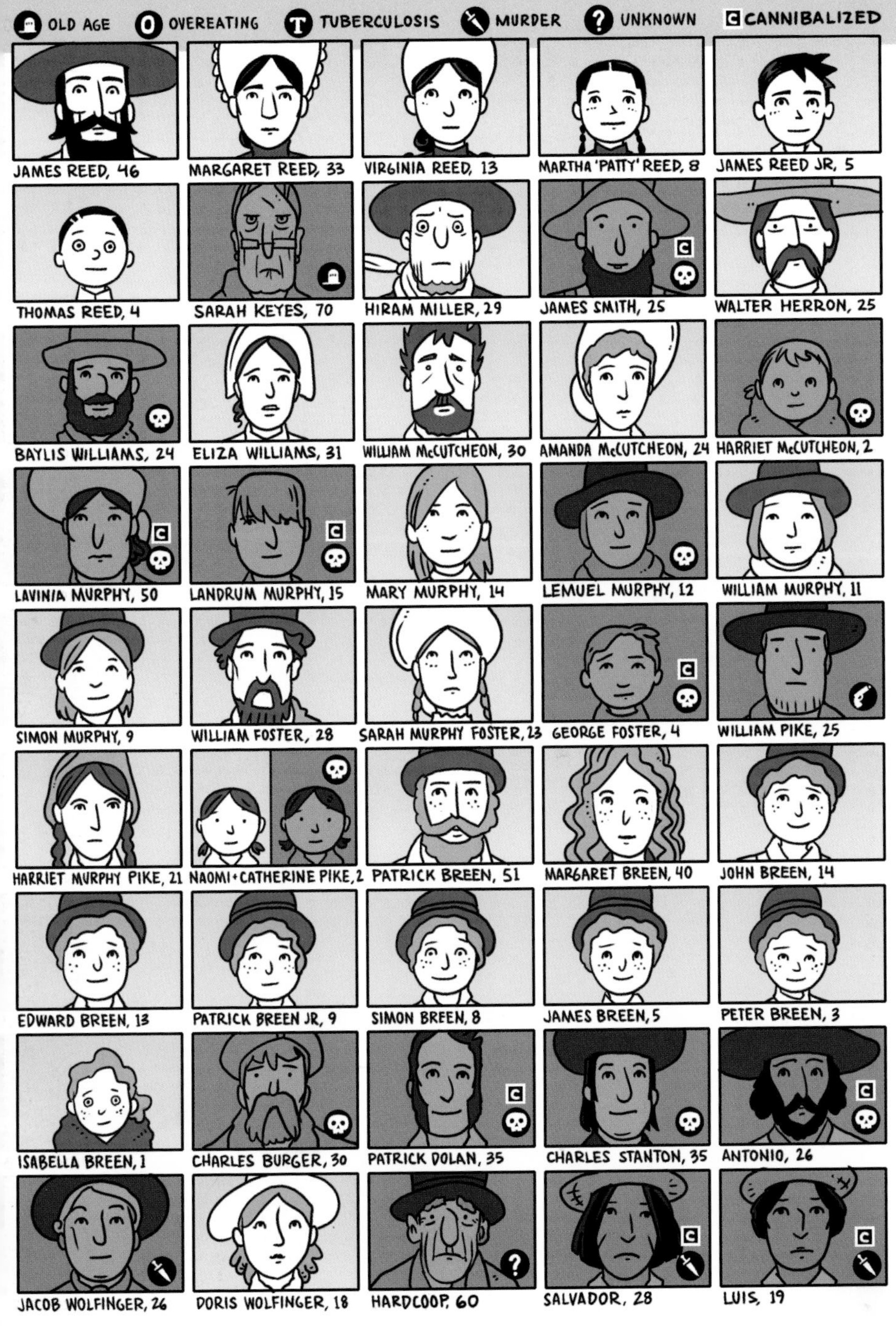
OLD AGE
OVEREATING
TUBERCULOSIS
MURDER
UNKNOWN
CANNIBALIZED
JAMES REED, 46
MARGARET REED, 33
VIRGINIA REED, 13
MARTHA 'PATTY' REED, 8
JAMES REED JR, 5
THOMAS REED, 4
SARAH KEYES, 70
HIRAM MILLER, 29
JAMES SMITH, 25
WALTER HERRON, 25
BAYLIS WILLIAMS, 24
ELIZA WILLIAMS, 31
WILLIAM McCUTCHEON, 30
AMANDA McCUTCHEON, 24
HARRIET McCUTCHEON, 2
LAVINIA MURPHY, 50
LANDRUM MURPHY, 15
MARY MURPHY, 14
LEMUEL MURPHY, 12
WILLIAM MURPHY, 11
SIMON MURPHY, 9
WILLIAM FOSTER, 28
SARAH MURPHY FOSTER, 23
GEORGE FOSTER, 4
WILLIAM PIKE, 25
HARRIET MURPHY PIKE, 21
NAOMI+CATHERINE PIKE, 2
PATRICK BREEN, 51
MARGARET BREEN, 40
JOHN BREEN, 14
EDWARD BREEN, 13
PATRICK BREEN JR, 9
SIMON BREEN, 8
JAMES BREEN, 5
PETER BREEN, 3
ISABELLA BREEN, 1
CHARLES BURGER, 30
PATRICK DOLAN, 35
CHARLES STANTON, 35
ANTONIO, 26
JACOB WOLFINGER, 26
DORIS WOLFINGER, 18
HARDCOOP, 60
SALVADOR, 28
LUIS, 19

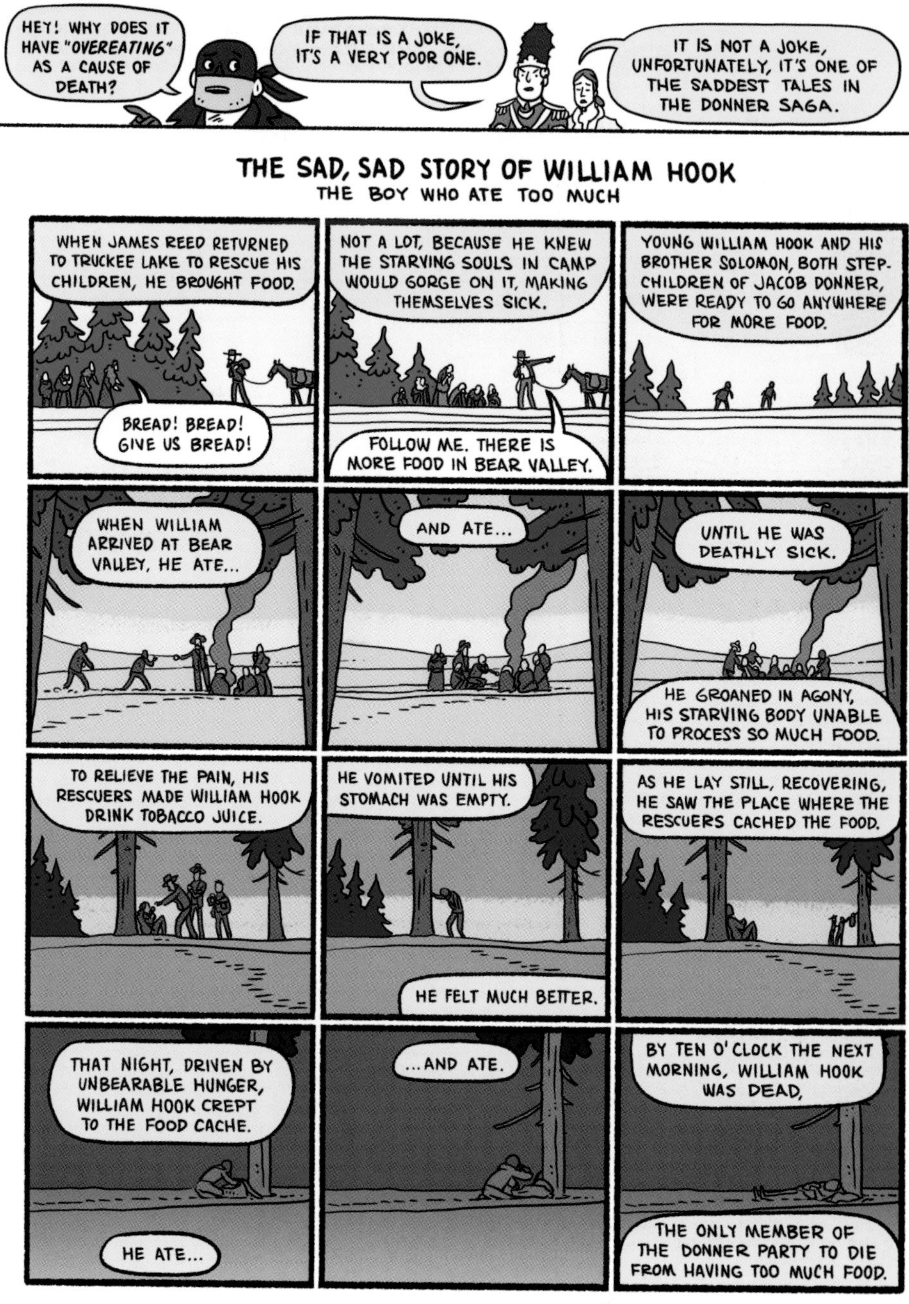
HEY! WHY DOES IT HAVE "OVEREATING" AS A CAUSE OF DEATH?
IF THAT IS A JOKE, IT'S A VERY POOR ONE.
IT IS NOT A JOKE, UNFORTUNATELY, IT'S ONE OF THE SADDEST TALES IN THE DONNER SAGA.
THE SAD, SAD STORY OF WILLIAM HOOK
THE BOY WHO ATE TOO MUCH
WHEN JAMES REED RETURNED TO TRUCKEE LAKE TO RESCUE HIS CHILDREN, HE BROUGHT FOOD.
BREAD! BREAD! GIVE US BREAD!
NOT A LOT, BECAUSE HE KNEW THE STARVING SOULS IN CAMP WOULD GORGE ON IT, MAKING THEMSELVES SICK.
FOLLOW ME. THERE IS MORE FOOD IN BEAR VALLEY.
YOUNG WILLIAM HOOK AND HIS BROTHER SOLOMON, BOTH STEP-CHILDREN OF JACOB DONNER, WERE READY TO GO ANYWHERE FOR MORE FOOD.
WHEN WILLIAM ARRIVED AT BEAR VALLEY, HE ATE...
AND ATE...
UNTIL HE WAS DEATHLY SICK.
HE GROANED IN AGONY, HIS STARVING BODY UNABLE TO PROCESS SO MUCH FOOD.
TO RELIEVE THE PAIN, HIS RESCUERS MADE WILLIAM HOOK DRINK TOBACCO JUICE.
HE VOMITED UNTIL HIS STOMACH WAS EMPTY.
HE FELT MUCH BETTER.
AS HE LAY STILL, RECOVERING, HE SAW THE PLACE WHERE THE RESCUERS CACHED THE FOOD.
THAT NIGHT, DRIVEN BY UNBEARABLE HUNGER, WILLIAM HOOK CREPT TO THE FOOD CACHE.
HE ATE...
...AND ATE.
BY TEN O'CLOCK THE NEXT MORNING, WILLIAM HOOK WAS DEAD,
THE ONLY MEMBER OF THE DONNER PARTY TO DIE FROM HAVING TOO MUCH FOOD.

JAMES AND MARGARET REED

THE REED FAMILY SETTLED IN SAN JOSE, WHERE JAMES BECAME A RANCHER. HE ALSO SAT ON THE FIRST TOWN COUNCIL AND WAS CHIEF OF POLICE.

VIRGINIA WROTE A MEMOIR OF HER JOURNEY CALLED *'ACROSS THE PLAINS IN THE DONNER PARTY 1846'*. HER DESCRIPTIONS WERE USED EXTENSIVELY WHEN RESEARCHING THIS BOOK. BILL THE PONY, SCARING SIOUX BRAVES WITH A TELESCOPE, TAKING HER FATHER'S GUNS --THESE ARE STORIES FROM VIRGINIA'S TALE.

PATTY'S TINY DOLL, NAMED "DOLLY", ALSO SURVIVED THE TRIP. DOLLY CAN BE SEEN AT SUTTER'S FORT STATE HISTORIC PARK, CA.

MARTHA "PATTY" REED

THERE WERE TWO DONNER FAMILIES--THE **GEORGE** DONNER FAMILY AND THE **JACOB** DONNER FAMILY. THE ONLY DONNERS TO MAKE IT SAFELY OVER THE PASS WERE ORPHANS; ALL FOUR DONNER PARENTS DIED AT TRUCKEE LAKE. THE DONNER ORPHANS FOUND FAMILIES IN CALIFORNIA TO LIVE WITH. MARY AND FRANCES DONNER LIVED WITH THE REEDS IN SAN JOSE. THE DONNER NAME IS NOW A PERMANENT PART OF THE LANDSCAPE OF THE AMERICAN WEST; DONNER LAKE AND DONNER PASS ARE JUST TWO OF MANY LOCATIONS NAMED FOR THE FAMILY.

ALL OF THE BREENS SURVIVED. ALL SEVEN CHILDREN, RANGING FROM AGES 1 TO 14, MADE IT THROUGH THE DEADLY WINTER OF 1846-47. THEY ARRIVED AT SUTTER'S FORT WITH NOTHING BUT THE CLOTHES ON THEIR BACKS. THEY WERE THE FIRST AMERICANS TO SETTLE IN SAN JUAN BAUTISTA. THEY LIVED HAPPILY EVER AFTER.

"I WAS BORN UNDER AN EVIL STAR!" LEWIS KESEBERG WOULD LATER SAY OF HIS ORDEAL WITH THE DONNER PARTY. THE FINAL MEMBER TO BE RESCUED FROM TRUCKEE LAKE, HE WAS OFTEN PAINTED BY THE MEDIA AS A VILLAIN, ESPECIALLY CONCERNING THE MYSTERIOUS FATE OF TAMSEN DONNER. SOME STORIES CLAIM HE MURDERED AND ATE HER. HE WAS PLAGUED BY CANNIBAL JOKES AND RUMORS FOR THE REST OF HIS LIFE. HIS BAD LUCK CONTINUED WHEN HIS BUSINESS, A HOTEL/RESTAURANT CALLED THE LADY ADAMS, BURNED DOWN AND HIS SECOND BUSINESS, A BREWERY, WAS DESTROYED IN A FLOOD.

"DOLLY"
(FOR MORE ON DOLLY, SEE PAGE 60.)

LEWIS KESEBERG

TO THE END OF HIS DAYS, **LANSFORD HASTINGS** INSISTED THAT HIS CUTOFF WAS THE SUPERIOR, EASIER ROUTE TO CALIFORNIA. AFTER FIGHTING IN THE MEXICAN-AMERICAN WAR, HE OFFERED TO GUIDE OTHER PIONEER GROUPS TO THE WEST. NOBODY ACCEPTED. DURING THE CIVIL WAR, HE HATCHED A PLOT TO JOIN CALIFORNIA WITH THE **SOUTH**. NOBODY ACCEPTED THAT, EITHER. HE HAD PLANS TO SET UP A COLONY IN BRAZIL FOR EXPATRIATE CONFEDERATES. ONCE AGAIN, NOBODY ACCEPTED. HE DIED ON A SHIP EN ROUTE TO BRAZIL.

CALABRO, MARIAN *THE PERILOUS JOURNEY OF THE DONNER PARTY* NEW YORK: CLARION, 1999

ALTER, J. CECIL *JIM BRIDGER*. NORMAN: UNIVERSITY OF OKLAHOMA PRESS, 1962

MULLEN JR., FRANK
THE DONNER PARTY CHRONICLES: A DAY BY DAY ACCOUNT OF A DOOMED WAGON TRAIN
RENO: A HALCYON IMPRINT OF THE NEVADA HUMANITIES COMMITTEE, 1997

HAFEN, LeROY R., ed. *TRAPPERS OF THE FAR WEST: SIXTEEN BIOGRAPHICAL SKETCHES*
LINCOLN: UNIVERSITY OF NEBRASKA PRESS, 1983

HOUGHTON, ELIZA POOR DONNER,
THE EXPEDITION OF THE DONNER PARTY AND ITS TRAGIC FATE CHICAGO: A.C. McCLURG, 1911

JOHNSON, KRISTEN, ed. *UNFORTUNATE EMIGRANTS: NARRATIVES OF THE DONNER PARTY*
LOGAN: UTAH STATE UNIVERSITY PRESS, 1996

JONES, EVAN *TRAPPERS AND MOUNTAIN MEN* NEW YORK: AMERICAN HERITAGE, 1961

McGLASHAN, C.F.
HISTORY OF THE DONNER PARTY: A TRAGEDY OF THE SIERRA
TRUCKEE, CALIF.: CROWLEY & McGLASHAN, 1879

MILLS, BRONWYN *THE MEXICAN WAR*
NEW YORK: FACTS ON FILE, 1992

NARDO, DON. *THE MEXICAN-AMERICAN WAR*
SAN DIEGO: LUCENT BOOKS, 1991

RARICK, ETHAN
DESPERATE PASSAGE: THE DONNER PARTY'S PERILOUS JOURNEY WEST
NEW YORK: OXFORD UNIVERSITY PRESS, 2008

STEWART, GEORGE R. *ORDEAL BY HUNGER: THE STORY OF THE DONNER PARTY* NEW YORK: HOLT, 1936

TUNIS, EDWIN *FRONTIER LIVING* CLEVELAND, WORLD PUB., 1961

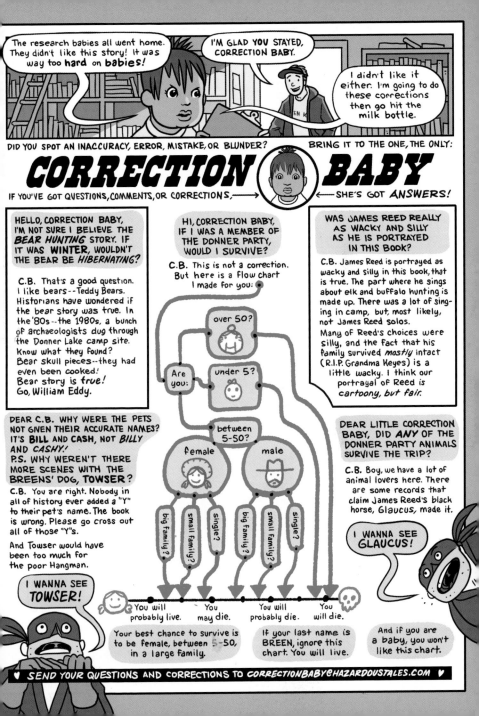

The research babies all went home. They didn't like this story! It was way too hard on **babies**!

I'M GLAD **YOU** STAYED, CORRECTION BABY.

I didn't like it either. I'm going to do these corrections then go hit the milk bottle.

DID YOU SPOT AN INACCURACY, ERROR, MISTAKE, OR BLUNDER?   BRING IT TO THE ONE, THE ONLY:

CORRECTION BABY

IF YOU'VE GOT QUESTIONS, COMMENTS, OR CORRECTIONS, ——→   ←—— SHE'S GOT **ANSWERS!**

HELLO, CORRECTION BABY, I'M NOT SURE I BELIEVE THE **BEAR HUNTING** STORY. IF IT WAS **WINTER**, WOULDN'T THE BEAR BE *HIBERNATING*?

C.B. That's a good question. I like bears--Teddy Bears. Historians have wondered if the bear story was true. In the '80s--the 1980s, a bunch of archaeologists dug through the Donner Lake camp site. Know what they found? Bear skull pieces--they had even been cooked! Bear story is *true!* Go, William Eddy.

DEAR C.B. WHY WERE THE PETS NOT GIVEN THEIR ACCURATE NAMES? IT'S **BILL** AND **CASH**, NOT **BILLY** AND **CASHY!** P.S. WHY WEREN'T THERE MORE SCENES WITH THE BREENS' DOG, TOWSER?

C.B. You are right. Nobody in all of history ever added a "Y" to their pet's name. The book is wrong. Please go cross out all of those "Y"s.

And Towser would have been too much for the poor Hangman.

I WANNA SEE **TOWSER!**

HI, CORRECTION BABY, IF I WAS A MEMBER OF THE DONNER PARTY, WOULD I SURVIVE?

C.B. This is not a correction. But here is a flow chart I made for you:

Are you:
- over 50?
- under 5?
- between 5-50?
  - female
    - big family?
    - small family?
    - single?
  - male
    - big family?
    - small family?
    - single?

You will probably live.   You may die.   You will probably die.   You will die.

Your best chance to survive is to be female, between 5-50, in a large family.

If your last name is BREEN, ignore this chart. You will live.

And if you are a baby, you won't like this chart.

WAS JAMES REED REALLY AS WACKY AND SILLY AS HE IS PORTRAYED IN THIS BOOK?

C.B. James Reed is portrayed as wacky and silly in this book, that is true. The part where he sings about elk and buffalo hunting is made up. There was a lot of singing in camp, but, most likely, not James Reed solos. Many of Reed's choices were silly, and the fact that his family survived *mostly* intact (R.I.P. Grandma Keyes) is a little wacky. I think our portrayal of Reed is *cartoony, but fair.*

DEAR LITTLE CORRECTION BABY, DID *ANY* OF THE DONNER PARTY ANIMALS SURVIVE THE TRIP?

C.B. Boy, we have a lot of animal lovers here. There are some records that claim James Reed's black horse, Glaucus, made it.

I WANNA SEE GLAUCUS!

♥ SEND YOUR QUESTIONS AND CORRECTIONS TO *CORRECTIONBABY@HAZARDOUSTALES.COM* ♥

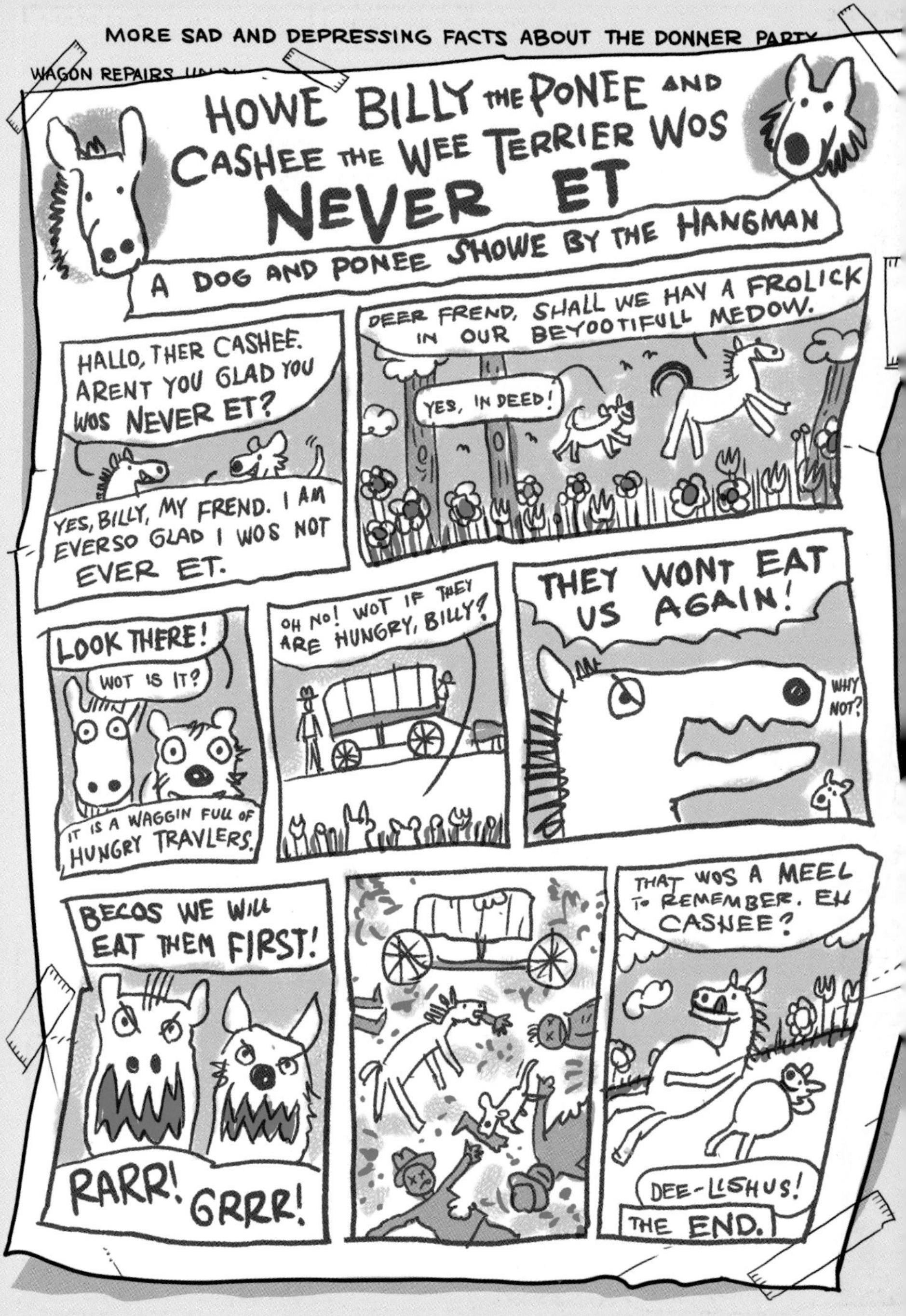
MORE SAD AND DEPRESSING FACTS ABOUT THE DONNER PARTY
WAGON REPAIRS
HOWE BILLY THE PONEE AND CASHEE THE WEE TERRIER WOS NEVER ET
SHOWE BY THE HANGMAN
A DOG AND PONEE SHOWE BY THE HANGMAN
HALLO, THER CASHEE. ARENT YOU GLAD YOU WOS NEVER ET?
YES, BILLY, MY FREND. I AM EVERSO GLAD I WOS NOT EVER ET.
DEER FREND, SHALL WE HAY A FROLICK IN OUR BEYOOTIFULL MEDOW.
YES, IN DEED!
LOOK THERE!
WOT IS IT?
IT IS A WAGGIN FULL OF HUNGRY TRAVLERS.
OH NO! WOT IF THEY ARE HUNGRY, BILLY?
THEY WONT EAT US AGAIN!
WHY NOT?
BECOS WE WILL EAT THEM FIRST!
RARR! GRRR!
THAT WOS A MEEL TO REMEMBER. EH CASHEE?
DEE-LISHUS!
THE END.

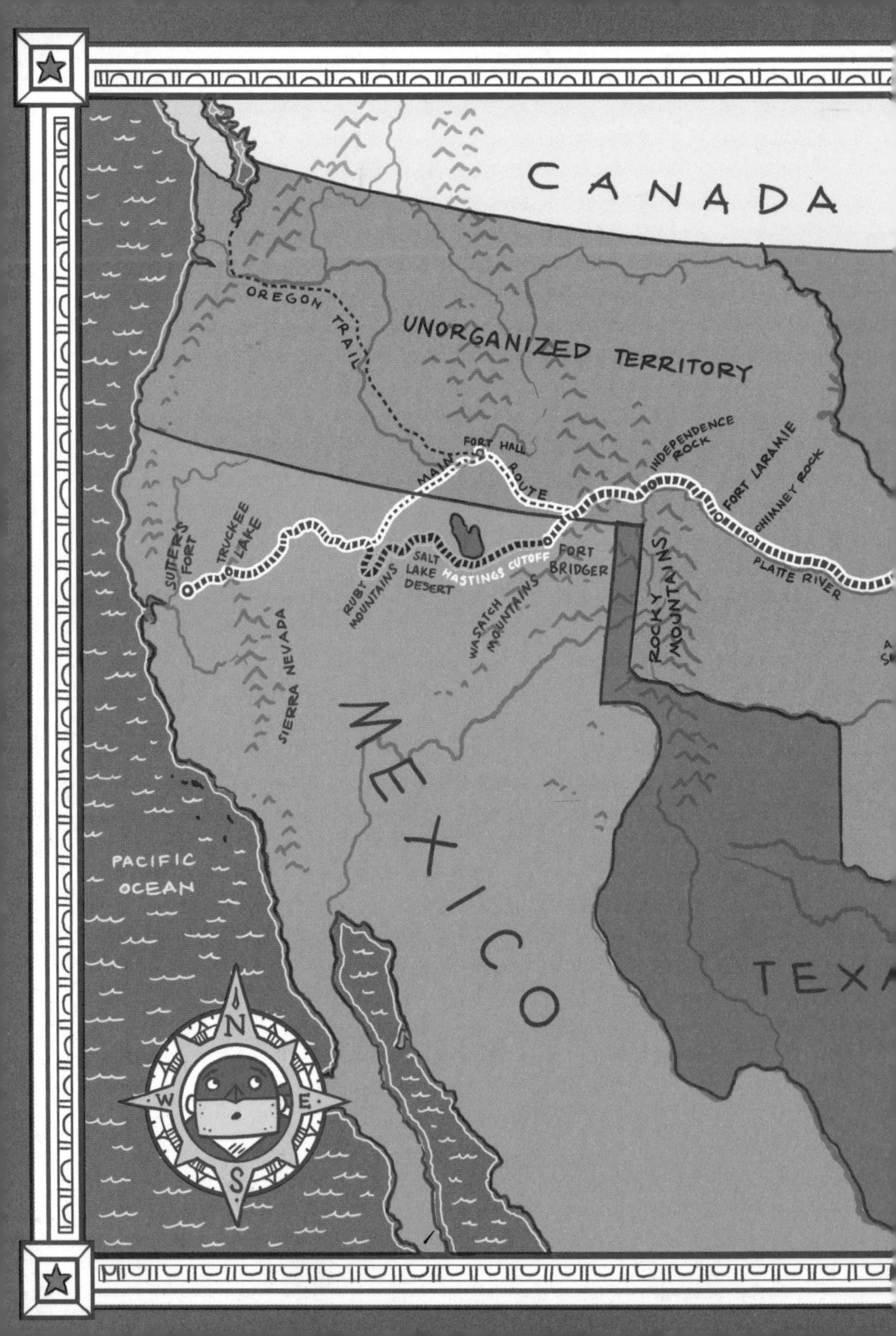

CANADA
OREGON TRAIL
UNORGANIZED TERRITORY
FORT HALL
MAIN ROUTE
INDEPENDENCE ROCK
FORT LARAMIE
CHIMNEY ROCK
PLATTE RIVER
SUTTER'S FORT
TRUCKEE LAKE
RUBY MOUNTAINS
SALT LAKE DESERT
HASTINGS CUTOFF
FORT BRIDGER
WASATCH MOUNTAINS
ROCKY MOUNTAINS
SIERRA NEVADA
MEXICO
PACIFIC OCEAN
TEXA
N
S
E
W